The Purgatory Principle
for Protestants

How God's Purifying Judgment
and Mercy
Answer Injustice

Kenneth Wilson, M.D., D.Phil.

Regula Fidei Press
Montgomery, Texas

Library of Congress Cataloging-in-Publication Data

ISBN 979-8-89259-000-6

1. Purgatory 2. Punishment 3. Justice 4. Theology

Table of Contents

Dedicated to all of my brothers at FM

as together we pursue

our transformational destiny

of being conformed into the image of Christ.

I have attempted to balance academic information with a more

pastoral care approach in the latter sections of this book.

Whether I have succeeded or not, the reader may determine.

Because few readers complete an entire book in one session,

both scripture passages and concepts are purposefully

repeated.

Scriptures are quoted in many different versions for

inclusivity.

Preface

The topic of this book unsettles Protestants. The mention of purgatory produces an involuntary knee-jerk rejection—it's a Catholic myth. This was my view until I read through the writings of the early church fathers as they explained scripture. I realized that Roman Catholics are not the only ones who rely upon tradition. Protestants also hold many dogmas as sacred that cannot be identified in scripture. Critically, traditions alter the way we read and interpret scripture. Those traditions can blind us to what is actually present.

This book will not argue for a traditional medieval Roman Catholic view of purgatory wherein sinners are tormented for hundreds of years in a place called Purgatory. In fact, I will discuss what I view as problems with that understanding. But I will also contend that Protestants have missed a critical component of theology by following the traditions of Martin Luther, and especially John Calvin. For over twenty years I have been instructing students about balancing God's mercy and judgment. The Old Testament and the New Testament constantly refer to both God's merciful love and God's discipline for the goal of holiness. According to Romans 8:29, God has predestined the process of his children being transformed into the image of Christ. The questions remain: how and when will that transformation occur? Is it instantaneous or a process?

I will suggest that most Protestant theologies contain an inherent injustice. Only balancing God's mercy with judgment after death can answer that injustice. I doubt that Protestants, Orthodox Christians, or Roman Catholics will embrace this proposed theology *en masse* (pun intended). But for those who are able to turn down the volume of their own tradition temporarily, perhaps they might hear a more coherent theology. I pray this will entice them to experience God more intimately as we are transformed into the image of Christ.

Abbreviations

Scripture

Gen	Genesis
Lev	Leviticus
Deut	Deuteronomy
1 Sam	1 Samuel
2 Sam	2 Samuel
1 Chr	1 Chronicles
Ps	Psalm/Psalms
Prov	Proverbs
Isa	Isaiah
Jer	Jeremiah
Lam	Lamentations
Ezek	Ezekiel
Dan	Daniel
Zeph	Zephaniah
Mal	Malachi
Matt	Matthew
Rom / R.	Romans
1 Cor/C.	1 Corinthians
2 Cor/C.	2 Corinthians
Gal	Galatians
Eph	Ephesians
Phil	Philippians
Col	Colossians
1 Thess	1 Thessalonians
1 Tim	1 Timothy
2 Tim	2 Timothy
Heb	Hebrews
Jas	James
1 Pet	1 Peter
2 Pet	2 Peter
Rev	Revelation

Bible Versions

AMP	Amplified Bible
ASV	American Standard Version
CEB	Common English Bible
CSB	Christian Standard Bible
CEV	Contemporary English Version
DRA	Douay-Rheims Bible
ESV	English Standard Version
HCSB	Holman Christian Standard Bible
JUB	Jerusalem Bible
KJV	King James Version
NASB	New American Standard Bible
NASB95	New American Standard Bible 1995
NCB	New Century Bible
NET	New English Translation
NIV	New International Version
NIV84	New International Version 1984
NJB	New Jerusalem Bible
NKJV	New King James Version
NLT	New Living Translation
NRSV	New Revised Standard Version
NRSVC	New Revised Standard Version Catholic
RSV	Revised Standard Version
SBLGNT	The Greek New Testament: SBL Edition
YLT	Young's Literal Translation

Ancient Writings

2 Esd	2 Esdras
2 Macc	2 Maccabees
Apoc. Bar.	Apocalypse of Baruch (also Apoc. Br.)
CCC	Catechism of the Catholic Church
Dial	Dialogues, Gregory the Great
Did	Didache
Exp. in Prim. Reg.	Commentary on First Kings
Fifth Hom. Psa	Fifth Homily in the Psalms
Herm. Mand.	Shepherd of Hermes, Mandates
Herm. Sim.	Shepherd of Hermes, Similitudes
Hom. in Evang.	Homilies on the Gospel

Hom in 1 Cor	Homily in 1 Corinthians
Homil. Lucam	Homlies in Luke
J.W.	Jewish Wars
Syr. X.4	Syriac 10.4
NT	New Testament
OT	Old Testament
PG	Patrologia Graeca
Pol. Phil.	Polycarp, Epistle to the Philippians
R. H. /RosHas.	Rosh Hashanah
Sir	Sirach
SCG	Summa contra Gentiles
Smyr	Letter to the Smyrneans
ST	Summa Theologiae
Symp.	Symposium, Xenophon
Syr. Bar.	Syriac Baruch
Test Abr. (T.Ab.)	Testament of Abraham
TSanhedrin	Tosephta Sanhedrin
Tosef., Sanh	Tosephta Sanhedrin
Vulg.	Vulgate
Wsd	Wisdom of Solomon
Zohar Chadash (Rus)	Kallabah Zohar Chadash, Ruth

Modern Literature

AYB	Anchor Yale Bible Commentary
BAGD	A Greek–English Lexicon of the New Testament and Other Early Christian Literature, 2nd edn.
BDAG	A Greek–English Lexicon of the New Testament and Other Early Christian Literature, 3rd edn.
JBL	Journal of Biblical Literature
MM	James Moulton & George Milligan, The Vocabulary of the Greek New Testament, 1914–1929
TDNT	Theological Dictionary of the New Testament

Introduction

The Roman Catholic doctrine of indulgences emboldened Martin Luther to pen his ninety-five theses in Wittenberg in 1517, thereby inciting the Protestant Reformation. Yet, it was only near the end of his life that Luther (a Catholic Augustinian monk) abandoned the doctrine of purgatory.[1] It remained for Calvin to pronounce the death-sentence: "Purgatory is a deadly fiction of Satan, which nullifies the cross of Christ, inflicts unbearable contempt upon God's mercy, and overturns and destroys our faith."[2] By adhering to *sola Scriptura*, the Reformers accused Rome of teaching as doctrines of God the mere commandments of men (Matt 15:9).[3] Purgatory failed

---

[1] F.L. Cross and Elizabeth Livingston, eds. "Purgatory," in *The Oxford Dictionary of the Christian Church*, 3rd edn. (Oxford University Press: Oxford, 2005),1359.

[2] John Calvin, *Calvin: Institutes of the Christian Religion,* John T. McNeill, ed., Trans. by Ford L. Battles in the Library of Christian Classics (Philadelphia, PA: The Westminster Press, 1960), III.5.6; *Corpus Reformatorum* 28 (1863), 732: "purgatorium exitiale satanae esse commentum quod Christi crucem evacuat, quod contumeliam Dei misericordiae no ferendum irrogat, quod fidem nostram labefacit et evertit."

[3] W. A. Lambert, "Doctrines of Men..." in *Works of Martin Luther with Introduction and Notes* (Philadelphia, PA: Holman Co. and Castle Press, 1915), 431–455; Martin Luther, *The Essential Luther* by Tryntje Helfferick, ed. and trans. (Indianapolis, IN: Hackett, 2018), 261; John Calvin, *Institutes* IV.7.25, where he argues the Pope is the Antichrist; Maarten Stolk, "Calvin and Rome" in Herman Selderhuis, ed. *The Calvin Handbook*. Gerrit Sheeres, trans. (Grand Rapids, MI: Eerdmans, 2009), 104–112.

their primary test.[4]

Protestant Christians asserted that Rome manufactured indulgences and merits of martyrs, along with arbitrary lengths of time in purgatory—these doctrines could not be found in the Scriptures. The battle for forensic justification by faith alone demanded a rejection of any human merits that had been invented to reach heaven. Most modern Protestants would agree with Calvin's statement that the cross of Christ would be nullified by a purgatorial punishment as a requirement for entering heaven.

But does Calvin's statement sufficiently answer the question? Most Christians will admit that God disciplines and punishes his children on earth. Could God discipline or punish a Christian after death? If Christians must confess sins to be forgiven (1 John 1:9) and God disciplines his earthly children (Heb 12:5–11), how can we claim Jesus Christ paid ALL penalties or consequences for sin? If the Reformers reacted righteously against the abuses, did they neglect or reject an essential truth in the process of eliminating corrupted tradition? Is it possible for Protestant Christians to believe in postmortem purgation and punishment of the justified Christian while rejecting the medieval Catholic tradition of purgatory? I suggest the answer is, "Yes." If so, how does this correlate with Protestant imputed righteousness and forensic justification?

---

[4] The Roman Catholic Church accepts 2 Maccabees as part of the biblical canon, as will be discussed later.

Protestants for Purgatory

Numerous early church authors, including Augustine, used scripture to support the temporary punishment of righteous persons after death. Even more modern Protestant authors like Kittel warn, "The doctrine of judgment by works is the constant presupposition of the doctrine of justification by faith. Without it, the latter loses its seriousness and depth."[5] The famous Reformed theologian, Louis Berkhof contended, "there is no indication whatsoever that this [judgment of works] will be limited to the wicked."[6] The Protestant scholar Jerry Walls defends purgatory as essential in transforming Christians into God's likeness while maintaining freedom of choice (free will).[7]

It will come as a surprise for most evangelical Christians to learn C.S. Lewis believed in a type of Purgatory:

> I believe in Purgatory. Mind you, the Reformers had good reasons for throwing doubt on 'the Romish doctrine concerning Purgatory' as that Romish doctrine had then become. I don't mean merely the commercial scandal. ... Its pains do not bring us nearer to God, but make us forget Him. It is not a

---

[5] Gerhard Kittel and Gerhard Friedrich, eds. Vol. 3, "*κρίνω*," *Theological Dictionary of the New Testament*, 10th edn. (Grand Rapids, MI: Eerdmans, 1984), 938, footnote 68.

[6] Louis Berkhof, *Systematic Theology* (1938; reprint, Grand Rapids, MI: Eerdmans, 1982), 732–3.

[7] Jerry Walls, *Purgatory: The Logic of Total Transformation* (New York: Oxford University Press, 2012), 177–181.

place of purification but purely of retributive punishment.

Our souls *demand* Purgatory, don't they? Would it not break the heart if God said to us, 'It is true, my son, that your breath smells and your rags drip with mud and slime, but we are charitable here and no one will upbraid you with these things, nor draw away from you. Enter into the joy' ?

Should we not reply, 'With submission sir, and if there is no objection, I'd *rather* be cleaned first.'

'It may hurt, you know'—'Even so, sir.'

I assume that the process of purification will normally involve suffering. Partly from tradition; partly because most real good that has been done me in this life has involved it. But I don't think suffering is the purpose of the purgation. I can well believe that people neither much worse nor much better than I will suffer less than I or more. 'No nonsense about merit.' The treatment given will be the one required, whether it hurts little or much. (italics original)[8]

I concur with Lewis that the purpose of purgatory is not suffering, nor even retributive punishment (primarily). Rather, the purpose is God's mercy removing residual sinful patterns of

---

[8] C.S. Lewis, *Letters to Malcolm, Chiefly on Prayer* (United Kingdom: Harcourt Brace, 1963; reprint New York: HarperCollins, 1991), 144–46.

thinking and attitudes from the self. The process may be likened to a field hospital during wartime. The deeper the fragments of sin have penetrated into the body, the deeper the Surgeon must dig to remove them. Consequently, the deeper the surgical exploration, the more the patient experiences intense pain. Extracting shrapnel from beneath the skin will hurt, but removing shrapnel from deep inside an infected muscle along with fractured bone fragments will be excruciating. The more Christians have allowed sin to penetrate, permeate, and fester within the self, the more pain will be experienced.

Overview

This work will suggest Protestant Christians can indeed sustain a biblical belief in a postmortem purgation of sin and punishment, while avoiding the medieval Roman Catholic doctrine of purgatory; yet still embrace imputed righteousness and forensic justification. We will examine why God's purifying judgment after death is both biblical and essential to answering injustice. In contrast, most Protestant theologies inherently and unknowingly impugn the holy justice of God. This book will explain why and how this has happened.

We will first examine the historical beliefs in first century Judaism, then Roman Catholic purgatory, alongside Eastern Orthodox teachings, and finally Protestant views. We will evaluate the arguments of Protestants against posthumous punishment, then explain why these Protestant arguments are not valid. This will be followed by examining the Scriptures for evidences of a posthumous punishment, hidden to most Protestants through tradition We then review what the early church fathers and modern authors have written, explicating the implications of this doctrine. Postmortem purification of Christians has been classified as retributive versus restorative. We explore these competing concepts and discuss their implications. Practical examples will assist us in seeing an inherent injustice if God does not judge residual sin and character deficiencies. Without contradiction, even the Protestant "justification by faith alone" can be upheld while allowing a theology that God judges Christians' works with resulting payment (reward) or punishment of his children as a merciful God.

Most Christians will read this book with a strong bias toward their own tradition. I venture that of all the major traditional Christian groups—Roman Catholics, the Orthodox, and the Protestants—none will be completely satisfied with my conclusions on posthumous punishment by a merciful God. Nevertheless, explanations from Jewish rabbis, Catholic Popes, Orthodox theologians, and Protestant scholars will assist us in discovering a possible common ground. The common goal should be our transformation into the likeness of Christ.

We begin with a brief overview of the beliefs about God's dealings with persons after death in ancient Judaism during the time of Jesus and his apostles.

Chapter 1
Ancient Judaism's Views on Purgatory

Many readers will wonder why a book on God's punishment of *Christians* after death would begin with *Jewish* beliefs in ancient Judaism. Christianity began as a sect of Judaism. The underlying beliefs and traditions of the Jews influenced early Christianity. Jesus of Nazareth was a Jew. The Apostle Paul and the other apostles were all Jewish. The earliest Christian church was Jewish.[1] Schiffman notes, "In these years what would later be called the 'church' was in reality a Jewish sect."[2] Cohen explained, "Early Christianity ceased to be a Jewish sect when it ceased to observe Jewish practices."[3] Bauckham reminds us, "The first Christians did not derive their understanding of the afterlife from any specific Jewish group, such as the Pharisees or Essenes, but shared the views which had become general in the Judaism of their time."[4]

Therefore, it behooves us to possess at least some understanding of the ancient Jewish beliefs on the afterlife. This

---

[1] Peter Richardson, *Israel in the Apostolic Church* (Cambridge: Cambridge University Press, 1969), 195; cf., Acts 2.

[2] Lawrence Schiffman, *From Text to Tradition: A History of Second Temple & Rabbinic Judaism* (Hoboken, NJ: Ktav Publishing, 1991), 149.

[3] Shaye Cohen, *From the Maccabees to the Mishnah*, 2nd edn. (Louisville, KY: Westminster John Knox Press, 2006), 161.

[4] Richard Bauckham, *The Jewish World Around the New Testament* (Grand Rapids, MI: Baker Academic, 2008), 256.

does not imply that Jesus and the Apostles embraced the popular teachings of their period. Jesus frequently spoke of the kingdom of heaven and Gehenna. He often taught of payment for obedience and punishment for disobedience. But from what we have recorded in scripture, Jesus never mentioned a specific place called Purgatory. As we will see, this contrasts to the views of his era, views he repeatedly did not shy away from refuting.

Ancient Judaism taught Purgatory

The ancient Jewish religion taught a suffering after death prior to bodily resurrection. Rabbi Shammai (first century) taught the existence of Paradise, Gehenna, and an intermediate place for purging of sin.[5] Regarding the latter, "those whose virtues and sins counterbalance one another shall go down to Gehenna and float up and down until they rise purified; for of them it is said: 'I will bring the third part into the fire and refine them as silver is refined, and try them as gold is tried' [Zech. xiii. 9.]; also, 'He [the Lord] bringeth down to Sheol and bringeth up again'" (I Sam. ii. 6). Students of Hillel deemed God so merciful that "the intermediates do not descend into Gehenna" (Tosef., Sanh. xiii. 3).[6] So there was difference of opinion among leading first century rabbis.

---

[5] See the Babylonian Talmud, Rosh Hashanah 16b-17a.

[6] Kaufmann Kohler, "Purgatory," *Jewish Encyclopedia*, 1901–1907.

Regarding the length of time which purgatory lasts, Rabbi Akiva ben Yosef (ca.100 CE) opined twelve months, while Rabbi Johanan ben Nuri (ca.135 CE) limited purgatory to forty-nine days. Eternal torment in Gehenna was reserved for the great seducers and blasphemers (Tosef., Sanh. xiii. 4-5; R. H. 16b). Rosenthal suggests that although the rabbis were not in agreement about the length of stay in Gehenna or purgatory: "Part purgatory, part hell, part passageway, Gehenom becomes a place for punishment and redemption."[7]

The *Tanna Devei Eliyahu* records Rabbi Yochanan ben Zakkai (a first century rabbi) encountering a wicked man who is physically dead but walking. He is gathering wood for the fire intended for purgatorial suffering (burning in pain). The suffering will cease when the dead man's living son begins his religious studies at the age of five. When the child responds, "Bless Hashem [THE Name] Who is blessed," 'I will be released from judgment in Gehinnom.'"

In *Testament of Abraham* (ca.120 CE), a person's life is evaluated after death for righteous deeds and sins. A scale is used and then those works are tried by fire. If the deeds are burned then the soul goes to "the place of the wicked, a most bitter house of correction" (Recension A, XIII). Abraham asks

---

[7] Rachel Rosenthal, "Between This World and the Next: Rabbinic Visions of Purgatory" from Jewish Theological Seminary; https://www.jtsa.edu/torah/rabbinic-visions-of-purgatory/ ; Accessed 6 February 2023.

about a soul caught in the middle between paradise and the place of the wicked; because, his evil deeds are equal to his good deeds. Abraham offers intercessory prayer (along with the *Archistrategos* Michael) for that soul for the purpose of releasing it unto paradise prior to the "Judge of all" coming. One more good deed is lacking to release the soul to paradise. The person is subsequently allowed to enter Paradise through those prayers (XIV).[8]

The Zohar Chadash (*Rus* Ch.2) discusses Rabbi Zemira'ah helping to deliver a very wicked man from posthumous suffering by teaching Torah to his still living wicked son. Not only was his suffering lessened as his son progressed in his studies, the deceased was eventually admitted to the Garden of Eden among the righteous when the son began rabbinical studies.[9]

Gehenna (Purgatory) as a Physical Place

Gehenna as a physical location on earth for punishment of the deceased by fire is evident in numerous quotations.

> And Rabbi Yirmeya ben Elazar also said: There are three entrances to Gehenna, one in the wilderness,

---

[8] *The Testament of Abraham, Greek Recensions* in Texts & Translations, Pseudepigrapha Series 2, trans. Michael Stone (Missoula, MT: Society of Biblical Literature, 1972), 35–37.

[9] Bais Yechiel, *Above All Else: The Chofetz Chaim Anthology on TORAH STUDY*, vol.2, trans. Gavriel Rubin (Jerusalem: Feldheim Publishers, 2006), 147–148.

one in the sea, and one in Jerusalem. There is one entrance in the wilderness, as it is written with regard to Korah and his company: "And they, and all that appertained to them, went down alive into the pit [She'ol], and the earth closed upon them, and they perished from among the congregation" (Numbers 16:33). In the sea there is a second entrance to Gehenna, as it is written about Jonah in the fish's belly: "Out of the belly of the netherworld [She'ol] I cried, and You did hear my voice" (Jonah 2:3). And there is a third entrance to Gehenna in Jerusalem, as it is written: "Says the Lord, Whose fire is in Zion, and Whose furnace is in Jerusalem" (Isaiah 31:9). And it was taught in the school of Rabbi Yishmael: "Whose fire is in Zion," this is Gehenna; and "Whose furnace is in Jerusalem," this is an entrance to Gehenna. (Eruvin 19a)

Pirkei D'Rabbi Eliezer (10) also claims, "The whale that swallowed Jonah showed him [the entrance to] Gehinom." Midrash Rabba (Gen 48:8) states "G-d opened a hole into Gehinom that boiled all the water covering the earth." Shabbat 39a explains the hot springs in Tiberius are heated when they flow past Gehenna's entrance. "Rabbi Yosei said to them: 'That is not so. That incident involved derivatives of fire, as the hot springs of Tiberias are hot because they pass over the entrance to Gehenna. They are heated by hellfire, which is a bona fide underground fire.'"[10]

One rabbi opined that Jews would not be hurt by the fire of Gehenna if Abraham rescued them from that place.

> However, that which is written: "Those who pass through the valley of weeping" (Psalms 84:7), which implies that the sinners nonetheless descend to Gehenna, should be explained as follows: There it speaks of those who are liable at that time for punishment in Gehenna, but our father Abraham comes and raises them up and receives them. He does not leave the circumcised behind and allow them to enter Gehenna, except for a Jew who had relations with a gentile woman, in punishment for which his foreskin is drawn, and our father Abraham does not recognize him as one of his descendants. (Eruvin 19a)

A Cambridge Tyndale scholar has provided his analysis of Jewish thought during the time of Christ's ministry. Instone-Brewer argues that Jesus and the Gospels offer only two options in the afterlife—an eternal hell or blissful heaven, thereby rejecting an intermediate place of purgatory.

---

[10] See also Eliezer Danzinger, "Is there any sort of Purgatory or Satan in Jewish teachings?" *Chabad.org* https://www.chabad.org/library/article_cdo/aid/512017/jewish/Is-there-any-sort-of-Purgatory-or-Satan-in-Jewish-teachings.htm#footnote1a512017 ; Accessed 15 May 2023.

Rabbinic literature indicates that the theology of hell was subject to debate and development during the early first century. The Pharisaic/rabbinic schools concluded that God's judgment would divide people into three groups: the good, the evil and the in-between. They agreed that this in-between group would go to heaven, but some of them (including Shammaites) thought they would visit hell for some punishment first. Others (including Hillelites) believed the in-between group would not fully enjoy the benefits of heaven, at least for some time.

The literature of Qumran and the Gospels both emphatically rejected these new ideas in the rabbinic theology of hell. Both sets of literature emphasized that there were only two groups at judgment day, and that the effects of hell are eternal because the destruction is utterly complete. The gospels added a new teaching: that ordinary Jews can go to hell if they do not repent, and that even gross sinners can go to heaven if they repent.[11]

His assessment, in my view, is accurate. The rabbis taught a literal physical location together with determined times of

---

[11] David Instone-Brewer, "Chapter 14: Eternal Punishment in First Century Jewish Thought" in eds. Christopher Date and Ron Highfield, *A Consuming Passion: Essays on Hell and Immortality in Honor of Edward Fudge* (Eugene, OR: Pickwick Publications, 2015), 215–243 at 241. See also School Disputes in *Tosephta Sanhedrin* 13.3.

temporary punishment, similar to the medieval Roman Catholics. This physical place cannot be found in the Hebrew or Christian scriptures (without allegorizing). To my knowledge, there is no evidence for any ancient teaching that purgatory was a *permanent* alternate destination from paradise or Gehenna. Nevertheless, outside of the Gospels, the NT epistles repeatedly warn God's own children of his temporary judgment upon their sin that cannot be reasonably limited to this life on earth without impugning God's justice (as we will later discover).

The Omission of a Temporary Gehenna

As he was dying, Rabbi Yohanan ben Zakkai (ca.70 CE) expressed his concern over his eternal state.

> But now that I am being brought before the King of kings of kings, the Holy One, blessed be he, who endures forever and ever, who, should he be angry with me, will be angry forever, and if he should imprison me, will imprison me forever, and if he should put me to death, whose sentence of death is for eternity, and whom I cannot appease with the right words or bribe with money, and not only so, but before me are two paths, one to the Garden of Eden and the other to Gehenna, and I do not know by which path I shall be brought, and should I not weep?" They said to him, "Our master, bless us." He said to them, "May it be God's will that the fear of Heaven be upon you as much as the fear of mortal

man." His disciples said, "Just so much?" He said to them, "Would that it were that much." (Mishnah, Berakhot 4:2, I.2)

This rabbi does not mention Gehenna as purgatory. Should this be surprising since we have evidence that belief in a temporary intermediate state was commonplace during this period? No. He expressed anxiety over possible *eternal* punishment, not temporary punishment. For these first century rabbis, only two *permanent eternal* destinations existed.

This might be compared to someone asking me what I did on Friday night. I would respond, 'I went to watch my favorite sports team play their best ballgame of the year.' I would not mention that on the way to the game I stopped at a fast food restaurant for a quick meal. The emphasis is on the major event. Similarly, Jesus and the Gospels speak of *eternal* destinies, not *temporary* purification or punishment after death. The epistles (written later) explain numerous detailed doctrines in the teachings of Jesus that were not recorded in the gospels.

Atonement for the Dead

This concept does not appear in early Judaism until the Midrash. The Sifré to Deuteronomy (Tannaitic Midrash, ca.280–300) mentions atonement for the dead:

And the Cohanim say (*Ibid.* 8) "Forgive Your people, Israel, which You have redeemed, O L-rd."

אשר פדית ה'. מלמד שכפרה זו מכפרת על יוצאי מצרים
"which You have redeemed": This teaches that this
atonement atones for those that left Egypt.

כפר לעמך. אלו החיים. "Forgive Your people": These
are the living;

אשר פדית, אלו המתים, מגיד שהמתים צריכים כפרה. נמצינו
למדים ששופך דמים חוטא עד יוצאי מצרים,

These are the dead, whereby we are taught that the
dead, too, require atonement, and that this atonement
atones until the exodus from Egypt, and that the
spiller of blood sins (retroactively) until the exodus
from Egypt. (Sifrei Devarim 21:7 [210])

There is no evidence that the Jews viewed 2 Maccabees 12 as
demonstrating atonement for the dead, so this will be discussed
later.

Modern Judaism

Wolfson describes the modern Jewish memorial service.

Originally, Yizkor was recited only on Yom Kippur.
Its primary purpose was to honor the deceased by
committing to giving *tzedakah* [charity] in their
memory, on the theory that the good deeds of the
survivors elevate the souls of the departed. It also

enhanced the chances for personal atonement by doing a deed of lovingkindness.[12]

Jews pray for the dead. "Yizkor is a prayer that is said on the anniversary of a death. It is a time to remember those who have died, and to give thanks for their lives; it also serves as an opportunity to ask God for forgiveness for any wrongs they may have committed while they were alive."[13]

"The *Kel Maleh Rachamim* [Prayer of Mercy] is a plea that the soul of the loved one be granted proper rest. Its recitation is a central part of a modern Jewish funeral or memorial service. It's also recited or sung at grave visitations and anniversaries of a death."[14] The Prayer of Mercy for the deceased asks:

> G-d, full of mercy, who dwells in the heights, provide a sure rest upon the Divine Presence's wings, within the range of the holy, pure and glorious, whose shining resemble the sky's, to the soul of [name of the person], [son/daughter] of [name of the person's

---

[12] Ron Wolfson, "Yizkor: The Jewish Memorial Service" https://www.myjewishlearning.com/article/yizkor-the-memorial-service/ ; Accessed 14 May 2023.

[13] Churchreaders, "Jewish Prayers for the Dead in English," https://churchreaders.com/jewish-prayer-for-the-dead-in-english/ ; Accessed 24 July 2022.

[14] "Jewish Funeral Prayers and Quotes," https://www.dignitymemorial.com/support-friends-and-family/jewish-funeral-prayers ; Accessed 14 May 2023.

father] for a charity was given to the memory of [his/her] soul. [For the sake of the charity which they gave to commemorate her soul, let her rest be in the Garden of Eden.] Therefore, the Master of Mercy will protect [him/her] forever, from behind the hiding of his wings, and will tie [his/her] soul with the rope of life. The Everlasting is [his/her] heritage, and [he/she] shall rest peacefully upon [his/her] bed [lying place]; and let us say: Amen.[15]

Conclusion

Rabbinic Judaism during the time of Jesus' ministry taught a literal physical location of eternal bliss or punishment (Paradise or Gehenna). There also existed a temporary place of purification or punishment, either in a separate distinct Gehenna (purgatory) or a temporary stay in the eternal Gehenna (hell). Specific lengths of stay in "purgatory" for sins were opined by some rabbis. Evidence exists that prayers were made for the dead and these prayers were believed to assist the deceased in attaining a better afterlife. Atonement for the deceased is also attested by the third century. This was the Jewish culture in which Jesus of Nazareth and his apostles lived and taught.

---

[15] *Kel Maleh Rachamim* (Prayer of Mercy) https://www.shiva.com/learning-center/prayers/kel-maleh-rachamim ; Accessed 14 May 2023.

Chapter 2

The Roman Catholic Doctrine of Purgatory

Early Catholicism

The most ancient writers in the Catholic church taught that Christians were purged of sin by God. This involved suffering for unforgiven sins after death.[1] (Because many of the early church fathers supported this view, this topic will be detailed in a later chapter.) These early views could be considered consistent with the modern Roman Catholic purgatory, but these earliest writers did not include specific lengths of time suffering for particular sins. Formal indulgences were absent.

The earliest comment on Christian punishment after death comes from Tertullian (ca.200) referencing Matthew 5:25–26. "Settle matters quickly with your adversary who is taking you to court. Do it while you are still together on the way, or your adversary may hand you over to the judge, and the judge may hand you over to the officer, and you may be thrown into prison. Truly I tell you, you will not get out until you have paid the last penny." (NET) Tertullian believed this passage proved Jesus taught posthumous punishment.

---

[1] "Purgatory," *The Oxford Dictionary*, 1358.

> Inasmuch as we understand "the prison" pointed out
> in the Gospel to be Hades, and as we also interpret
> "the uttermost farthing" to mean the very smallest
> offense which has to be recompensed there before the
> resurrection, no one will hesitate to believe that the
> soul undergoes in Hades some compensatory
> discipline, without prejudice to the full process of the
> resurrection, when the recompense will be
> administered through the flesh besides. (Tertullian, *A
> Treatise on the Soul*, 58)

Prison has been compared to the use of the same Greek word (φυλακῇ) in 1 Peter 3:19 about the deceased in Sheol (the place of the dead). Tertullian uses this passage to teach a preliminary expiatory suffering prior to the final judgment in the resurrected body.

The Decian persecution (250 CE) caused many Christians to obtain a *libellus*, an official signed document stating that the bearer had sacrificed to the Roman gods in front of the Roman magistrate in compliance with Roman law. Christians who did not sacrifice were martyred (e.g., Pope Fabian), imprisoned, or went into hiding (e.g., Cyprian of Carthage). Christians who sacrificed were called *lapsi* and were denied readmittance into the Christian community. Specific severe acts of penance were required for that Christian who denied Christ. This led to the *lapsi* obtaining a second *libellus*, allegedly signed by a Christian martyr, remitting the punishment of that sin and allowing readmittance to the Church. This appears to be the first time something similar to an indulgence can be found within Christianity.[2] But it must be noted that these *libelli* were not official and were not Catholic indulgences in the modern sense. Earliest Christianity does not mention specific indulgences that remove God's temporal punishment on sin for living and dead Christians.[3]

Penance

In contrast, penance was practiced from the beginning of the church. The focus of penance was reconciliation to the life of the community. Less serious sins required confession and penance until the sinner was publicly restored back into the community by the bishop (Ignatius, *Philad.*3.2, 8.1; Polycarp, *Phil.* 8.1).[4] Christians who committed a more serious sin were allowed to participate in the meeting but removed prior to

---

[2] Tertullian (ca.200) does mention obtaining "peace" from martyrs in prison that could be transferred to others (*To Martyrs*; *Ad martyres*, *Patrologia Latina* 1, 016–0220).

[3] According to the *Catechism of the Catholic Church*, an indulgence is "a remission before God of the temporal punishment due to sins whose guilt has already been forgiven, which the faithful Christian who is duly disposed gains under certain prescribed conditions through the action of the Church which, as the minister of redemption, dispenses and applies with authority the treasury of the satisfactions of Christ and all of the saints. An indulgence is partial or plenary according as it removes either part or all of the temporal punishment due to sin. Indulgences may be applied to the living or the dead" (Part 2, Section 2, Chapter 2, Article 4, X. Indulgences). See Apostolic Constitution of Pope Paul VI, *Indulgentiarum doctrina*: *Whereby the Revision of Sacred Indulgences is Promulgated*, Norms 1, 2, and 3, (1966).

[4] L. Michael White, "Penance," in Everett Ferguson, ed. *Encyclopedia of Early Christianity*, 2nd edn. (New York: Routledge, 1999), 891.

partaking of the Eucharist (Ignatius, *Smyr.* 4.1).[5] Tertullian, a lawyer and early church father, introduced the legal basis for penance in a Latin word play. Since Christ's death obtained forgiveness of sins by compensation to God, a release from the penalty (*poena*) of sin could occur by the compensatory exchange of penitence (*paenitentium*) by the sinner (*On Repentance*; *De poenitentia* 6).[6] This became the basis for a release from temporal punishment.

But some sins like murder and adultery were too serious to allow penance—God would need to decide that person's fate (Tertullian, *De paenitentia* 5).[7] A second baptism may have even been practiced as part of penance.[8] After the Decian persecution in 250 CE, specific prescribed acts of penance for readmittance to the Church were commonplace and often extreme. Local bishops disagreed as to whether penance could be performed only once (e.g., Hippolytus, Clement of Alexandria) or numerous times after the initial Christian baptism that washed away sin.[9]

---

[5] Henry Chadwick, *The Early Church* (New York: Dorset Press, 1967), 32–33.

[6] White, "Penance," 891.

[7] J. Patout Burns, "On Rebaptism: Social Organization in the Third Century Church," *JECS* 1 (1993): 367–403.

[8] Allan Fitzgerald, "Penance," in Susan Harvey and David Hunter, eds. *The Oxford Handbook of Christian Studies* (Oxford: Oxford University Press, 2008), 796–7; Tertullian, *De paenitentia* 7–10.

[9] White, "Penance," 891.

It was not until 517 at the Council of Epaone (eastern France) that these extreme penances were reduced. Later, Irish priests developed handbooks recommending milder specific acts for penance that allowed sinners to return to full participation in the Christian community. This was named *tariffed penance* in the Penitential Books which contained detailed taxes or tariffs prescribed for each sin.[10] When Gregory the Great died in 604, the Catholic penitential system contained most of its modern elements, including the three stages of "conversion in the mind, confession with the mouth, and vindication from sin" (*Exp. in Prim. Reg.* 6.2). Gregory more formally established that penance would continue after death (in a type of purgatory) by adopting St. Augustine's distinction that baptism was for original sin in infants while penance was for post-baptismal sin in older children and adults (*Hom. in Evang.* 19.4; *Dial.* 4.25, 39, 48, 56).

The "penitential works" were prayer, fasting, and almsgiving. These could be interpreted as indications of the reversal of the sin and also as the "means of punishment" (satisfaction) that the penitent voluntarily accepted in order to replace any need for divine punishment. Citing Matthew 12:32 as evidence, Gregory the Great (540–604 CE) was the first to

---

[10] Cyril Vogel, "Penitence," in Angelo Di Berardino, ed. *Encyclopedia of the Early Church.* Vol. 2, trans. Adrian Walford (Cambridge: James Clarke & Co., 1992); Diarmond MacCullough, *A History of Christianity* (London: Penguin Books, 2009), 333.

provide an explanation for praying for the dead in purgatory during the official services. In Matthew 12:32 Christ warns, "Whoever speaks a word against the Son of Man will be forgiven. But whoever speaks against the Holy Spirit will not be forgiven, either in this age or in the age to come." (WEB) That some sins would not be forgiven in the age to come (Matt 12:32) implied some sins could be forgiven after death (through Christians praying for the dead).

Gregory followed Augustine's teaching, who emphasized the giving of alms to the poor in the name of the dead as a means of attaining divine mercy (because it was a form of repentance for those who remained alive). The "work of satisfaction" had to be done for the benefit of another Christian, who would then join the penitents in the plea for divine forgiveness. This almsgiving was not paid to the church but to God, by giving directly to the poor. (Matt 25:40) Gregory explained:

> But yet we must believe that before the day of judgment there is a Purgatory fire for certain small sins: because our Saviour saith, *that he which speaketh blasphemy against the h[H]oly Ghost, that it shall not be forgiven him, neither in this world, nor in the world to come.* **Out of which sentence we learn, that some sins are forgiven in this world, and some other may be pardoned in the next**: for that which is denied concerning one sin, is

consequently understood to be granted touching some other. But yet this, as I said, we have not to believe but only concerning little and very small sins, as, for example, daily idle talk, immoderate laughter, negligence in the care of our family (which kind of offences scarce can they avoid, that know in what sort sin is to be shunned), ignorant errors in matters of no great weight: all which sins be punished after death, if men procured not pardon and remission for them in their lifetime: for when St. Paul saith, that *Christ is the foundation:* and by and by addeth: *And if any man build upon this foundation gold, silver, precious stones, wood, hay, stubble: the work of every one, of what kind it is, the fire shall try. If any man's work abide which he built thereupon, he shall receive reward; if any man's work burn, he shall suffer detriment, but himself shall be saved, yet so as by fire.* For although these words may be understood of the fire of tribulation, which men suffer in this world: yet if any will interpret them of the fire of Purgatory, which shall be in the next life: then must he carefully consider, that the Apostle said not that he may be saved by fire, that buildeth upon this foundation **iron, brass, or lead, that is, the greater sort of sins**, and therefore more hard, and consequently not remissible in that place: but wood, hay, stubble, that is, little and very light sins, which the fire doth easily consume. Yet we have here

> further to consider, that none can be there purged, no,
> not for the least sins that be, unless in his lifetime he
> deserved by virtuous works to find such favour in that
> place. (*Dial.* 4, 39; bold added)[11]

Moreira identified Bede the Venerable (ca.725) as a key figure in placing purgatory as an official orthodox doctrine of the Church. "This was Bede's contribution: to frame purgatory as an orthodox response to heresy."[12] This theology would be strengthened in the Crusades.

Middle Ages and the Reformation

In 1063, the First Crusade prompted Pope Alexander II to pronounce a remission of punishment if Christians fought the Moors. Under Pope Urban II in 1095, the first plenary (complete or full) indulgence was created.[13] A plenary indulgence removes all temporal punishment of the sinner by God rather than only a partial removal. Christians who confessed sins in the sacrament of penance and then went to war as a crusader obtained full pardon from temporal punishment of sins after death. This continued in subsequent crusades with other popes

---

[11] Gregory changes Paul's words by substituting "iron, brass, or lead" for "gold, silver, precious stones (χρυσόν, ἄργυρον, λίθους τιμίους)." His claim from this text that greater sins are not forgivable versus lesser sins that are forgivable after death is not found in the text itself.

[12] Isabel Moreira, *Heaven's Purge: Purgatory in Late Antiquity* (New York: Oxford University Press, 2010), 159.

[13] sv. "plenary indulgence," *The Oxford Dictionary*, 1310.

such as Gregory VIII in 1187, who authored the bull *Audita tremendi*, pronouncing plenary indulgences for Christians who hired another person to fight the crusade for them.[14]

This practice follows the teaching of St. Anselm (1033–1109) of sinners paying the debt to God for violations of the commandments. Both martyrs and saints had performed an excess of good works they could share with others, because their violations had already been paid. This surplus "merit" of good works from a particular saint or martyr could benefit the penitent Christian who performed penitential works, if approved by the Pope, who opened this treasury of merit (excess good works) with his keys.

Thomas Aquinas wrote his *Summa Theologiae* from 1265–1274. The Supplement reads, "Wherefore those who deny Purgatory speak against the justice of God: for which reason such a statement is erroneous and contrary to faith. Hence Gregory of Nyssa, after the words quoted above, adds: 'This we preach, holding to the teaching of truth, and this is our belief; this the universal Church holds, by praying for the dead that they may be loosed from sins.' This cannot be understood except as referring to Purgatory: and whosoever resists the authority of the Church, incurs the note of heresy" (ST Supplement,

---

[14] Richard Price, "Informal Penance in Early Medieval Christendom," *Studies in Church History*, Vol.40: Retribution, Repentance, and Reconciliation (2004): 29–38.

Appendix II, Q3).[15] Aquinas made a distinction between the eternal fire of punishment in hell from the temporary purging fire of purgatory that existed in a different location.

Penance

The Catholic Church in the medieval and Reformation eras assigned definitive lengths of time in a location called purgatory for certain sins and corresponding reduction of time for certain indulgences. Penance penalties were often extreme. Dante's "Purgatorio" in *The Divine Comedy* (*ca.* 1308–1320) reinforces these ideas. Catherine of Genoa's (d.1515) *Treatise on Purgatory* received acclaim due to her own experience in a mystical visit—a direct encounter with purgatory.

> They cannot see that they are in pain because of their sin .... I believe no happiness can be found worthy to be compared with that of a soul in Purgatory except that of the saints in Paradise; and day by day this happiness grows as God flows into these souls, more and more as the hindrance to His entrance is consumed. Sin's rust is the hindrance, and the fire burns the rust away so that more and more the soul opens itself up to the divine inflowing. ... But, on the

---

[15] "Gregory of Nyssa understood after-death suffering as purificatory of the mind/soul to prepare it for the fuller knowledge of God." In personal communication 20 September 2023, Professor J. Patout Burns has kindly noted this misunderstanding by Aquinas when referring to Gregory of Nyssa's opinions because he used incomplete treatises or paraphrased Aquinas.

other hand, they endure a pain so extreme that no tongue can be found to tell it. (*Treatise on Purgatory* I–II)

"Professional pardoners" selling indulgences in the sixteenth century led to such abuse and misconduct that it incited the Protestant Reformation by Martin Luther. The Council of Trent responded with its famous Decree on Justification: "If anyone says that after the reception of the grace of justification the guilt is so remitted and the debt of eternal punishment so blotted out to every repentant sinner, that no debt of temporal punishment remains to be discharged either in this world or in purgatory before the gates of heaven can be opened, let him be anathema."[16]

In 1567, Pope Pius V finally prohibited the sale of indulgences for money.[17] The Pope then approved the Council of Trent's revision of indulgences that included offering indulgences to persons indirectly.

Modern Catholicism

First collected in 1807, a handbook on indulgences named the *Raccolta* (Collection) was printed for lay persons to have a definitive list of all of the indulgences offered by

---

[16] Council of Trent, Sixth Session, 13 January 1547, can. 30 from *The Canons and Decrees of the Council of Trent*, trans. H. J. Schroeder (Rockford, Ill.: TAN Books and Publishers, 1978).

[17] "Indulgences," *The Oxford Dictionary*, 835.

previous Popes.[18] This included prayers and pious works along with assigned lengths of time remitted for each act. For example, reciting the "Our Father" seven times and one "Ave Maria" on the same day would remove one hundred earthly days from purgatory. When the Anglican priest and theologian John Henry Newman converted to Catholicism, an influential fictional poem about purgatory was produced named *The Dream of Gerontius* (1865). This was even set to music by the famous English composer Edward Elgar. "In the early 20th century, St. Pius X [d. 1914] connected a partial indulgence to kissing the [Pope's] Fisherman's Ring."[19] In 1967, Pope Paul VI wrote *Indulgentiarum Doctrina*: "If the faithful offer indulgences in suffrage for the dead, they cultivate charity in an excellent way and while raising their minds to heaven, they bring a wiser order into the things of this world." Indulgences are still provided to reduce the time of posthumous suffering through acts such as reciting specified prayers or visiting holy sites. Specific practices can be found in the 1999 *Manual of Indulgences*. Only the payment of debt can be influenced by indulgences. The second requirement—the pain of personal

---

[18] William Kent, "Indulgences," in *The Catholic Encyclopedia*, Vol. 7. (New York: Robert Appleton Company, 1910); http://www.newadvent.org/cathen/07783a.htm ; Accessed 16 November 2022; See also *Oxford Dictionary Church*, "Raccolta," 1370.

[19] *The Catholic World Report*, "Why do people kiss the pope's ring?" March 27, 2019. https://www.catholicworldreport.com/2019/03/27/why-do-people-kiss-the-popes-ring/; Accessed 16 November 2022.

purification occurring naturally during the healing from disordered affections—is remedial and not influenced by indulgences.

The Protestant talking points against purgatory often exceed formal Catholic teaching. The massive *Catechism of the Catholic Church* contains only three short paragraphs on purgatory, including two citations from early church fathers (ECFs), and these are quite general in nature.[20]

> 1030 All who die in God's grace and friendship, but still imperfectly purified, are indeed assured of their eternal salvation; but after death they undergo purification, so as to achieve the holiness necessary to enter the joy of heaven.

> 1031 The Church gives the name Purgatory to this final purification of the elect, which is entirely different from the punishment of the damned. The Church formulated her doctrine of faith on Purgatory especially at the Councils of Florence and Trent. The tradition of the Church, by reference to certain texts of Scripture, speaks of a cleansing fire:

>> As for certain lesser faults, we must believe that, before the Final Judgment, there is a purifying fire. He who is truth says that

---

[20] *Catechism of the Catholic Church*, 2nd edn. (Vatican: Libreria Editrice Vaticana, 2019), 268–69 (1030–1032).

whoever utters blasphemy against the Holy Spirit will be pardoned neither in this age nor in the age to come [Matt 12:31]. From this sentence we understand that certain offenses can be forgiven in this age, but certain others in the age to come. [St. Gregory the Great, *Dial* 4:39, PL 77:396]

1032 This teaching is also based on the practice of prayer for the dead, already mentioned in Sacred Scripture: "Therefore Judas Maccabeus made atonement for the dead, that they might be delivered from their sin." [2 Macc 12:46] From the beginning the Church has honored the memory of the dead and offered prayers in suffrage for them, above all the Eucharistic sacrifice, so that, thus purified, they may attain the beatific vision of God. The Church also commends almsgiving, indulgences, and works of penance undertaken on behalf of the dead:

Let us help and commemorate them. If Job's sons were purified by their father's sacrifice [Job 1:5], why would we doubt that our offerings for the dead bring them some consolation? Let us not hesitate to help those who have died and to offer our prayers for them. [St. John Chrysostom, Hom in 1 Cor 41.5 (on 1 Cor 15:46); PG 61:361]

Therefore, there are three possible outcomes of persons' futures upon death. Those few persons who vehemently reject God go directly to Hell, those few in intimate communion with God proceed directly to heaven, and the vast majority of people must be cleansed before entering God's presence. Purgatory is not a permanent intermediate place between hell and heaven. All persons who enter purgatory will eventually enter heaven. For Catholics, "Justification is not only the remission of sins, but also the sanctification and renewal of the interior man." (CCC 2nd edn., 3.3.2, 1989). This purifying of Christians must be accomplished either in this life or the next. Both are usually required.

The 2005 *Compendium of the Catechism of the Catholic Church* 210 and 211 teach, "Purgatory is the state of those who die in God's friendship, assured of their eternal salvation, but who still have need of purification to enter into the happiness of heaven." "Because of the communion of saints, the faithful who are still pilgrims on earth are able to help the souls in purgatory by offering prayers in suffrage for them, especially the Eucharistic sacrifice. They also help them by almsgiving, indulgences, and works of penance." Yet, if someone commits a mortal sin this demands the eternal punishment of Hell without any possible recourse.

The purgatorial purification does not occur as a result of God's vengeance but occurs as a natural result of sin itself. Pope Benedict XVI wrote: "Purgatory is not, as Tertullian thought, some kind of supra-worldly concentration camp where man is forced to undergo punishment in a more or less arbitrary fashion. Rather it is the inwardly necessary process of transformation in which a person becomes capable of Christ, capable of God, and thus capable of unity with the whole communion of saints."[21] This follows Pope Paul VI in his *Indulgentiarum Doctrina* of 1967, confirming that neither scripture nor tradition define specific lengths or periods of suffering.[22]

In 1968, to counteract the widespread abuse of indulgences, Pope Paul VI established the *Enchiridion Indulgentiarum* (Handbook of Indulgences) which limited and codified only certain indulgences with prayers accompanied by good works of piety, charity, and penance. Both partial and plenary indulgences appear. The *Enchiridion of Indulgences* decreased the number of various indulgences from 491 to 70 and specifically clarifies, "without any determination of days or years."[23] Pope John Paul II on August 4, 1999 explained that

---

[21] Joseph Ratzinger (Pope Benedict XVI) *Eschatologie–Tod und ewiges Leben* (Regensburg: Friedrich Pustet, 1977), repr. as *Eschatology: Death and the Eternal Life* 2nd edn., trans. Michael Waldstein (Washington, DC: CUA Press, 2007), 230.

[22] Pope Paul VI, *Indulgentiarum Doctrina* 12 (1967), https://www.vatican.va/content/paul-vi/en/apost_constitutions/documents/hf_p-vi_apc_01011967_indulgentiarum-doctrina.html ; Accessed 19 February 2019.

[23] *Enchiridion of Indulgences* (1968): 6, "Norms on Indulgences 5" citing "N. 4 of The Doctrine of Indulgences."

purgatory, "does not indicate a place, but a condition of existence. Those who, after death, exist in a state of purification, are already in the love of Christ who removes from them the remnants of imperfection." [24] This concerns the corrective removal of disordered affections adhering to the person that must be purged and purified prior to intimacy with God.

Modern Catholicism teaches that indulgences do not forgive the guilt of sin, nor do they deliver from eternal punishment. That must have already occurred in the sacraments of confession and penance. Rather, indulgences assist in the purification and correction of the sinner rather than the payment of a debt. Performing these good works is equivalent to the Protestant sanctification process. Indulgences do not guarantee a soul's salvation or permit future sin without consequences. The Church recognizes that it has no jurisdiction over deceased Christians. Therefore, indulgences on behalf of the dead merely request God to accept them, rather than guaranteeing God will lessen or waive punishment.

Penance

One difference between modern and ancient penance concerns the private nature of modern penance versus public penance required in ancient times. Also, the penitential acts required of

---

[24] Pope John Paul II, http://w2.vatican.va/content/john-paul-ii/en/audiences/1999/documents/hf_jp-ii_aud_04081999.html ; Accessed 19 February 2019.

the penitent today are less extreme (no flagellation) and monetary gifts can redeem penitential acts, which was unknown in early Christianity. Modern specified indulgences were absent, as were specified lengths of time in purgatory being remitted. Early Christians often wrote about a purgatorial fire purging Christians of sin sometime between death and resurrection, or at the judgment. The lengths of time during which a person suffered punishment were usually unspecified, but some authors mention a range from instantaneous to weeks. Le Goff claims that prior to 1107 CE there was no formal doctrine of a place called Purgatory.[25] However, the practices of praying for the dead, penance for post-baptismal sins, and the widespread expectation of Christians that after death they would suffer God's fire for purging of sin were all common ancient Christian concepts.

Modern Roman Catholic purgatory has reverted to its earliest forms as an unspecified process of purifying the Christian of sins in preparation to experience God fully. Purgatory is a process—not a place. The sacrifice of Jesus Christ has provided forgiveness of sin preventing a residency in hell. However, the process of actually purging the sin and repaying the sinner for good works and evil works remains at the judgment so that the person may experience the beatific vision (heaven to Protestants). In the words of Pope Benedict

---

[25] Jacques Le Goff, *The Birth of Purgatory*, trans. Arthur Goldhammer (Chicago: University of Chicago Press, 1984), 135.

XVI,

Paul begins by saying that Christian life is built upon a common foundation: Jesus Christ. This foundation endures. If we have stood firm on this foundation and built our life upon it, we know that it cannot be taken away from us even in death. Then Paul continues: "Now if any one builds on the foundation with gold, silver, precious stones, wood, hay, straw—each man's work will become manifest; for the Day will disclose it, because it will be revealed with fire, and the fire will test what sort of work each one has done. If the work which any man has built on the foundation survives, he will receive a reward. If any man's work is burned up, he will suffer loss, though he himself will be saved, but only as through fire" (*1 Cor* 3:12-15). In this text, it is in any case evident that our salvation can take different forms, that some of what is built may be burned down, that in order to be saved we personally have to pass through "fire" so as to become fully open to receiving God and able to take our place at the table of the eternal marriage-feast.[26]

He elaborated on this idea with the fire not arising from a purgatorial location but rather the fire being Christ himself.

---

[26] Pope Benedict XVI, *Spe salvi* (Encyclical Letter of November 30, 2007), 46.

Some recent theologians are of the opinion that the fire which both burns and saves is Christ himself, the Judge and Saviour. The encounter with him is the decisive act of judgment. Before his gaze all falsehood melts away. This encounter with him, as it burns us, transforms and frees us, allowing us to become truly ourselves. All that we build during our lives can prove to be mere straw, pure bluster, and it collapses. Yet in the pain of this encounter, when the impurity and sickness of our lives become evident to us, there lies salvation. His gaze, the touch of his heart heals us through an undeniably painful transformation "as through fire". But it is a blessed pain, in which the holy power of his love sears through us like a flame, enabling us to become totally ourselves and thus totally of God. In this way the inter-relation between justice and grace also becomes clear: the way we live our lives is not immaterial, but our defilement does not stain us for ever if we have at least continued to reach out towards Christ, towards truth and towards love. Indeed, it has already been burned away through Christ's Passion. At the moment of judgment we experience and we absorb the overwhelming power of his love over all the evil in the world and in ourselves. The pain of love becomes our salvation and our joy. (*Spe salvi*)

Conclusion

The modern Roman Catholic teachings on purgatory are often mischaracterized by many Protestants. We will see that both the Scriptures and historical theology support some type of purging of sin for Christians after death.

Prayers for the dead may not secure forgiveness or eternal bliss for the departed. They are an expression of love because the loved one continues to exist while those who remain grieve. The United States Conference of Catholic Bishops states:

> Because of our belief not only in the immortality of the soul, but also in the resurrection of the body, the Church professes hope in the face of death, and acts with charity in the funeral rites. The Church provides a number of prayers for the faithful to offer both to accompany the dying of a loved one and to strengthen our faith upon their death. Through private prayer and public funeral rites we strengthen our faith and hope, comfort those who mourn, and bury the bodily remains of the deceased with care befitting what was the Temple of the Holy Spirit.[27]

> Remember our brothers and sisters who have gone to their rest in the hope of rising again; bring them and

---

[27] USCCB, "Bereavement and Funerals," https://www.usccb.org/prayer-and-worship/sacraments-and-sacramentals/bereavement-and-funerals ; Accessed 9 May 2023.

all the departed into the light of your presence (Eucharistic Prayer II, Commemoration of the Dead).

Look with love on our dying brother (sister) and make him (her) one with your Son in his suffering and death that, sealed with the blood of Christ, he (she) may come before you free from sin (Mass for the Dying, Opening Prayer).

Lord Jesus, holy and compassionate, forgive **N. [Name]** his (her) sins. By dying you opened the gates of life for those who believe in you: do not let our brother (sister) be parted from you, but by your glorious power give him (her) light, joy, and peace in heaven, where you live for ever and ever.[28]

Praying for the dead accentuates the reality of the afterlife while providing comfort to the grieving. To modify the infamous rhyme of Luther's nemesis, Johann Tetzel (1465–1519), "As soon as a prayer in the parish pew rings/ the soul from purgatory springs." Modern Roman Catholics do not subscribe to that caricature. A more detailed evaluation of the Roman Catholic position appears in Chapter 7.

We now explore the views of the Orthodox Church.

---

[28] Catholic News Agency, "Prayers for the Dead," https://www.catholicnewsagency.com/resource/243349/prayers-for-the-dead ; Accessed 9 May 2023.

Chapter 3
The Eastern Orthodox
Doctrine of Purgatory

In the Eastern Orthodox Church there does not exist a Roman Curia that helps define doctrine or policy uniformly for the Church; nor, is there any papal primacy and infallibility. Therefore, the Eastern church allows more diverse doctrinal beliefs. But regarding purgatory, Louth explained, "The notion of purgatory, as a kind of third place in the afterlife alongside heaven and hell, has never had any place in Orthodox theology".[1] Nevertheless, we find a purification of the soul after death, prayers for the dead, penance, absolution of sins, and a type of indulgences that are (or were) practiced.

The Early Orthodox

The Eastern Church from the earliest times believed all Christians require constant purging of sin. The famous ascetic John Chrysostom (ca.407) taught that even the Apostles and the Blessed Virgin Mary were in need of prayers to continue their

---

[1] Andrew Louth, "Chapter 12: Eastern Orthodox Eschatology," in Jerry Walls, ed. *The Oxford Handbook of Orthodox Eschatology* (Oxford: Oxford University Press: 2008), 233–247 at 242.

perpetual ascent into god-likeness in character after death.[2] In addition, the Eastern Church differs from the Latin Church in regard to the latter's individualistic approach. The East embraces a more communal view. The living and the dead offer prayers by (and for) the corporate bride and body of Christ in their perpetual ascent to God toward deification. Deification is not the Mormon concept of becoming gods but rather participating in the divine nature (2 Pet 1:4).[3] Every Christian—living or dead—should pray earnestly for every other Christian until the entire Church as one in communion with Christ achieves this blessedness. Outside of this singular eschatological foundation, the Orthodox Church holds no specific doctrines on the afterlife, preferring to be silent when Scripture is silent. Beliefs are more emersed and expressed in traditional practice.

Nevertheless, historically there were two primary popular interpretations of what type of judgment occurs upon death. The first is the "tollhouse" model wherein each soul ascends through multiple levels in the afterlife, where demons tax the soul by accusing persons of their sins. Each level must be met with corresponding repentance or good works to counter

---

[2] John Meyendorff, *Byzantine Theology: Historical Trends and Doctrinal Themes* (New York: Fordham University Press, 1974; repr. 1979), 221. He cites Mark of Ephesus who cites Chrysostom's Eucharistic liturgy.

[3] For a thorough discussion on the Christian concept of deification see Norman Russell, *The Doctrine of Deification in the Greek Patristic Tradition* (Oxford: Oxford University Press, 2004).

those accusations lest the demons drag the soul down to hell. The second view is a deathbed judgment. On the deathbed, both demons and angels arrive to make claim on the soul. The opposing forces fight by citing sins versus good deeds to determine who may escort the soul to its final destiny. The alternate deathbed scenario is a simple balance scale that weighs the good and the bad. There are also instances where the two models are combined, such as a homily attributed to Cyril of Alexandria (ca.425), but this probably dates from about the sixth century.[4]

Some persons within the Eastern Church subscribed to Origin's (ca.250) interpretation of John 14:30, that upon death the demons as "toll (tax) collectors" met the soul in the air, scrutinizing it and attempting to take it with them to hell (*Fifth Hom. Psa.* 36; PG 12:1366; also PG 88:812). *The Life of Antony* by Athanasius (ca.360) supported a view that each tollhouse highlighted a particular sin such as fornication or lying, possibly originally incited by the *Apocalypse of Paul* (Nag Hammadi). Basil of Caesarea (d.379) encouraged his parishioners to envision their souls metaphorically as being weighed on balance scales with demons waiting on one side and angels on the other (PG 31:432). A wide variety of theological works ensued with

---

[4] Vasileios Marinis, *Death and the Afterlife in Byzantium: The Fate of the Soul in Theology, Liturgy, and Art* (New York: Cambridge University Press, 2017), 15–24.

variations on this theme.[5]

"The most influential text about the geography of the afterlife in Byzantium is pseudo-Athanasias's *Quaestiones ad Antiochum ducem*."[6] The righteous await God's final judgment in Paradise (as does the thief on the cross beside Christ) while the wicked await it in Hades. There is no actual blessing in Paradise or torment in Hades, but rather a joyous expectation for the righteous and fearful anticipation for the wicked. As in ancient Jewish literature, Hades (Sheol) is merely the place of all of the dead, not Hell.

Middle Orthodox

One text can exemplify this period. Written ca.950, the *Life of Basil the Younger* provides a detailed account of the deathbed experience of Basil's servant Theodora. Near her last breath, two horrible demons immediately circle her bed carrying documents listing all of her sins. Theodora then sees two angels debating those demons. Death (personified) arrives tearing her soul from her body by dislocating all of her joints and reconfiguring her body to force out the soul. The demons attack Theodora while angels search for her good works to counter each accusation of sin. Only when Basil appears offering the

---

[5] E.g., *Lausiac History 69* (ca.420), *Ladder to Paradise* (ca.630), Maximus the Confessor (d.662) PG 77: 1072–1089, *Life of John Eleemon* (ca.700), Anastasios of Sinai (ca.700), and *Oneirocriticon of Achmet* (10th cent.).

[6] Marinus, *Afterlife in Byzantium*, 25.

gold of his own good deeds on behalf of Theodora do the demons leave. The belief was that every Christian upon baptism (like Theodora), received a guardian angel to record good deeds and a demon who kept track of all sins.

Theodora ascends through twenty tollhouses where the resident demon focuses on one (or two) particular sin(s), demanding that particular debt be paid, while extracting fear and pain. By the fifth tollhouse Theodora has already spent all of her good deeds compensating for her sins, so the angels must use Basil's golden spiritual wealth to pay these debts and allow her ascent to continue. Had Theodora confessed her sins to a spiritual father, enacted the repentance demanded, and received forgiveness from the spiritual father, then the Holy Spirit would have wiped her slate clean of that sin. The demon would not have had a record of it. The only possible exception to this clean slate was the horrendous sin of fornication. This was the tollhouse sin that condemned the most souls to Hell. Theodora finally arrives in Paradise and Abraham's abode where she awaits the Last Judgment at God's throne.

Late Byzantium

The East's confrontation with the West's formalized doctrine of purgatory (late twelfth and thirteenth centuries) led to a rejection of what was viewed as a false doctrine. A written encounter of the Eastern Orthodox metropolitan George Bardanes (d.ca.1240) with the Roman Catholic Fra Bartolomeo demonstrates this Eastern Orthodox dismissal of purgatory as a doctrine.[7]

Even the question of purgatory did not carry the same significance in the Eastern Orthodox Church as in the Latin west. Because Orthodox doctrine rejected the Latin "satisfaction" of the justice of God, there was no need for the sinner to undergo retributive punishment and purging to satisfy God's justice. However, whether forced or by choice, the Byzantine emperor Michael VIII Paleologos in 1274 signed a Confession of Faith at the Council of Lyons admitting this justice component existed in a purgatorial fire, along with numerous other Latin preferred doctrines. (The Roman Catholic crusaders that plumaged Constantinople seventy years prior may have influenced these uncharacteristic concessions.)

The Council of Florence in 1439 attempted to reconcile the Eastern Orthodox and Roman Catholic Church from the Great Schism that had occurred almost 400 years earlier in 1054.[8] The topics of contention were the *Filioque* (procession of the Holy Spirit from both the Father and the Son), papal supremacy, and purgatory. The *Filioque* controversy appears to have reached a genuine resolution by stating the Holy Spirit proceeds from the Father "and also the Son." But Pope Eugenius

---

[7] Martiniano P. Roncaglia, *George Bardanès, Métropolite de Corfou et Barthélemy de l'Ordre franciscain* (N.p.: Rome, 1953), 56–71.

[8] Mark Noll, *Turning Points: Decisive Moments in the History of Christianity*, 2nd edn. (Grand Rapids: Baker Academic, 2000), 132–39.

IV's bull *Laetentur Coeli (Let the Heavens Rejoice)* appeared prematurely.[9]

The disagreement over purgatory produced a compromise. "We confess that the souls of good men receive the full reward, and those of sinners full punishment, whereas those in a middle condition are subjected to agonies in prison; but what is the exact cause of their miseries, whether it be fire or darkness or anything else, we cannot positively affirm."[10] But the Patriarch of Byzantium died suddenly while attending the meeting and the Byzantine Emperor refused to accept any Latin teaching on purgatory.

The Eastern capitulation on papal supremacy and purgatory were most likely a reluctant political compromise for military reasons, orchestrated by the Byzantine emperor John VIII Palaiologos, attempting to convince Rome to protect Byzantium from the invading Muslims (that conquered it fourteen years later).[11] The council even resorted to offering

---

[9] *Oxford Dictionary of the Christian Church*, 948. A papal bull is an official document or letter sealed with special lead seal (Latin, *bulla*).

[10] Dorotheus of Mitylene, *The History of the Council of Florence*, J.M. Nealle, ed, trans. Basil Popoff (London: Joseph Masters, 1861), 142–49.

[11] Joseph Gill, "Florence, Council of," in *New Catholic Encyclopedia*, 2nd edn. (Detroit: Thomson Gale, 2003), 5:770–72; Louis Bréhier, "Attempts at Reunion of the Greek and Latin Churches," *Cambridge Medieval History* 4 (1936) 594-62; Marcel Viller, "La Question de l'Union des Églises entre Grecs et Latins depuis le concile de Lyon jusqu'à celui de Florence (1274–1438), *Revue d'histoire ecclésiastique* 17.2 (1921) 260–305, 515-532; *Council of Florence*, 162–3, 166. The Pope promised military aid. Anthony of Heraclea stated he signed involuntarily.

bribes to appease dissenters.[12]

The Russian Orthodox Church immediately rejected this acquiescence by Constantinople to Rome, as did many Greeks. Mark of Ephesus adamantly refuted the Pope's claims because the Pope was "exalting himself equal to God." As Popoff stated, "Peace was proclaimed between the Churches, but nothing peaceful was there in the spirit of the reconciled parties."[13] The attitude of the Byzantine Emperor and Orthodox bishops upon returning home was: "We have sold our faith, we have exchanged Orthodoxy for heterodoxy, and losing our former pure faith have become azymites. May our hands that have signed the unjust decree be cut off! May our tongues which have spoken consent with Latins be plucked out!"[14] The majority of Orthodox churches into the modern period have refused to acknowledge this forced reconciliation.

Modern Orthodox

The absolution of sins occurs differently in the East than the West. The Orthodox confession need not be made to a priest or clergyman. Rather, it is performed in private prayer, implying

---

[12] Syr. X.4, *Council of Florence*, 154.

[13] *Council of Florence*, 156.

[14] *Council of Florence*, 164. An azymite is a person who uses unleavened bread for the Eucharist. It was a pejorative term used by the Orthodox against the Latin Catholics.

that "remission of sins is attributed to God Himself." [15] Nevertheless, lay persons since the fifteenth century have confessed to priests. The purpose of confession and penance was not to provide satisfaction in judgment for a legal crime against God (as in the West), but rather to heal the sick sinner from Satan's influence. [16] Even sacramental penance after formal excommunication (for a mortal sin such as murder) changed after the fourth century from public penance to a private confession. This was followed by a prayer of absolution by a priest.[17]

Indulgences are not called by that name, but certificates of absolution seemed to convey the same purpose for the living and the dead. In 1727 at the Council of Constantinople, the Eastern Church wrote that instead of using the Latin term indulgences, the Greeks would call them "permissive letters." These certificates were discontinued centuries ago in most places but persisted in Greece until the mid-twentieth century.[18]

The Orthodox Church prays for deceased Christians because death cannot separate those "in Christ" from God or each other. The collective communal understanding of the

---

[15] A. I. Almazov, *Tainaia Ispoved' v pravoislovnoi vostochnoi tserkvi III* (Np.: Odessa, 1894), 149–50.

[16] Meyendorff, *Byzantine Theology*, 196.

[17] Meyendorff, *Byzantine Theology*, 195.

[18] See "Индульгенции" (Indulgence) at православная энциклопедия https://www.pravenc.ru/text/389591.html#part_10 ; (*Orthodox Encyclopedia*); Accessed 17 November 2022.

Church implies we must pray for all members of the Church, whether alive or dead, until the entire Body of Christ achieves deification. "Individual persons cannot arrive at perfection without the realization of the fundamental unity of human nature. Love of God is necessarily bound up in the love of one's fellow-man. This perfect love will make a man like Christ...."[19] This must be a voluntary transformation into Christ's likeness, continuing constantly until the judgment on the last day.

St. Isaac the Syrian (ca.617–700) emphasized,

> Repentance is fitting at all times and for all persons. To sinners as well as to the righteous who look for salvation. There are no bounds to perfection, for even the perfection of the most perfect is nought but imperfection. Hence, until the moment of death neither the time nor the works of repentance can ever be complete.[20]

Eastern theology does not focus on individual "salvation" as in Western theology, but on corporate transformation of Christ's bride into the very nature of Christ himself (deification).[21] For example, Evagrius Ponticus (ca.345–399) identified the marks of the perfect monk. He is one who "'will after God, count all

---

[19] Vladimir Lossky, *The Mystical Theology of the Eastern Church* (Crestwood, NY: St. Vladimir's Seminary Press, 1976), 214.

[20] St. Isaac the Syrian, *Theotoki*, ed. LV, 325.

[21] Cf., 2 Pet. 1:4, "that you might become partakers of the divine nature."

men as God Himself.' The person of another will appear as the image of God to him who can detach himself from his individual limitations, in order to rediscover the nature common to all, and to realize by so doing his own nature."[22]

Although it is true that "it is appointed for man once to die and after that the judgment" (Heb 9:27), that judgment need not be immediate at death, since death does not prevent the now sinless soul from continual growth into participation of God's nature. Adam was created "very good" by God (some Christians would even say "perfect"). But even prior to this primal sin, Adam was not perfect in the Orthodox understanding. The Holy Spirit works to produce the divine nature in those who are willing (2 Pet 1:4). Just like the divine Christ became human by choice, humans were created to become divine by free choice. This means a move toward deification, or assuming God's nature (not ontological replication).[23]

Irenaeus of Lyons (ca.185) wrote: "For this is why the Word became man, and the Son of God became the Son of man: so that man, by entering into communion with the Word and thus receiving divine sonship, might become a son of God."[24] Athanasius (296–373) repeated this in a condensed version,

---

[22] Lossky, *Mystical Theology*, 122.

[23] St. John Damascene, *De fide ortho* II.12 (P.G. 94, 924A). See Lossky, *Mystical Theology*, 126.

[24] Irenaeus, *Adversus Haereses* V, preface (PG 7, 1120).

"For he was made man that we might be made God." [25]

Modern Orthodox doctrine continues to teach this theosis. "Prayer, fasting, and other works are not the purpose of life, but they are the '*necessary means* for the achievement of the purpose.'"[26] The Holy Spirit produces the divine nature in Christians as they cooperate. It seems it may require all of eternity to achieve that divine plan (Rom 8:29).[27] This may be what I appreciate the most about Orthodox theology. Our goal is not "reaching heaven." Our goal is total conformation and transformation to God's nature.

The Orthodox Church does not teach a specific location like purgatory for purging sin. Louth specifically rejects a purgatorial fire with expiatory suffering in the purification of souls in the afterlife.[28] However, prior Orthodox theologians (particularly in the seventeenth and eighteenth centuries), did debate the reality of a satisfaction for sins through suffering after death.

Recent scholarship has identified the current East-West

---

[25] Athanasius, *On the Incarnation* (*De incarnatione* 54.3). This is not the Mormon concept of individual mini-gods but rather a community of participatory love unified with the only God and sharing his divine nature, all within God's grace.

[26] Christoforos Stavropoulos, *Partakers of the Divine Nature*, trans. S. Harakas (Minneapolis, MN: Light and Life Publishing Co., 1976), 33.

[27] Nicolas Zernov, *Eastern Christendom: A Study of the Origin and Development of the Eastern Orthodox Church* (London: Weidenfeld & Nicolson, 1961), 235.

[28] Louth, "Eastern Orthodox Eschatology," 243.

dichotomy ("exemplified" by the Orthodox theologian Gregory Palamas versus the Roman Catholic theologian Thomas Aquinas) as a modern (mis)construction. The writings of the Byzantine period demonstrate that Palamas and his colleagues were appreciative of the scholarship of Aquinas since he possessed an excellent knowledge of Greek philosophy, the Greek language, and Patristics. It was not until the early nineteenth century that the current negative view of Aquinas by the Orthodox became the standard.[29] More unity between the Catholic and Orthodox may be forthcoming.

---

[29] Marcus Plested, *Orthodox Readings of Aquinas* (Oxford: Oxford University Press, 2012), 220–28.

Chapter 4
The Protestant Rejection of Purgatory

This section will discuss Protestant theology during the Reformation, Enlightenment, and then modern Protestant thought. Protestants have no centralized clerical oversight that governs doctrine, resulting in numerous diverging opinions on many issues. However, most Protestants reject purgatory.

The Protestant Reformation

The quotation by John Calvin (1509–1564) in the Introduction summarizes the Protestant response to Roman Catholic purgatory: "Purgatory is a deadly fiction of Satan, which nullifies the cross of Christ, inflicts unbearable contempt upon God's mercy, and overturns and destroys our faith."[1] Calvin continued, "[If] the blood of Christ is the sole satisfaction for the sins of believers, the sole expiation, the sole purgation, what remains but to say that purgatory is simply a dreadful blasphemy against Christ?"[2]

This was an alteration in the prior theology of Martin

---

[1] John Calvin, *Calvin: Institutes of the Christian Religion,* John T. McNeill, ed., Trans. by Ford L. Battles in the Library of Christian Classics (Philadelphia, PA: The Westminster Press, 1960), III.5.6.

[2] John Calvin, *Institutes* III.5.6.

Luther (1483–1546), an Augustinian monk and leader of the Protestant Reformation. When Luther posted his ninety-five theses, he still accepted the doctrine of purgatory. Luther retained this Roman Catholic belief in purgatory for decades. "The existence of a purgatory I have never denied. I still hold that it exists, as I have written and admitted many times, though I have found no way of proving it incontrovertibly from Scripture or reason." (*Defense and Explanation of All the Articles*, 1521). Luther only retracted this view fifteen years later in the Schmalkaldic Articles (1536).[3]

> Therefore purgatory, and every solemnity, rite, and commerce connected with it, is to be regarded as nothing but a specter of the devil. … Our Papists, however, cite such statements [opinions] of men in order that men should believe in their horrible, blasphemous, and cursed traffic in masses for souls in purgatory [or in sacrifices for the dead and oblations], etc. But they will never prove these things from Augustine. Now, when they have abolished the traffic in masses for purgatory, of which Augustine never dreamt, we will then discuss with them

---

[3] "Purgatory," *The Oxford Dictionary*, 1359. Note that of the nine Lutheran confessions only the Smalcald/Schmalkald Articles discuss purgatory. These others include *The Three Ecumenical or Universal Creeds, The Augsburg Confession, The Defense of the Augsburg Confession, The Large Catechism, The Small Catechism, The Smalcald Articles, Treatise on the Power and Primacy of the Pope, The Epitome of the Formula of Concord,* and *The Solid Declaration of the Formula of Concord.*

whether the expressions of Augustine without Scripture [being without the warrant of the Word] are to be admitted, and whether the dead should be remembered at the Eucharist. (2.2 "Of the Mass")[4]

Luther appeared to be more concerned with the ritual abuse of purgatory during the Catholic mass than its existence as a doctrine. His *Confession Concerning Christ's Supper* states: "As for the dead, since Scripture gives us no information on the subject, I regard it as no sin to pray with free devotion in this or some similar fashion: 'Dear God, if this soul is in a condition accessible to mercy be thou gracious to it.' And when this has been done once or twice, let it suffice."[5] Yet, Luther mocked the priest who "prays for those who repose in the sleep of peace and rest in Christ and have the sign of faith. If that is true, why should you pray for them? Are you not a madman and a fool?"[6] As a result of Luther's attack, prayers for the dead were abandoned during Protestant services.

In the later 1531 edition of that same Augsburg Confession, a sentence on purgatorial satisfaction was added

---

[4] Martin Luther, *Triglot Concordia: The Symbolical Books of the Ev. Lutheran Church*, trans. by F. Bente and W. H. T. Dau (St. Louis: Concordia Publishing House, 1921), 453–529.

[5] Martin Luther, *Luther's Works: The American Edition* vol.37, Jaroslav Pelikan and Helmut Lehmann, eds. (Minneapolis, MN: Fortress Press and St. Louis, MO: Concordia Publishing, 1955–1986), 369.

[6] Luther, *Luther's Works* 36: 321.

that was absent in the original 1530 text.[7] "Also rejected are those who teach that 'canonical satisfactions' [satisfactions required by canon law] are necessary to pay for eternal torment or purgatory." (XII. Concerning Repentance, italics original) The *Apology of the Augsburg Confession* also rails against abuse of the mass rather than merely against prayers for the dead.

> The adversaries also falsely cite against us the condemnation of Aerius, who, they say, was condemned for the reason that he denied that in the Mass an offering is made for the living and the dead. They frequently use this dexterous turn, cite the ancient heresies, and falsely compare our cause with these in order by this comparison to crush us. [The asses are not ashamed of any lies. Nor do they know who Aerius was and what he taught.] Epiphanius testifies that Aerius held that prayers for the dead are useless. With this he finds fault. Neither do we favor Aerius, but we on our part are contending with you who are defending a heresy manifestly conflicting with the prophets, apostles, and holy Fathers,

---

[7] Satisfactions are the third step for a penitent. "There are three essential 'acts' required of the penitent: an act of contrition, the act of confessing one's sin, and the act of making satisfaction which is commonly called the 'penance'." Vatican News, "The Act of Contrition and the Sacrament of Reconciliation," 17 December 2018; See also https://www.vaticannews.va/en/church/news/2018-12/the-act-of-contrition-sacrament-reconciliation-confession.html; Accessed 9 May 2023.

namely, that the Mass justifies ex opere operato,[8] that it merits the remission of guilt and punishment even for the unjust, to whom it is applied, if they do not present an obstacle. Of these pernicious errors, which detract from the glory of Christ's passion, and entirely overthrow the doctrine concerning the righteousness of faith, we disapprove. (Art. XXIV [XII]: 96, Of the Masses for the Dead.)

This work further explains that satisfactions meant for temporal church discipline have been conflated with satisfying God in purgatory by the Romanists. [9] Luther ultimately rejected purgatory.

John Calvin similarly decried what the Church had done to purgatory and prayers for the dead when responding to Cardinal Jacopo Sadoleto (who himself had admitted Catholic abuses).

As to purgatory, we know that ancient churches made some mention of the dead in their prayers, but it was done seldom and soberly, and consisted only of a few words. It was, in short, a mention in which it was obvious that nothing more was meant than to attest in passing the affection which was felt toward the dead.

---

[8] *Ex opere operato* is Latin for "by the work worked." This means the sacraments confer God's grace when the sign/sacrament is validly effected. God's own power confers his grace as a result of the recipient's activity without concern for any merit on the part of either the recipient or priest.

[9] Article XIIb (VI): "Of Confession and Satisfaction," 17–24.

As yet, the architects were unborn, by whom your
purgatory was built; and who afterwards enlarged it
to such a width, and raised it to such a height, that it
now forms the chief prop of your kingdom. You
yourself know what a hydra of errors thence
emerged; you know what tricks superstition has at its
own hand devised, wherewith to disport itself; you
know how many impostures avarice has here
fabricated, in order to milk men of every class; you
know how great detriment it has done to piety. (Letter
to Cardinal Sadoleto, September 1, 1539)

Calvin provides more explanation in his *Institutes of the
Christian Religion.*

Let us grant, however, that all this might have been
tolerated for a time as a thing of no great moment; yet
when the expiation of sins is sought elsewhere than
in the blood of Christ, and satisfaction is transferred
to others, silence were most perilous. We are bound,
therefore, to raise our voice to its highest pitch, and
cry aloud that purgatory is a deadly device of Satan;
that it makes void the cross of Christ; that it offers
intolerable insult to the divine mercy; that it
undermines and overthrows our faith. For what is this
purgatory but the satisfaction for sin paid after death
by the souls of the dead? Hence when this idea of
satisfaction is refuted, purgatory itself is forthwith
completely overturned. But if it is perfectly clear,

from what was lately said, that the blood of Christ is
the only satisfaction, expiation, and cleansing for the
sins of believers, what remains but to hold that
purgatory is mere blasphemy, horrid blasphemy
against Christ? I say nothing of the sacrilege by
which it is daily defended, the offenses which it
begets in religion, and the other innumerable evils
which we see teeming forth from that fountain of
impiety. (*Inst.* III.5.6)

The Enlightenment

The founder of the Methodists, John Wesley (1703–1791),
defined perfection as "the humble, gentle, patient love of God,
and our neighbour, ruling our tempers, words, and actions."[10]
He explained all Christians reach this perfection at "the instant
of death, the moment before the soul leaves the body" if not
years or decades prior.[11] In contrast to the earlier Reformers
who taught sin was inevitable until death, Wesley viewed entire
sanctification in holiness (Christian perfection) as possible prior
to death.[12] Many Christians understand Wesley's position to be
a rather optimistic assessment of the capacity for human
progress in sanctification (i.e., justification for Catholics) while

---

[10] John Wesley, *Brief Thoughts on Christian Perfection* (Np.: London, 1767), 61.

[11] John Wesley, *Christian Perfection* (Sections 26–281).

[12] This was not absolute perfection but a relative one. See John Wesley, *A Plain Account of Christian Perfection* 26.4.

still on earth.

The more typical Protestant concept of justification by faith is a forensic declaration of righteousness imputed solely by Christ. This follows Luther's famous phrase "simul iustus et peccator" (simultaneously justified and a sinner). God looks at the sacrifice of Jesus Christ and declares the sinner not guilty.

The progressive work to become more like Christ is an issue of sanctification, separate from justification. John Wesley founded a magazine entitled *Arminian Magazine*. Methodist or Wesleyan theology is Arminian in nature as opposed to Calvinistic. Modern Wesleyans trace their beliefs to Wesley's theology.

Modern Protestant Scholars Reject Purgatory

N.T. Wright exemplifies scholarly arguments against purgatory, explaining that deceased Christians are in an intermediate state only because they await resurrection of their physical bodies to be reunited on a physical earth where Jesus Christ will reign as King. "The idea that Christians need to suffer punishment for their sins in a postmortem purgatory, or anywhere else, reveals a straightforward failure to grasp the very heart of what was achieved on the cross."[13] He teaches our current sufferings in this earthly life function as a purgatory to cleanse us of sin as

---

[13] N.T. Wright, *For All the Saints: Remembering the Christian Departed* (Harrisburg, PA: Morehouse, 2004), 30.

we pass to our glorious future.[14] Wright understands Romans 6:6–7 as teaching the death of the body enacts the death of sin in that body. At death, the sinner "literally is justified from sin."[15]

Popular Evangelical Preachers Denounce Purgatory

Pastor John MacArthur writes, "The Catholic doctrine of purgatory offers false hope to people hoping to atone for their own sins on the other side of the grave. Rome's warped and perverted view of justification will undoubtedly usher into eternal torment many who expected to have more time to achieve perfection."[16]

John Piper argues:

> But here's the assumption that [C.S.] Lewis and the Catholic Church bring to the situation: their assumption is that it requires another process, beyond the process of this life, to get abiding sin out of our lives. Now, why would they assume that? Since we had a relatively long process of purification or sanctification in this life by the Holy Spirit, and it did not perfect us, we realize it's going to take a divine stroke or word of purification by the hand of God or

---

[14] Wright, *All the Saints*, 34.

[15] Wright, *All the Saints*, 32.

[16] John MacArthur, "The False Hope of Purgatory," in Fulfilling the Promises https://fulfillingthepromises.com/the-false-hope-of-purgatory-by-john-macarthur/ ; Accessed 26 November 2022

the word of God, the way Jesus purified people instantaneously with a word, in order to finish this purifying work. Why would we not rather assume that God does it first progressively in this life, and then at the end finishes it instantaneously?

The same thing is confirmed in 2 Corinthians 5:6–9, only it's even clearer. He says, "We are always of good courage. We know that while we are at home in the body we are away from the Lord. . . . We would rather be away from the body and at home with the Lord. So whether we are at home or away, we make it our aim to please him."

I don't know how it could be much clearer than to say that "away from the body" is "at home with the Lord." That's our immediate hope — not any intervening purgatory between being away from the body and being at home with the Lord. To be away from the body is to be at home with the Lord, which, Paul says, is far better. ... [Cites 1 Cor 6:6–9; 1 Cor 15:51–52]

Now, that instantaneous change of our bodies at the resurrection is a better, more biblical picture of what happens to the imperfect soul at death. In a moment,

> in the twinkling of an eye, God says to us, just like
> Jesus said to the leper in Luke 5:13, "Be clean." [17\]

But despite these protests by Protestant preachers, according to a 2017 Pew Research Poll, a majority of modern U.S. Protestants have reverted to Roman Catholic doctrines over which the Reformers separated from Rome.

> Meanwhile, 52% say Christians should look both to the Bible and to the church's official teachings and tradition for guidance, the position held by the Catholic Church during the time of the Reformation and today. When these two questions are combined, the survey shows that just three-in-ten U.S. Protestants believe in both *sola fide* and *sola scriptura*. One third of Protestants (35%) affirm one but not the other, and 36% do not believe in either sola fide or sola scriptura. [...] In the U.S. today, seven-in-ten Catholics say they believe in purgatory. Black Protestants are closely divided on this question. By contrast, most white evangelical Protestants (72%) and white mainline Protestants (66%) say they do not believe in purgatory.[7] [Footnote 7. Among all evangelical Protestants, including both whites and racial and ethnic

---

[17] John Piper, "What Does the Bible Say about Purgatory?" Ask Pastor John , May 17, 2021, Episode 1627 https://www.desiringgod.org/interviews/what-does-the-bible-say-about-purgatory ; Accessed 14 June 2023.

minorities, 28% say they believe in purgatory while 68% do not. Among all mainline Protestants, including both whites and nonwhites, 35% believe in purgatory and 61% do not].[18]

On the question of purgatory in this poll, it is surprising that over one-fourth of white evangelical Protestants and almost one-third of white mainline Protestants believe in purgatory. The prominent voices attacking purgatory have possibly not been convincing to many Protestants.

Modern Protestant Arguments against Purgatory

The previously quoted comments by C.S. Lewis affirming his belief in purgatory—while rejecting the older Roman Catholic caricature of it—deserve our attention. But, we first examine the reasons modern Protestants have dismissed the doctrine of purgatory. The first section will discuss Protestant arguments and the second will detail scriptures used as proof-texts.

Justification as Absolute

The most common argument against believers receiving any

---

[18] Pew Research Center, "U.S. Protestants Are Not Defined by Reformation-Era Controversies 500 Years Later," August 31, 2017. *Sola scriptura* means only the Bible (not church tradition) is the source of truth and practice, while *sola fide* means faith alone (without good works) can justify a person to be declared a righteous child of God. https://www.pewresearch.org/religion/2017/08/31/u-s-protestants-are-not-defined-by-reformation-era-controversies-500-years-later/ ; Accessed 3 June 2023.

punishment after death utilizes a particular view of the doctrine of justification. Since Christ paid for all of our sins, a regenerate person (Christian) should never fear any further penalty or consequence for sin. Christ imputes his own righteousness to the sinner. By faith alone, all sins have been forgiven unconditionally.

But does this necessarily absolve the Christian from all future punishment? Many authors claim any further punishment of a justified person creates a double jeopardy problem.[19] This means if justification in Christ has paid the penalty for our sin, then God would be unjust to demand a second punishment, penalty, or consequence of any kind. The sinner would be forced to pay twice for the same sin. Numerous scriptures are quoted as evidence.

Purgatory is not found in the Bible

Protestants argue that one cannot find "purgatory" in scripture. The primary Roman Catholic verse used to support purgatory (2 Maccabees 12) is not part of the Protestant canon of scripture. Therefore, purgatory should be rejected.

---

[19] Double jeopardy is the concept that a person cannot be tried twice for the same crime, as prohibited in the Fifth Amendment to the U.S. Constitution. Theological "attorneys" would use the legal defense of *autrefois acquit* (formerly acquitted) by Christ. This is a variant of the classical double jeopardy argument used to explain limited expiation or refute universalism. Cf., Oliver Crisp, *Deviant Calvinism: Broadening Reformed Theology* (Minneapolis, MN: Fortress Press, 2014), 214.

No intermediate place exists

When a person dies, the soul goes immediately to heaven or hell (2 Cor 5:8). Upon death the person is immediately judged by God (Heb 9:7). There is no place called purgatory to which a person goes prior to being judged by God.

Biblical Proof-texts

- "As far as the east is from the west, so far has He removed our transgressions from us." (Ps 103:12)
- "He will again have compassion on us, and will subdue our iniquities, You will cast all our sins into the depths of the sea." (Micah 7:19)
- "Now all things are of God, who has reconciled us to Himself through Jesus Christ, and has given us the ministry of reconciliation, that is, God was in Christ reconciling the world unto Himself, not imputing their trespasses to them, and has committed to us the word of reconciliation." (2 Cor 5:18)
- "For all have sinned and fall short of the glory of God, being justified freely by His grace through the redemption that is in Christ Jesus, whom God set forth as a propitiation by His blood, through faith to demonstrate His righteousness, because in His forbearance God had passed over the sins that were previously committed." (Rom 3:23–25)

These proof-text passages will be explained in the next chapter.

These same Protestant arguments against purgatory have been defended for centuries. One good resource is Charles Hodge's *Systematic Theology*, completed in 1873.[20] Modern Protestant leaders express the same opinions.

Appeal to the Judgment Seat of Christ as solely for rewards

Most Protestants view the Great White Throne Judgment and the Judgment Seat of Christ as the same event. But a specific group of evangelical Christians claims the βῆμα (Judgment Seat) of Christ exists solely as a reward seat for Christians, not a judgment seat. *The Moody Handbook of Theology* posits:

> The judgment seat of Christ is mentioned in Romans 14:10, 1 Corinthians 3:9-15, and 2 Corinthians 5:10. It does not denote a judgment concerning eternal destiny but rather rewarding church age believers for faithfulness. The term *judgment seat* (Gk. *bema*) is taken from the Grecian games where successful athletes were rewarded for victory in athletic contests. Paul used that figure to denote the giving of rewards to church age believers.[21]

This agrees with Dallas Theological Seminary's first President L. S. Chafer. "Although his sins have been brought up at the

---

[20] Charles Hodge, *Systematic Theology*, vol. 3 (repr. Grand Rapids: Eerdmans, 1993), 749–70.

[21] Paul Enns, *The Moody Handbook of Theology* (Moody Press: Chicago, 1989), 392.

cross and will not be brought up again, at the judgment seat of Christ his works or service must be judged."[22] Walvoord, the second DTS president, wrote: "Although some have attempted to make this a Protestant purgatory, i.e., a time of punishment for unconfessed sin, it seems clear from the general doctrine of justification by faith that no condemnation is possible for one who is in Christ. ... The penalty is limited to the loss of reward'" [23] Hoyt expressed the view of many evangelical Christians regarding postmortem punishment.

> There will be no need for forensic punishment, for Christ has forever borne all of God's wrath toward the believer's sins. ... However, Scripture teaches that for the believer God's *justice* has already been fully and forever satisfied at the Cross in relation to the believer's sins. If God were to punish the believer judicially for his sins for which Christ has already rendered payment, He would be requiring two payments for sin and would therefore be unjust.[24]

This modern "rewards only" judgment error is currently espoused by Robert (Bob) Wilkin and his Grace Evangelical

---

[22] Lewis S. Chafer, *Systematic Theology*, Vol. 7 (Dallas Seminary Press: Dallas, Texas, 11th printing, 1973 edn.), 215.

[23] John Walvoord "The Future Work of Christ Part II: The Church in Heaven," *BSac* 123:490 (Apr 66): 100.

[24] Samuel L. Hoyt, "The Judgment Seat of Christ in Theological Perspective—Part 1: The Judgment Seat of Christ and Unconfessed Sins," *BSac* 137 (Jan 80): 32–41.

Society. This group claims the only negative consequences a believing Christian would experience for a murder is shame, rebuke, and disapproval resulting in loss of inheritance (reigning) in the kingdom of God.[25] The justified Christian is guaranteed heaven without punishment, regardless of behavior or even apostasy. Their heretical view of how a person becomes justified (becomes a Christian) has eclipsed their untenable "rewards only" error.[26] Because this is such a minority view, the more extensive explanation and rebuttal has been placed in Appendix B for those who are interested. We now critique the ubiquitous Protestant rejection in the next chapter.

---

[25] Dwight Hunt, "1–2 Corinthians" in *The Grace New Testament Commentary*, Vol.2 (Denton, Texas: Grace Evangelical Society, 2010), 786; Bob Wilkin, "Can Believers Get Away with Murder?" May 3, 2021 GES Blog. See also Wilkin, "Will the Bad Deeds of Believers be Considered at the Judgement Seat of Christ?" March 1, 2015 GES Blog. Bob Wilkin, "Christians will be Judged According to their Works at the *Rewards* Judgment, but *Not* at the *Final* Judgment," in *Four Views of the Role of Works at the Final Judgment*, eds. Alan Stanley and Stanley Gundry (Grand Rapids: Zondervan, 2013), 25–50. James Dunn appropriately refuted Wilkin: "In this case the problem is that so many New Testament texts envisage that Christians will be subjected to divine judgment before the throne of God or of his Christ." James Dunn, "Response to Robert N. Wilkin," *Four Views*, 51.

[26] Kenneth Wilson, *Heresy of the Grace Evangelical Society: Become a Christian without Faith in Jesus as God and Savior* (Montgomery, TX: Regula Fidei Press, 2020). Wilkin's GES group could qualify as a cult. See the six characteristics that typify a cult in Ron Rhodes, *The Challenge of the Cults and New Religions: The Essential Guide to Their History, Their Doctrine, and Our Response* (Grand Rapids: Zondervan, 2001), 31–34. These six are authoritarian leadership, exclusivism, isolationism, opposition to independent thinking, fear of being "disfellowshipped" and threats of Satanic attack if one questions the authority figure or leaves the cult. All six are not required to be a cult.

Chapter 5
Critique of the Protestant View

Most Protestants do not possess a proper understanding of the Roman Catholic doctrine of purgatory. Therefore, many of their usual arguments against it are not valid.

"No middle place between heaven and hell"

Although the medieval view of Purgatory did entail a physical location as represented in Dante's *Inferno and Purgatorio*, the modern Catholic view of Purgatory rejects spatial requirements. Previous popes specifically stated that purgatory is a process, not a place.[1] The official teaching (*Catechesis*) of the Roman Catholic Church does not teach purgatory to be a place. So, if purgatory is not a place, then it should be obvious that neither is purgatory a place where persons spend eternity if they are not bad enough for Hell or good enough for Heaven. That is not a Catholic understanding. Purgatory is not a middle place between Heaven and Hell as some Protestants claim.

"Suffering in Purgatory violates Scripture"

Many Christians think that there will be no more suffering after

---

[1] Pope John Paul II and Pope Benedict XVI, previously cited.

a person dies. They base this idea on Rev 21:4. "He will wipe every tear from their eyes. There will be no more death or mourning or crying or pain, for the old order of things has passed away." (NIV) Unfortunately, this text cannot support that view. The context immediately prior (v.1) designates this time as the new heavens and the new earth after the first heaven and earth pass away. The new heavens and new earth have not yet arrived. This means a deceased Christian may still experience pain or mourning before this future event occurs. It does not *prove* pain or suffering occur, but merely disproves the theory (on the basis of this verse) that death means the end of all suffering or pain. Not until the new heavens and new earth arrive will pain and tears cease to exist. There is no Scripture to defend a claim of the absence of tears, pain, or suffering upon physical death. This could possibly be assumed because these are more physical descriptions, but suffering is not always physical.

"Purgatory does not appear in Scripture"

The word *purgatory* cannot be found in the Bible. Does this prove the concept does not exist in Scripture? No. The word *Trinity* cannot be found in scripture, yet Christians believe the Father, Son, and Holy Spirit comprise three persons in one God. They understand the Trinity exists based upon numerous Scripture passages that support the idea that each person of the one God is fully God.

The same may be concluded with the word purgatory. The word *purgatory* does not appear but a purging of God's people of sin must occur before entering the presence of Holy God. Could it be that whatever sanctification has not been completed on earth must be completed prior to entering the presence of God? Or, do we assume every Christin achieves the same degree of complete sanctification while on earth? Glorification after death must be (questionably) assumed to be an instantaneous, painless process.

"Suffering for hundreds of years is not in Scripture"

This statement is true but irrelevant. The medieval Catholic Church did assign centuries of relief from suffering through indulgences. Some modern Catholics attempt to argue that indulgences only applied to earthly penance; but, few people live hundreds of years on earth, and Dante's "Purgatorio" was popular at the time. The typical defensive move is to use the three chronologies of Aquinas, including that our earthly time need not correspond to God's time because he is omnitemporal. Wisely, the modern Roman Catholic Church does not place a length of suffering in purgatory. Some Catholic authors even claim that the purification process could be almost instantaneous.[2]

---

[2] E.g., Joseph Ratzinger, *Eschatology: Death and the Eternal Life*, 2nd edn., trans. Michael Waldstein (Washington, DC: The Catholic University of America Press, 1988), 230. This was written while he was a cardinal. He later became Pope Benedict XVI.

Likewise, most Protestants teach an instantaneous transformation of the Christian into perfection upon death. However, earthly time and the measurement of time after death may be different. Even if instantaneous, a nano-second face to face with Holy God who is a consuming fire (Heb 12:18–29) could be an inexpressibly traumatic experience that burns away evil works and un-Christlike character. Time is not a limitation to an omnitemporal God.

"Immediate union with Christ occurs at death"

Protestants cite numerous scriptures claiming these teach immediate union with Christ upon death. These include Heb 9:27, "And inasmuch as it is appointed for men to die once and after this *comes* judgment." (NASB) After death God judges people. Nothing infers when that judgment will occur. If I say, "I am going to eat ice cream after I arrive home," that does not mean I will immediately open the freezer and eat ice cream. I may want to eat dinner *prior* to eating desert tonight. I may want to spend time with my wife discussing her day. Claiming that this verse proves an immediate blissful abode with Christ cannot withstand scrutiny. Additionally, "after that the judgment" does not sound particularly blissful. Judgment comes prior to Christ's embrace. How is that immediate union?

Another passage cited by Protestants is 2 Cor 5:6–8. "So we are always of good courage. We know that while we are at home in the body we are away from the Lord, for we walk by faith, not by sight. Yes, we are of good courage, and we would rather be away from the body and at home with the Lord." (ESV) Many authors miss the context by neglecting the verses that follow: "So whether we are at home or away, we make it our aim to please him. For we must all appear before the judgment seat of Christ, so that each one may receive what is due for what he has done in the body, whether good or evil." (2 Cor 5:9–10) Death inevitably produces a meeting with God, but again, no time frame is provided. Christ's judgment seat does not appear to generate bravery unless you are pleasing the Lord by obeying him (1 John 2:28). Judgment precedes union.[3]

Phil 1:21–24 has also been used. "For to me to live is Christ, and to die is gain. But if to live in the flesh,—*if* this shall bring fruit from my work, then what I shall choose I know not. But I am in a strait betwixt the two, having the desire to depart and be with Christ; for it is very far better: yet to abide in the flesh is more needful for your sake." (ASV) Paul's desire to be with Christ after death in no way proves he is ushered directly into Christ's arms upon dying. A judgment must precede it. This verse does not support immediate bliss with Christ after death.

In Rev 6:9–11, Christian martyrs plead with God for judgment upon their killers. "And when he opened the fifth seal, I saw underneath the altar the souls of them that had been slain for the word of God, and for the testimony which they held: and

---

[3] The judgment seat of Christ may occur at each individual's death rather than postponed until the Great White Throne judgment.

they cried with a great voice, saying, 'How long, O Master, the holy and true, dost thou not judge and avenge our blood on them that dwell on the earth?'" (DRA) This is one of the stronger arguments but still falls short. Scripture does not tell us anything about what transpired between death and the martyrs being under the altar. No immediacy exists. This does not imply soul sleep, although bodily sleep is evident elsewhere (e.g., 1 Cor 11:29–30; 1 Thess 4:13–18).

Similarly, the saints who are martyred in the Great Tribulation indeed stand before God to serve Him. But the text does not state they went immediately to God's throne.

> After these things I looked, and behold, a great multitude which no one could number, of all nations, tribes, peoples, and tongues, standing before the throne and before the Lamb, clothed with white robes. … So he said to me, "These are the ones who come out of the great tribulation [τῆς θλίψεως τῆς μεγάλης], and washed their robes and made them white in the blood of the Lamb. Therefore they are before the throne of God, and serve Him day and night in His temple." (Rev 7:9–15, NKJV)

The words of Christ to the thief (Luke 23:34) could possibly limit a delay into Christ's presence to a single day. "Then he said, 'Jesus, remember me when You come into Your kingdom!' And He said to him, 'I assure you: Today you will be with Me in paradise.'" (HCSB) This assumes that Paradise was incorporated into "Heaven" after Christ's resurrection. It cannot be proven. It also assumes the thief experienced immediate bliss instead of a preceding judgment "today." It is unlikely the thief entered Paradise bypassing Christ's judgment of his works, since Scripture teaches judgment must occur. Therefore, no Scripture states that immediately upon death we are at peace with Christ. In fact, repeatedly in scripture, a judgment of our deeds occurs prior to that intimacy with Christ.

"Passages on punishment refer to non-Christians"

As we will see, numerous scriptures teach God's judgment on the Christian after death. However, some Christian groups relegate these passages to unbelievers or false Christians (based upon their theological presuppositions).

The previously cited 1 Cor 11:29–30 states, "For a person who eats and drinks without discerning the body of the Lord is eating and drinking judgment on himself. That is why many of you are weak and ill, and a number of you have fallen asleep." Paul does not question their genuine Christianity but rebukes their sin. They were selfishly feasting and drinking, thereby taking the Eucharist (Lord's Supper) in an unworthy manner, so brought upon themselves the judgment of physical death (1 Cor 11:27–34). The likelihood of "many" within the early church signing up to be persecuted and martyred as false Christians seems absurd. God punishes Corinthian Christians for their sin. Despite "Jesus paid it all" these Christians are punished by God with sickness and physical death.

To the Colossians, Paul instructs, "and all, whatever ye may do—out of soul work—as to the Lord, and not to men, having known that from the Lord ye shall receive the recompense of the inheritance—for the Lord Christ ye serve; and he who is doing unrighteously shall receive what he did unrighteously, and there is no acceptance of persons." (Col 3:23–25, YLT) No evidence exists here for a theologically contrived distinction between Christians and non-Christians. The audience is Christian and all receive payment (ἀνταπόδοσιν). Christians serving the Lord Christ are paid an inheritance while those Christians doing evil will also receive payment for it (punishment).

Many other passages can be brought forth as evidence that God punishes his children. This punishment of Christians will be covered in detail in a later section.

"Purgatory demands double payment for sins"

Protestants argue that Christ paid for all sins. Purgatory suggests Christ's all sufficient sacrifice was not enough payment. If purgatory is true, this means a Christian must pay for his own sins to avoid Hell. This may be the most misunderstood aspect of Roman Catholic doctrine by Protestants. Catholics do not teach that Christ's sacrifice was insufficient. The payment of the Lord Jesus Christ was totally sufficient to pay for the sins of the whole world (1 John 2:2). According to Catholic doctrine, no person who believes in Christ will suffer in Hell. That eternal penalty of sin was paid.[4]

However, the temporal penalty of sin remains. The passages previously cited in 1 Cor 11:29–30 and Col 3:23–25 demonstrate that God punishes "justified" Christians, even with illness and physical death. In Acts 5:1–11, Ananias and Saphira, after gifting money (a partial amount) to the Jerusalem church for their property they had sold, physically dropped dead for lying to the Holy Spirit.[5]

To understand this additional temporal penalty, one must understand the difference between payment for the eternal consequences of sin versus the temporal consequences of sin. Christ already paid the eternal consequences of sin (eternal separation from God). But all Christians remain liable for the temporal consequences of sin (temporary punishment of the

---

[4] *Catechism of the Catholic Church* 1030 "All who die in God's grace and friendship, but still imperfectly purified, are indeed assured of their eternal salvation; but after death they undergo purification, so as to achieve the holiness necessary to enter the joy of heaven." Note that Hodge correctly limits the Catholic understanding of Christ's sacrifice for sin to deliverance from eternal damnation. See Hodge, *Systematic Theology*, vol. 3, 750.

[5] Again, certain Protestant groups claim these two must have been non-Christians since they did not persevere in good works. This claim derives from Augustine's pagan influences through Calvin. See Kenneth M. Wilson, "Chapter 6: Calvinism is Augustinianism," in *Calvinism: A Biblical and Theological Critique*, eds. David Allen and Steve Lemke (Nashville, TN: B & H Publishing, 2022), 213–237; Kenneth M. Wilson, "Reading James 2:18–20 with Anti-Donatist Eyes: Untangling Augustine's Exegetical Legacy," *Journal of Biblical Literature* 139.2 (2020): 389–410; Kenneth Wilson, *Augustine's Conversion from Traditional Free Choice to "Non-free Free Will": A Comprehensive Methodology*, Studien Und Texte Zu Antike Und Christentum 111 (Tübingen: Mohr Siebeck, 2018).

Christian). The comparison may be made to the legal system with the infamous trials of football star O. J. Simpson. Simpson was acquitted of murdering his ex-wife and her boyfriend in criminal court (because the prosecuting attorney foolishly tried to force a glove onto an athlete's hand). So, O. J. Simpson walked—"Get Out of Jail Free"—in criminal court. But then Simpson stood trial in civil court for monetary damages for the same murder of his ex-wife and her boyfriend.

This civil jury found him liable to pay those damages for the very same murders: the jury was convinced Simpson murdered them.[6] For the exact same offense, Simpson stood trial in two different types of courts with two different verdicts. In the first (criminal) court he was judged innocent of the murders, so he walked away free. In the second (civil) court, he was found financially liable for the murders and had to pay damages.

Since Christ paid for all sin, then is God unjust to punish sinners again?—of course not. Christ's sacrifice is the first court that sets persons free to walk out from hell "free." The eternal consequences were already paid by Christ. In the second court, Christians must pay or be paid for what has been done in the body. Temporal consequences remain. God can punish Christian sinners in any way he deems appropriate as long as Christians are not permanently separated from him eternally.

---

[6] Britannica. https://www.britannica.com/event/O-J-Simpson-trial ; Accessed 1 December 2022.

We have seen that God punishes his children while on earth. Therefore, Christ cannot have removed ALL consequences for sin. Why do Protestants build an artificial barrier between God punishing his children in this life versus the next life? According to scripture, not all of the punishment for sin was removed by Christ's death.

"Purgatory is a second chance for heaven after death"

Roman Catholics do not believe purgatory offers a second chance. Only persons who believe in Jesus Christ enter purgatory. Those who reject Christ are admitted to hell. Very few Christians are so pure that they enter heaven immediately after death. Virtually all Christians enter purgatory to purify them for entrance to the beatific vision (experiencing God in heaven). The claim is false: Purgatory is not a second chance.

Evaluating Biblical Proof-texts

There are numerous passages used by Protestants attempting to refute posthumous punishment. Many of these are listed below.

Psalm 103:12

"As far as the east is from the west, *so* far has He removed our transgressions from us." The irony of this passage being used as a proof-text is that it was written by King David. This is the man who committed adultery, then murdered the husband trying to cover up his first sin of adultery. God told David through the prophet Nathan that his sin was forgiven: he would not die. But, the child conceived would die and David's own children would fight against him and would publicly disgrace him (2 Sam 11–12). Yes, the sin was forgiven but God still punished David.

Micah 7:19

"He will again have compassion on us, and will subdue our iniquities. You will cast all our sins into the depths of the sea." (NKJV) Once again we have irony because Micah has been characterized as a prophet of doom. The majority of this book prophesies God's coming judgment, even on Jerusalem. In context, the sins of the Jewish nation (not individual people) are discarded.

> Who is a God like you, pardoning iniquity and passing over transgression for the remnant of his inheritance? He does not retain his anger forever, because he delights in steadfast love. He will again have compassion on us; he will tread our iniquities underfoot. You will cast all our sins into the depths of the sea. You will show faithfulness to Jacob and steadfast love to Abraham, as you have sworn to our fathers from the days of old. (Micah 7:18–20; NKJV)

Just as Micah prophesied, God's judgment did indeed come quickly upon that nation by the Assyrians, then the Babylonians, punishing the nation for sin.

2 Corinthians 5:18

> Now all things are of God, who has reconciled us to Himself through Jesus Christ, and has given us the ministry of reconciliation, that is, God was in Christ reconciling the world unto Himself, not imputing their trespasses to them, and has committed to us the word of reconciliation. (NKJV)

Because Christ reconciled the world, God does not write trespasses on the ledger sheet in hell of a person who believes in Jesus Christ. The barrier eternally separating God from humanity eternally due to sin has been destroyed. However, sin remains in Christians that creates a barrier to intimacy experientially on earth. In 1 John 1:9, we read, "If we confess our sins, he is faithful and just to forgive us *our* sins and to cleanse us from all unrighteousness." (JUB) If Christ no longer imputes any sin, then why must Christians confess that sin in order to be cleansed? God's condition for us to be forgiven for our sin is a change of heart by confession. Even after Christ's sacrifice, forgiveness for God's child is still conditional. Failure to confess exposes a wrong heart. It does not incur hell but hinders intimacy with God both now and after death.

Romans 3:23–25

> For all have sinned and fall short of the glory of God, and are justified by his grace as a gift, through the redemption that is in Christ Jesus, whom God put

> forward as a propitiation by his blood, to be received
> by faith. This was to show God's righteousness,
> because in his divine forbearance he had passed over
> former sins. (ESV)

Similar to the previous verse, God has passed over (or, not imputed) prior sins. This concerns an eternal destiny, not ongoing conformity to Christ's character. Conformity requires confession when obedience falters. A change of heart places us back into God's merciful embrace.

None of these Protestant passages preclude God from punishing his children. Some of the very verses allegedly "proving" no consequences for sin actually prove the opposite. God forgives then punishes.

Conclusion

In summary, the Protestant arguments against God punishing Christians after death cannot stand the test of scrutiny. Theological bias allows persons to merely assume these are valid arguments from scripture. The medieval caricature of purgatory was indeed a "deadly fiction of Satan." The abuses and man-made fabrications about purgatory were indeed fictitious dirty bathwater to discard. But John Calvin threw out the baby with the bathwater.[7] The consistent biblical theme of

---

[7] This was the conclusion of the Scottish Protestant theologian Peter Forsyth, *This Life and the Next* (Boston: The Pilgrim Press, 1948), 37.

God's judgment of his own children is the clean baby. It is time to re-examine the Holy Scriptures—scriptures that repeatedly describe God's judgment upon his children—with an open mind. We will do this in Chapter 8. Next, we critique the Orthodox view.

Chapter 6
Critique of the Orthodox View

As explained in Chapter 2, no official doctrine exists regarding purgatory in the Eastern Orthodox Church. The Orthodox reject the idea that Christians will be in a specific location for posthumous punishment, nor do they believe in expiatory suffering for sin after death. This will considerably shorten the discussion in this chapter.

In my opinion, the key elements of the Orthodox Church about the afterlife are the sanctification of the entire church corporately, conformation to Christ without expiatory suffering, and the progressive growth in the likeness of God eternally (even following physical death). The Western mindset has historically emphasized the individual rather than the community, although that is fortunately beginning to change. Yet, both Catholics and Protestants may remain somewhat puzzled by the Orthodox teaching of the church being sanctified as a unified body of Christ.

Corporate Sanctification

The progressive conformation to the divine nature, the character of Jesus Christ, is the process of salvation. This cannot be accomplished without participation in the life of the church.

"Orthodoxy believes that the Christian Faith and the Church are inseparable. It is impossible to know Christ, to share in the life of the Holy Trinity, or to be considered a Christian, apart from the Church."[1]

In 2 Pet 1:3–11, Christians who have already been purified from their sins are exhorted to become partakers of the divine nature by practicing virtues instead of being corrupted by worldly lusts. Practicing virtues does not gain entrance into God's kingdom. Rather, it guarantees an abundant (extravagant) entrance. Those who lack these virtues will not have an extravagant entrance. There appears to be a difference among individual Christians in their conformation to the likeness of Christ while on this earth that may continue after death.

> Seeing that His divine power has granted to us everything pertaining to life and godliness, through the true knowledge of Him who called us by His own glory and excellence. For by these He has granted to us His precious and magnificent promises, so that by them you **may become** partakers of *the* divine nature, having escaped the corruption that is in the world by lust. Now for this very reason also, applying all diligence, in your faith supply moral excellence, and in *your* moral excellence, knowledge, and in *your*

---

[1] Rev. Fr. Thomas Fitzgerald, "Teachings of the Orthodox Church," Greek Orthodox Diocese of America 6/11/1990. https://www.goarch.org/-/teachings-of-the-orthodox-church ; Accessed 5 June 2023.

knowledge, self-control, and in *your* self-control, perseverance, and in *your* perseverance, godliness, and in *your* godliness, brotherly kindness, and in *your* brotherly kindness, love. For if these *qualities* are yours and are increasing, they render you neither useless nor unfruitful in the true knowledge of our Lord Jesus Christ. For he who lacks these *qualities* is blind *or* short-sighted, having forgotten *his* purification from his former sins. Therefore, brethren, be all the more diligent to make certain about His calling and choosing you; for as long as you practice these things, you will never stumble; for in this way the entrance into the eternal kingdom of our Lord and Savior Jesus Christ will be abundantly supplied to you. (2 Pet 1:3–11, NASB95; bold mine)

The "**may become**" emphasizes a possibility to be realized by our choices. If Christians vary in sanctification levels, being more or less like Christ in character on earth, then it seems reasonable to conclude that some Christians will require more conformity after death than others. Supporting each other and praying for each other to become more like Christ corporately seems reasonable.

Furthermore, the Church prepares *herself* with righteous acts (even if God enables us). In Rev 19:7 we read, "Let us rejoice and exult, and give him the glory, for the marriage of the Lamb has come, and his **Bride has made herself ready**; it was granted her to clothe herself with fine linen, bright and pure—

for the fine linen is **the righteous deeds of the saints**." (ESV; bold mine). Most Protestants assume the wedding garment is the imputed righteousness of Christ obtained freely by faith. That is not what the text states. Christians must actually become righteous in character ("righteous *deeds* of the saints") to participate in this wedding of the corporate Church to Christ. (For Protestants, this makes it unlikely that the wedding represents heaven.) More probably it is a special honor provided only to those who purposefully conformed themselves to Christ's image while on earth, rather than waiting until after death for God finish it with much transformation being required. Every Christian will be conformed to Christ's image (Rom 8:29). The question is when and to what degree that conformity occurs.

Deification as Intimacy with God

Western Christians often emphasize the personal aspect of God as Father and Jesus as Friend to the exclusion of the transcendent nature. This might be true for some Roman Catholics, but especially characterizes most Protestant evangelicals. Gregory of Nyssa (d.ca.395) explained that the uncreated monad of the Father-Son-Holy Spirit energies all simultaneously flow transcendent and immensely personal. The human participatory intimacy into the divine nature will require eternity—yet, never to be perfectly obtained.[2] If this is true, and it seems so to me, then humans can never achieve absolute perfection, even when standing sinless in the presence of Jesus Christ. Further transformation into the divine nature continues eternally even without the issue of sin.

Lossky emphasizes freedom of choice in this process.

> God becomes *powerless* before human freedom; He cannot violate it since it flows from His own omnipotence. Certainly man was created by the will of God alone; but he cannot be deified by it alone. A single will for creation, but two for deification. A single will to raise up the image, but two to make the image into a likeness. (italics original)[3]

Deification requires our choice and effort. "After the Fall, human history is a long shipwreck awaiting rescue; but the port of salvation is not the goal; it is the possibility for the shipwrecked to resume his journey whose sole goal is union with God."[4] The eternal obstacle for humanity is exercising dependence upon God's Spirit for deification by obedience in grace (mimicking Christ), rather than pursuing self-deification. Protestants get it wrong: The goal is not "getting to heaven."

---

[2] Vladimir Lossky, *Orthodox Theology: An Introduction*, trans. Ian and Ihita Kesarcodi-Watson (Crestwood, NY: St. Vladimir's Seminary Press, 2001), 33 (citing Gregory of Nyssa), 44–8.

[3] Lossky, *Orthodox Theology*, 73.

[4] Lossky, *Orthodox Theology*, 85.

Western Christianity understands salvation as rescue from sin's penalty of hell—eternal separation from God. Orthodox Christianity understands salvation as deification in reuniting our natures into eternal intimacy with God. In Western Christianity salvation is viewed as being in the same house with the Father. For the Orthodox, salvation is not merely residing in the same house with the Father: Salvation is experiencing intimate eternal love with the Father. This can only occur as our nature becomes more progressively conformed to Christ's nature. This is deification. Deification involves more than the absence of sin.

Posthumous Growth into God-likeness

Progressive conformation to God's likeness is often equated with the absence of sin. When we see Christ we will be like him without sin. "Beloved, we are God's children now. What we shall be has not yet been revealed. However, we do know that when he appears we shall be like him, for we shall see him as he really is. Everyone who has this hope in him keeps himself pure, just as he is pure." (1 John 3:2–3) The author speaks of sin and purification in the context, so being "like him" in this text most likely means the absence of sin.

But Scripture provides no basis for assuming that the absence of sin in Christians equals complete conformation to the character of Christ. The mere absence of sin does not adequately embrace the positive character of God. Perfected love will be one blessing to which I aspire. Clement of Alexandria (ca.190) explained, "According to another view, it is not he who merely controls his passions that is called a continent man, but he who has also achieved the mastery over good things, and has acquired surely the great accomplishments of science, from which he produces as fruits the activities of virtue." (*Stromata* 7.13)

Does that virtue occur instantaneously, or does the presence of God over "time" so saturate us that we become more and more like God? If the apostles Paul and James taught this as happening currently by looking into God's written Word (2 Cor 3:15–18; James 1:21–25), then perhaps it will also occur after death by looking directly into the face of the glorified Incarnate Word. It is reasonable to think that progressive conformation into the perfect character of Christ will require eternity. That is the Orthodox view.

Every child of God encounters God after death with a different level of conformity to Christ. Upon death, even in the absence of sin, there is a spectrum of individual intimacy or enjoyment of God's presence as that child looks into the Father's face. The more closely we have attained the likeness of Christ in character, the more we enjoy our intimacy with God.

Rejection of Expiatory Suffering

Orthodox theologians reject the concept that posthumous suffering is expiatory. The *Cambridge Dictionary* defines expiation as "the act of showing that you are sorry for bad behaviour by doing something or accepting punishment." The Greek Orthodox attitude toward suffering is instructive.

> Suffering is not a *problem,* but an unfathomable, theoretically incomprehensible *mystery.* We should not try to explain suffering or construct theories about the reasons for suffering in the world and systematic explanations that seek to reconcile innocent suffering with belief in a good and all powerful God The pervading presence of senseless suffering in the world falls outside the bounds of every rational system.[5]

For the Orthodox, suffering is inevitable but inexplicable.

> After his first fall, man himself departed in soul from God and became unreceptive to the grace of God which was opened to him; he ceased to listen to the divine voice addressed to him, and this led to the further deepening of sin in him…. Thus, original sin is understood by Orthodox theology as a sinful inclination which has entered into mankind and become its spiritual disease. […] With sin, death [physical] entered into the human race. Man was created immortal in his soul, and he could have

---

[5] Fr. Emmanuel Clapsis, "Suffering and the Crucified Christ," Greek Orthodox Diocese of America 8/17/2015 https://www.goarch.org/-/suffering-and-the-crucified-christ ; Accessed 5 June 2023.

remained immortal also in body if he had not fallen away from God.[6]

God's expulsion of Adam and Eve from the Garden of Eden and their process of dying physically was not solely punitive. As Irenaeus taught (ca.185), the expulsion was itself a grace to prevent an eternity spent estranged from God in a corrupted body.[7] Original sin did not produce damnable guilt upon all humans as in Augustine's 412 CE invention; and, within Orthodoxy, has often been termed the ancestral or primal sin to distinguish it from Augustine's novel "Original Sin" view.[8]

Conclusion

Therefore, the Orthodox view of praying for corporate sanctification and a further conformation into the likeness of God after death appear possible biblically. The rejection of purgatory as a particular place or location parallels the modern

---

[6] Michael Pomazansky, *Orthodox Dogmatic Theology: A Concise Exposition, trans. and ed.* Hieromonk Seraphim Rose (1963 as *Pravoslavnoye Dogmaticheskoye Bogoslaviye*; rev. 1973; repr. 3rd expanded edn. (Platina, CA: St. Herman of Alaska Brotherhood, 2009) https://www.intratext.com/IXT/ENG0824/_P1J.HTM ; Accessed 5 June 2023. The location is "Man's Fall into Sin": "God's Grace to Fallen Man."

[7] Irenaeus, *Adv. Haer.* 3.25.2; Cf., Craig Truglia, "The Orthodox Doctrine of Sin: A Comprehensive Treatment," at Orthodox Christian Theology, April 11, 2012 at https://orthodoxchristiantheology.com/2021/04/11/the-orthodox-doctrine-of-original-sin-a-comprehensive-treatment/; Accessed 5 June 2023.

[8] M.C. Steenberg, "Original Sin," in John McGuckin, ed. *The Concise Encyclopedia of Orthodox Christianity* (Oxford: Wiley Blackwell, 2014), 348–9. Wilson, *Augustine's Conversion*, 110–113, 117, 121, 128, 134, 159.

Catholic view. The rejection of expiatory suffering seems to have more of a philosophical basis since expiatory suffering for sin occurs repeatedly within scripture. This will be covered in the next chapter as we critique the Catholic view.

Chapter 7
Critique of the Roman Catholic View

Modern Catholics reject the concept of purgatory as a location of posthumous punishment. Even Catholics during the Counter Reformation admitted the abuses and corruption within the Church (e.g., Cardinal Sadoleto's letter to John Calvin). The distinguishing doctrine of the Roman Catholic Church concerns the expiatory nature of Christian suffering after death.

On Purgatory *by St. Bellarmine*

St. Bellarmine (1542–1621, Doctor of the Church) assumed Purgatory was a place. "Purgatory is a certain place in which, like a prison, souls which were not fully purged here on earth are purged after this life, that so purged they may undoubtedly avail to enter heaven, in which nothing tainted will enter. On this is the whole controversy."[1] His numerous OT passages supporting Purgatory were used by some early church fathers allegorically, but (in my opinion) are not convincing.[2]

Bellarmine's primary NT text is Matt 12:32, "Whoever

---

[1] Robert Bellarmine, *On Purgatory*, trans. Ryan Grant (Post Falls, ID: Mediatrix Press, 2017), 6.

[2] These include 2 Macc, Tobias 4:18, 1 Sam 31:13, 2 Sam 1:12, Ps 37 , Ps 65 (66):11, Isa 4:4 and 9:18, Micah 7:8, Zech 9:12, and Mal 3:3.

speaks a word against the Son of Man will be forgiven, but whoever speaks against the Holy Spirit will not be forgiven, either in this age or in the age to come." (NCB) St. Augustine, St. Gregory, St. Bede, and St. Bernard all used this text as evidence for the efficacy of prayers and offerings for the dead.[3] I agree with Bellarmine that there will punishment in the next life. However, I disagree that this particular verse demonstrates such an idea. An alternative explanation follows.

Matthew 12:32 Evaluated

Jesus warns that the blasphemy of the Holy Spirit will not be forgiven in this world or the next.[4] The context is the Pharisees who blasphemed the Holy Spirit by attributing to Beelzebul Jesus' miracle of demonic exorcism, performed through the power of the Holy Spirit (12:22–24). This horrendous sin of rejecting God's unprecedented divine power displayed through the incarnate Jesus could not be forgiven on this earth or

---

[3] Bellarmine, *Purgatory*, 26.

[4] Most all Protestant expositors claim this sin consists of a person firmly rejecting Jesus Christ, which is out of context. The text states that speaking against Christ will be forgiven. For a different approach see Scott N. Callaham, "Blasphemy against the Holy Spirit: Rejecting the Sign of the Covenant," Horizons in Biblical Theology, Online April 20, 2023. https://brill.com/view/journals/hbth/45/1/article-p37_3.xml; Accessed 3 June 2023. For what I view as a more contextually cogent answer see Duane Liftin, "Revisiting the Unpardonable Sin: Insight from an Unexpected Source," *JETS* 60.4 (2017): 713–32. BDAG, page 178 "Βλασφημεω" demonstrates this sin is a verbal attack of false attribution. Blasphemy is speaking an insult or a false attacking accusation. Blasphemy must be verbal. Therefore, this sin is verbal. Unbelief in Christ or rejection of Christ is not in view.

eternally. These Jews would be punished both on this earth (this age/life) and in the next age/life. Jesus prophesied the physical destruction of these rebellious people and their temple in 70 CE by General Titus, and their eternal damnation in the next life. "As a result, upon you will fall the guilt of all the innocent blood that has been shed upon the earth...." (23:35; cf., John 15:20–25) "You snakes! You brood of vipers! How can you escape being condemned to Gehenna?" (23:33, NCB) Jesus continues in Matt 24:2 to clarify this meaning: "Truly I tell you, not one stone will be left here upon another; all will be thrown down." That is why Peter warned the Jews of that generation to save themselves not from hell, but from that wicked generation (Acts 2:40). In 70 CE, Titus destroyed the temple and killed tens of thousands of Jews. This judgment occurred in *this* world.

But Jesus also warned the hypocritical Pharisees that they would not escape the condemnation of Gehenna (hell, Matt 23:33). That is in the *next* world. Therefore, Jesus is stating that when these Jews attributed to Satan the mighty miracles Jesus performed through the Holy Spirit, that the Jews of that generation would not have forgiveness either in this world or the next. It is a double condemnation—both now and eternally. The text says nothing about the possibility of sins being forgiven in the next world. It states only that the unique sin of attributing the Holy Spirit's earthly miracles through the incarnate Christ to Satan (verbally blaspheming the Holy Spirit and limited to that generation) will *not* be forgiven now or forever. One must engage in speculation to assume there is a forgiveness in the next world from this passage. A general forgiveness of sins in the next life through prayers and offerings must be found elsewhere.[5]

Bellarmine's analysis of 1 Cor 3:15 proves beneficial as he examines the various alternatives and opinions of authors.[6] This text will be discussed in the next chapter.

Expiatory Suffering after Death

Expiation is the act of purifying from sin, making atonement, or reparation for an offense. *The Cambridge Dictionary* defines expiation as "the act of showing that you are sorry for bad behavior by doing something or accepting punishment." The *Catholic Dictionary* states, "Atonement for some wrong-doing. It implies an attempt to undo the wrong that one has done, by suffering a penalty, by performing some penance, or by making reparation or redress. (Etym. Latin ex-, fully + piare, to propitiate: expiare, to atone for fully.)" Jurgie's definition explains, "Expiation is a debt for sins committed, which is paid by suffering; it is a reparation offered to the holiness and the

---

[5] As stated, the typical Protestant understanding that the blasphemy of the Holy Spirit is rejecting the person of Jesus fails to address the context. E.g., Wayne Grudem, *Systematic Theology* (Grand Rapids, MI: Zondervan, 1994), 506–9.

[6] Bellarmine, *Purgatory,* 31–53.

justice of God, offended by sin."[7] Thus, Jurgie's definition differs from the ancient Latin one wherein repentance is a change of heart by the sinner.

Protestants will object that Christ has already made atonement for our sin (1 John 2:2). What is not so clear is why we still need an "advocate" (παράκλητον) when we sin as Christians. Again, if "Jesus paid it all" then why must we confess our sins? "If we confess our sins, he is faithful and just and will forgive us our sins and purify us from all unrighteousness" (1 John 1:9, NIV). God's faithfulness to forgive our sin is conditional upon our change of heart by confessing that sin. What happens if we do not confess our sins? Do we go to Hell? Most Protestants would answer, "No." So what does occur if Christians do not confess sins?

Revisiting 1 John 1:9

Note that the "purify us from all unrighteousness" also appears in 1 John 1:7, but without any mention of confession. Instead, we are cleansed if "we walk in the light as he is in the light." This chapter and epistle emphasize practical holiness in becoming more like Christ in sanctification (i.e., Catholic justification). Most Protestants have been taught "cleanse/purify us from all unrighteousness" in 1:9 means God also forgives the sins we do not confess. But that is unlikely when we compare it

---

[7] Martin Jurgie, *Purgatory and the Means to Avoid It*, trans. Malachy G. Carroll from the 7th French edn. (Cork: The Mercier Press, 1949), 8.

with 1:7, where the same wording appears *without* confessing sin.

> "But if we walk in the light as He Himself is in the light, we have fellowship with one another, and the **blood of Jesus His Son cleanses us from all sin.**" (1 John 1:7, HCSB, bold mine)

> "If we confess our sins, He is faithful and righteous to forgive us our sins and **to cleanse us from all unrighteousness.**" (1 John 1:9, HCSB, bold mine)

In my view, the cleansing from sin/unrighteousness is not forgiveness. It is progressive practical conformity to Christ's character. The epistle emphasizes that Christians should be obedient. We should walk away from the world (1 John 2:15–17) and follow/obey Jesus Christ by walking in the light. Being obedient and confessing sin restores intimacy with God as he conforms us to the image of Christ. Forgiveness for unconfessed sin is not in view. Cleansing is conformity to Christ's character.

Punishment for the Sin of Unforgiveness

Jesus warned about unforgiveness toward another person. "But if you don't forgive others, your Father will not forgive your offenses." (Matt 6:15, CSB) These concepts are difficult to explain with "Jesus paid it all." If true, then God could not punish his children for ongoing sin. What happens when God does not forgive our sin? How can that be true if Jesus paid it all? There remains some type of negative consequence for the sin of not forgiving another person. It should not relate to being sent to hell, but should relate to something unpleasant either in this life or the next.[8]

Why does scripture emphasize forgiveness so much that God's forgiveness of our sin is conditional upon us forgiving others? Jesus explained this in Matthew 18:21–25. Peter, as a Christian (Matt 16:16), was told to forgive his brothers seventy-times-seven times. Jesus then warned Peter what would happen if he did not forgive others. "Then the angry king sent the man to prison to be tortured until he had paid his entire debt. That's what my heavenly Father will do to you if you refuse to forgive your brothers and sisters from your heart." (NLT) A Puritan pastor explained, "He that cannot forgive others breaks the bridge over which he must pass himself; for every man has need to be forgiven." (Thomas Fuller, 1608–1661)

Therefore, expiation *does not* concern hell. Expiation *does* concern sin in a Christian. No Christian goes to hell. But if God does not forgive that sin then something must be done with it—God will judge it. According to scripture, God will punish (even "torture") those Christians who do not forgive others.[9]

---

[8] Those whose view is that God always repays here on earth (direct retribution theology) need to read the book of Job. The "friends" were rebuked for falsely accusing Job of sin under this theological delusion.

[9] The phrase παρέδωκεν αὐτὸν τοῖς βασανισταῖς refers to a merciless jailor commonly associated with torture of prisoners; BDAG, βασανισμός "1. infliction of severe suffering or pain associated with torture or torment, *tormenting, torture* Rv 9:5b."

Review of the Two Courts of Law

Again, these are two separate courts of law. Suppose I steal a $2,000 computer from a store, then during the getaway my car dents a parked car. The criminal court will charge me with a Class A misdemeanor liable for up to a $4000 fine and/or up to one year in jail. So, I plead guilty to keep from going to jail but my brother must pay my $4000 fine since I have no money. I am free of the criminal charges—all is paid. However, the owner of the dented car witnessed the accident, took down my license plate number, and sues me in civil court for $4,000 in damages. I am still liable for the civil damages although the criminal charges have been paid by my brother. There are two different courts of law.

In the same way, God can forgive his child of all sin through the sacrificial payment of Christ. In criminal court, I am not going to hell. The penalty of eternal death has been forever paid. But, God can still have his child pay personally for sin in a civil family court.

Bellarmine's chapter on 1 Cor 15:29 argues that early Christians were being figuratively baptized for the dead through suffering in prayers and fastings for them (like the ancient Jews were accustomed to doing).[10] Baptism signifies the purging fire of suffering or judgment. We see this in Mark 10:38, "Can you drink the cup I drink or be baptized with the baptism I am

---

[10] Bellarmine, *Purgatory*, 59–61.

baptized with?" (NIV) In Luke 12:50, "But I have a baptism to undergo, and what constraint I am under until it is completed!" (NIV) In Matt 3:11–12, "He will baptize you with the Holy Spirit and fire. His winnowing fork is in his hand, and he will clear his threshing floor, gathering his wheat into the barn and burning up the chaff with unquenchable fire." (NIV)[11] Both *The Oxford Companion to the Bible* and *The Oxford Bible Commentary* interpret this phrase to mean some Corinthians were vicariously being water baptized for people who had died.[12] Fergusson discusses the proxy baptism for the deceased by the Valentinians, Cerinthians, Theodotus, and others designated as Gnostics.[13]

The statements of Jesus about handing over to the Judge until the last farthing is paid has been applied to Purgatory. Even Bellarmine admits the validity of Chrysostom's view: this is most probably limited to an earthly transaction ("reconciliation with a human adversary.")[14] However, Bellarmine compares Matthew 5:25 with Luke 12:58 where eight early church fathers

---

[11] The charismatic concept that this refers to tongues of fire (as in Acts 2) misses the context of judgment in verse 12.

[12] Bruce Metzger and Michael Coogan, eds. *The Oxford Companion to the Bible* (New York: Oxford University Press, 1993), 74; John Barton and John Muddiman, eds. *The Oxford Bible Commentary* (Oxford: Oxford University Press, 2001), 1131.

[13] Everett Ferguson, *Baptism in the Early Church: History, Theology, and Liturgy in the First Five Centuries* (Grand Rapids, MI: Eerdmans, 2009), 276–302.

[14] Bellarmine, *Purgatory*, 66.

allegorize it to mean Purgatory. This later tradition does not appear to be a strong argument.

Indulgences to lessen suffering

Indulgences do not save a person from Hell. Since the first centuries, the Roman Catholic Church has provided ways of lessening temporary suffering after death. This practice cannot be identified in scripture. It exists by tradition, based upon "biblical principles." [15] Since "only God can forgive sin," indulgences do not forgive sin. "An indulgence is a remission before God of the temporal punishment due to sins whose guilt has *already been forgiven*" (*Indulgentiarium Doctrina* 1). Rather, they lessen the consequences of sin on the sinner in the afterlife. "An indulgence is partial or plenary according as it removes either part or all of the temporal punishment due to sin" (*Indulgentiarium Doctrina* 2, 3). Christ paid the eternal punishment of hell. Indulgences pay the temporal (temporary) penalty of sin.

> In the Sacrament of Penance the guilt of sin is removed, and with it the eternal punishment due to mortal sin; but there still remains the temporal

---

[15] E.g., 2 Corinthians 2:6-11 is understood as Paul granting indulgences. See Dave Armstrong, "The Biblical Roots and History of Indulgences," *National Catholic Register*, 25 May 2018; https://www.ncregister.com/blog/the-biblical-roots-and-history-of-indulgences ; Accessed 9 May 2023. The objective support for this interpretation and praxis seems weak.

punishment required by Divine justice, and this requirement must be fulfilled either in the present life or in the world to come, i.e., in Purgatory. An indulgence offers the penitent sinner the means of discharging this debt during his life on earth.[16]

Vicarious sacrifice can be evidenced in the sufferings of Jesus Christ, so the principle is sound. The offering of indulgences for persons who are already deceased raises some questions. We do see Job offering sacrifices for sin on behalf of his living children. "And when the feast days had run their course, Job would send and sanctify them, and he would rise early in the morning and offer burnt offerings according to the number of them all; for Job said, 'It may be that my children have sinned, and cursed God in their hearts.' This is what Job always did." (Job 1:5, NRSV) Scripture does not speak to its validity.

The book of 2 Maccabees is in the Apocrypha, not the Pseudepigrapha. However, by the time of Augustine (ca.400) many churches were reading Maccabees as divine scripture.[17] The Septuagint versions (Greek translations of the Hebrew OT) can be obtained today with or without the Apocryphal writings. In contrast to the early Catholic Church, Jewish scholars have not been interested in this book, nor is it part of their Jewish

---

[16] William Kent, "Indulgences," *The Catholic Encyclopedia*, vol. 7 (New York: Robert Appleton Company, 1910).
http://www.newadvent.org/cathen/07783a.htm ; Accessed 9 May 2023.

[17] Augustine of Hippo, *City of God* (*Civ. Dei* 18.36).

canon of scripture.[18] The Roman Catholic Church accepts 2 Maccabees as part of the biblical canon, despite its rejection as Holy Scripture by Jews, Protestants, and Jerome—a Doctor of the Church and premier biblical scholar. It seems reasonable to think that the prayers for the dead by the early church found a source for their practice in 2 Maccabees, thus embracing it— despite its rejection as Jewish scripture.[19]

According to the text, these sacrifices for the dead were intended to help them at the resurrection, not while they were still dead. God had allowed these soldiers to be killed because they had taken "things consecrated to the idols of the Jamnites." This was forbidden by Jewish law, a deliberate sin that violated the first commandment of Moses. If these idol items had been taken merely for monetary value then these soldiers may not have been killed by God as a result of willful sin of idolatry. But, according to Catholic doctrine, these persons who were killed must have died in a state of grace (a positive intentional union with God and neighbor) at death to avoid hell and qualify for purgatory. So these Jews, if they had been Catholics, may not have qualified for purgatory. Even if one accepts 2

---

[18] Daniel R. Schwartz, *2 Maccabees. Commentaries on Early Jewish Literature* (Berlin/New York: Walter de Gruyter, 2008), "Reception and Text," 85–96. For a broader description of the Jewish canonical process see Martin Goodman, *A History of Judaism* (Princeton, NJ: Princeton University Press, 2018), 26–38.

[19] The Orthodox Church also accepts 2 Maccabees as canonical.

Maccabees as part of scripture these were Jews, not Christians.[20] Therefore, in my opinion, this is a questionable proof text for the Roman Catholic doctrine of indulgences for the dead.

The merits of saints might be endless, and the merits of Christ are certainly endless. Can a living person do a good work that can be credited to help a dead person? How do we know God (through the Pope) actually transfers those merits to the dead? This tradition is indeed ancient but lacking in biblical support. Nevertheless, the Church has declared this practice valid.

Tertullian used Matthew 5:25–26 to prove the prison of purgatory.[21] "Settle matters quickly with your adversary who is taking you to court. Do it while you are still together on the way, or your adversary may hand you over to the judge, and the judge may hand you over to the officer, and you may be thrown into prison. Truly I tell you, you will not get out until you have paid the last penny." (NET) There could be some merit to this understanding, but the immediate context (the sentence prior) argues for an earthly social understanding. "So if you are offering your gift at the altar and there remember that your brother has something against you, leave your gift there before

---

[20] Catholics suggest that it was the same God in the OT and NT, and the same Decalogue applies. Therefore, this principle of sacrifice for the dead can apply to Christians. I agree with the premise, but God changed his method of human interaction with the new covenant so sacrifices ceased. This fact should cause pause in forming a conclusion assuming that Jewish sacrifices for the dead apply to Christians.

[21] Tertullian, *Treatise on the Soul*, 58.

the altar and go. First be reconciled to your brother, and then come and offer your gift." (ESV) If the prior verse refers to social behavior now, then the next verse about the court is more likely to refer to earthly circumstances. The verses prior (5:21–22) and following (5:27–30) refer to judgment for anger, the council for insulting, and then the Gehenna of fire for calling a fellow Jew μωρός (fool). It appears moral behavior will be judged. The context suggests an earthly interaction that will ultimately be judged in the future kingdom. [22] The verses following (5:27–30) speak of Gehenna fire for mental adultery. Therefore, neither of these verses seem to support that Jesus taught on purgatory, although they might be construed this way.

Prayers for the Dead

This ancient practice has been explained by Burns as an expression of love for other Christians who have departed.

> Prayer for the dead is indeed an ancient practice of Christians, well evidenced in the literature. In context, it seems to be an extension of the prayer that was offered for a repenting sinner, undergoing the ritual required for major sins. As Christians had prayed for divine mercy upon their sinful fellows before death, they continued to do so after they had

---

[22] But see Nathan Eubank, "Prison, Penance or Purgatory: The Interpretation of Matthew 5.25-6 and Parallels," *New Testament Studies* 64.2 (April 2018): 162–177.

died. The divine judgment on these sinners was the focus of that prayer.[23]

The modern Catholic Church continues to provide indulgences for Catholics who pray for the dead.

> This year, the Vatican has decided once again to grant a plenary indulgence to Catholics who visit a cemetery to pray for the dead on any day in the month of November. In a typical year, the Church only grants this plenary indulgence for the souls in Purgatory to those who pray in a cemetery on Nov. 1-8, the week of the Solemnity of All Souls' Day. But last year the Apostolic Penitentiary issued a decree that extended the availability of certain plenary indulgences amid concerns about avoiding large gatherings of people in churches or cemeteries due to the COVID-19 pandemic.[24]

This view of posthumous punishment helps explain numerous scriptures that otherwise must either be relegated to non-Christian punishment or allegorized. We will explore these in the next chapter.

---

[23] Professor J. Patout Burns, personal communication, 10 October 2023. I thank him for this explanation.

[24] Courtney Mares, "Catholics can get an indulgence for the dead by praying at a cemetery any day this November," *Catholic News Agency*, Oct 28, 2021; https://www.catholicnewsagency.com/news/249426/catholics-can-get-an-indulgence-for-the-dead-by-praying-at-a-cemetery-any-day-this-november ; Accessed 11 May 2023.

Chapter 8

Evidences for a Christian

Posthumous Purification

Whether one is Roman Catholic, Orthodox, or Protestant, virtually all Christians agree that the holiness of God in a perfect afterlife requires that all persons entering his presence be purified. The disagreement occurs on how that purification happens. A first step is to understand God's punishment of his own children while they remain on earth.

God punishes his children on earth

Scripture demonstrates that God disciplines and punishes his children while they remain on earth. This nullifies the constant Protestant refrain that "Jesus paid it all" without exception. Roman Catholics, Orthodox, and Protestants all teach that Jesus Christ rescued us from eternal separation from God. Yes, Jesus paid it all in that sense. But God can, and still does, punish his children. So "Jesus paid it all" must be limited in application.

Both the OT and NT contain instances where God punished his children after forgiving their sins. When confronted by Nathan the prophet, King David confessed his sins of adultery and murder (2 Sam 12; Ps 51). Nathan's reply to David instructs us: "The Lord has put away your sin; you shall not die. However, because by this deed you have given great occasion to the enemies of the Lord to blaspheme, the child also *who* is born to you shall surely die" (2 Sam 12:13–14, NKJV). But God inflicted David with even further punishment. Bloodshed from the sword would afflict his household for his entire life (v.10), David's own family would become his adversaries, and his wives would be publicly scandalized by another man (v.11). David's confession of sin provided forgiveness and restored his intimacy with God—his repentance prevented physical death: but neither confession nor repentance absolved him from a future punishment for those sins.[1]

Isaiah warned that physical death would be the only means of atonement for the sins of God's people. "The LORD of hosts has revealed himself in my ears: 'Surely this iniquity will not be atoned for you until you die,' says the Lord GOD of hosts." (Isa 22:14, ESV)[2] The sins of God's children were so atrocious that no repentance would abate God's severe punishment.

Hebrews 12 is the most extended NT teaching on this topic of God's punishment.

---

[1] Some persons might consider these as a prophecy of the evil consequences (fallout) that would result from sin rather than punishment, but the death of David's child from Bathsheba does seem to be punishment.

[2] See also Isa 24:5–6, "The earth lies defiled under its inhabitants; for they have transgressed the laws, violated the statutes, broken the everlasting covenant. Therefore a curse devours the earth, and its inhabitants suffer for their guilt; therefore the inhabitants of the earth are scorched, and few men are left. (ESV)

And you have forgotten the exhortation that addresses you as sons: My son, do not take the Lord's discipline lightly or lose heart when you are reproved by him, for "The Lord disciplines [punishes] the one he loves and punishes [flogs, scourges] every son he receives." [the author quotes from Prov. 3:11–12][3]

Endure suffering as discipline: God is dealing with you as sons. For what son is there that a father does not discipline? But if you are without discipline—which all receive—then you are illegitimate children and not sons. Furthermore, we had human fathers discipline us, and we respected them. Shouldn't we submit even more to the Father of spirits and live? For they disciplined us for a short time based on what seemed good to them, but he does it for our benefit, so that we can share his holiness. No discipline seems enjoyable at the time, but painful. Later on, however, it yields the peaceful fruit of righteousness to those who have been trained by it. (Heb 12:5–11, CSB)

---

[3] BDAG connects ἐλεγχόμενος in both Pr 3:11 (LXX) and Heb 12:5 to punishment: "**4. to penalize for wrongdoing, *punish, discipline*** (Wsd 1:8; 12:2; Job 5:17 al.) **Hb 12:5** (Pr 3:11); (w. παιδεύειν, as Sir 18:13) **Rv 3:19.**— LLutkemeyer, CBQ 8, '46, 221–23.—B. 1442." Likewise, μαστιγοῖ means "**1. to beat with a whip or lash, *whip, flog, scourge*** a. of flogging as a punishment decreed by the synagogue (Dt 25:2f; s. the Mishna Tractate Sanhedrin-Makkoth, edited w. notes by SKrauss '33) w. acc. of pers. **Mt 10:17; 23:34.** Of the beating administered to Jesus **J 19:1.** (bold and italics original) The author of Hebrews uses **παιδεία** eight times from Chap. 5–11 with the concept of training. Protestants have chosen to sidestep punishment by God as a divine aspect of our transformation into holy people.

This passage references Job 5:17–18: "How happy is the one whom God reproves; therefore do not despise the discipline of the Almighty. For he wounds, but he binds up; he strikes, but his hands heal." (NRSVC) Yes, God punishes his children with discipline. Therefore, the blood of Christ does not remove all punishment for sin in this life. His sacrifice carries full efficacy for forgiving sin, but *total* dismissal of the consequence is limited to saving from the specific punishment of eternal death.

As we already discussed in 1 Cor 11:27–32, Christians were sick and dying as punishment for their sins.

> For this reason, whoever eats the bread or drinks the cup of the Lord in an unworthy manner will be guilty of the body and blood of the Lord. A person should examine himself first, and in this way let him eat the bread and drink of the cup. For the one who eats and drinks without careful regard for the body eats and drinks judgment against himself. That is why many of you are weak and sick, and quite a few are dead. But if we examined ourselves, we would not be judged. But when we are judged by the Lord, we are disciplined so that we may not be condemned with the world. (NET)

That discipline of Christians by God was a judgment that included illness and death. Those are punishments.

This parallels 1 John 5:16 "If anyone sees his brother committing a sin that does not bring death, he should ask, and

God will give life to him—to those who commit sin that doesn't bring death. There is sin that brings death. I am not saying he should pray about that." (1 John 5:16, HCSB) The death in context of a brother (or sister) should indicate physical death as in 1 Cor 11, not eternal death.[4] God uses physical death of his children as a punishment. Commentaries that find eternal death here impose their own theology while ignoring the ubiquitous Jewish prevalence of physical death for sin. See Appendix A for a more scholarly discussion.

The same principle applies in James 5:19–20. "My brethren, if one of you should stray from the truth and another succeeds in bringing him back, remember this: A person who brings back a sinner from erring ways will rescue his soul from death and cover a multitude of sins." The Greek σώσει ψυχὴν αὐτοῦ ἐκ θανάτου (save his soul/life from death) has often been understood as saving unto eternal life. However, this phrase appears only three times in the NT outside of the four Gospels. Interestingly, all are in Jewish epistles—Hebrews, 1 Peter, and James—and follow Jesus' uses in the Gospels. The ψυχὴ can mean the life of the person as in 1 Peter 3:20, "when once the longsuffering of God waited in the days of Noah, while the ark

---

[4] The NCV Bible imposes its theology when translating the text: "sinning (sin that does not lead to eternal death)" The NRSVA translates as "If you see your brother or sister committing what is not a mortal sin, you will ask, and God will give life to such a one—to those whose sin is not mortal. There is sin that is mortal; I do not say that you should pray about that."

was a preparing, wherein few, that is, eight souls [ψυχαί] were saved by water." (KJV) Too often our Christian interpretations neglect the Jewish concepts underlying the Christian teachings. God sometimes punishes Christians on earth with physical death. This death is punishment, not merely "discipline" or "child training" as most Protestants like to call it.

God did not send Christ to die so that we could "go to heaven," yet allow us to continue living sinful lives. God desires his children to live holy lives now—practical holiness in this life to imitate him. "Always live as God's holy people should, because God is the one who chose you, and he is holy. That's why the Scriptures say, 'I am the holy God, and you must be holy too.' You say that God is your Father, but God doesn't have favorites! **He judges all people by what they do.** So you must honor God while you live as strangers here on earth." (1 Pet 1:15–17, CEV, bold mine). God will discipline and punish so that it hurts in order to help us live holy lives.

The eternal penalty has been paid: the temporal penalty remains to encourage holiness. If God punishing us in this life does not violate Christ's all-sufficient sacrifice for sin, why should God's punishment in the afterlife do so? Both are temporal punishments—time limited, not eternal. Does Protestant justification absolve the Christian of all future punishment? I suggest the answer is a definite, "No." God punishes his children causing them pain on the earth in this life. We now turn to passages on God's punishment in the next life.

1 Corinthians 3:15

One of the key passages for purgatory used by the Roman Catholic Church is 1 Cor 3:15. The Orthodox Church rejects this purgatorial interpretation due to John Chrysostom's thoughts that this person goes to hell, with "saved" meaning he persists in eternal fire (rather than annihilation). Chrysostom writes,

> Now his meaning [on 1 Cor 3:15] is this: If any man have an ill life with a right faith, his faith shall not shelter him from punishment, his work being burnt up. The phrase, "shall be burned up," means, "shall not endure the violence of the fire." But just as if a man having golden armor on were to pass through a river of fire, he comes from crossing it all the brighter; but if he were to pass through it with hay, so far from profiting, he destroys himself besides; so also is the case in regard of men's works. For he doth not say this as if he were discoursing of material things being burnt up, but with a view of making their fear more intense, and of shewing how naked of all defense he is who abides in wickedness. Wherefore he said, "He shall suffer loss:" lo, here is one punishment: "but he himself shall be saved, but so as by fire;" lo, again, here is a second. And his meaning is, "He himself shall not perish in the same way as his works, passing into nought, but he shall abide in the fire." [53][6.] He calleth it, however, "Salvation," you will say; why, that is the cause of his adding, "so

as by fire:" since we also used to say, "It is preserved
in the fire," when we speak of those substances which
do not immediately burn up and become ashes. For
do not at sound of the word fire imagine that those
who are burning pass into annihilation. (*Homily 9* on
1 Cor 3)

Chrysostom argues "preserved in the fire" means eternal
suffering in fire rather than being annihilated. However,
Chrysostom seems to have missed the Jewish background of
Paul's reference. Townsend explains at length.

A neglected key to the exegesis of 1 Cor. 3:15 is to
be found in *Rosh ha-Shanah* 16b-17a *bar.*
(///'TSanhedrin 13:3). According to the *baraita* the
schools of Hillel and Shammai were in agreement
that on Judgment Day (יום הדין) the thoroughly
righteous (צדיקים גמורין) will be consigned to life
eternal and the thoroughly wicked (רשעים גמורין), to
Gehinnom; but concerning those who were in
between (בינונים), who were neither wholly good nor
wholly bad, the two schools differed. The followers
of Hillel reasoned that a gracious God would incline
the scales in favor of the (בינוניים). The Shammaites,
however, were not so lenient. They maintained that
the בינוניים would "go down to Gehinnom, 'chirp' (cf.
Isa. 29:4) and arise (לגיהנם ומצפצפין ועולין יוררין)."
Biblical support for this view was found primarily in
Zech. 13:9, according to which the LORD promises,

"And I will bring this third into the fire (באש) and will refine them as one refines silver and will test them as one tests gold. And they shall call on my name, and I will answer them." The parallelism between this Rabbinic passage and 1 Cor. 3:10-15 is striking. Like the *baraita,* Paul is speaking about בינוניים. These Corinthian teachers were not wholly evil, since they had done their building upon the foundation of Christ (vss. 10-12); yet they had not built well. Both Paul and the *baraita* speak in terms of refining gold and silver in the fire (vss. 12-14), although, in the case of the Apostle, his elaborate metaphor requires him to relate the refining reference to the works of each בינוני and not to the man himself. Also, unless one accepts Chrysostom's interpretation of σωθήσεται, both Paul and the Shammaites believed in the ultimate salvation of the בינוניים.

Finally there is the parallelism between the *baraita* and the statement in I Cor. 3:15 that the salvation of the בינוניים. will be "οὕτως δὲ ὡς διὰ πυρός." While it is possible that the Pauline statement is merely a figure of speech denoting a narrow escape, the Apostle's wording, taken more literally, does correspond surprisingly well with the Shammaitic belief that the בינוניים will pass through hell fire before their final salvation. Of course, in 1 Cor. 3 the Apostle has depicted the fires as the apocalyptic flames of the *eschaton* rather than the fires of

Gehinnom. This difference, however, is more apparent than real, since according to the *baraita* the fires of Gehinnom are also those of the Last Judgment.[5]

Additionally, Townsend provides evidence that Paul himself was probably a Shammaite Pharisee. Paul's father was also a Pharisee (Acts 23:6). I add that according to Acts 26:5, "They have known me for a long time and can testify, if they are willing, that according to the strictest sect of our religion, I lived as a Pharisee" (NIV84; κατὰ ἀκρίβειαν τοῦ πατρῴου νόμου, SBLGNT).[6] The strictest sect was that of Beit Shammai.[7] The comment in Acts 22:3, where Paul claims to have been educated by Gamaliel, has led some scholars to mistakenly believe he was of the Hillel sect. But Finkelstein has convincingly argued that "both Simeon ben Gamaliel I, and Gamaliel II, were

---

[5] John T. Townsend, "1 Corinthians 3:15 and the School of Shammai," HTR 61.3 (July 1968): 500–504. Townsend taught NT and Rabbinic literature at Harvard Divinity School.

[6] The Greek Orthodox NT (GOC) reads, ὅτι κατὰ τὴν ἀκριβεστάτην αἵρεσιν τῆς ἡμετέρας θρησκείας ἔζησα Φαρισαῖος.

[7] Marcus Jastrow, S. Mendelsohn, sv. "Bet Hillel and Bet Shammai," in *Jewish Encyclopedia*, "The Hillelites were, like the founder of their school (Ber. 60a; Shab. 31a; Ab. i. 12 *et seq.*), quiet, peace-loving men, accommodating themselves to circumstances and times, and being determined only upon fostering the Law and bringing man nearer to his God and to his neighbor. The Shammaites, on the other hand, stern and unbending like the originator of their school, emulated and even exceeded his severity. To them it seemed impossible to be sufficiently stringent in religious prohibitions." https://jewishencyclopedia.com/articles/13499-shammaites ; Accessed 19 May 2023. See also E.P. Sanders, *Judaism: Practice & Belief 63BCE–66CE* (London: SCM Press, 1992), 436–7.

Shammaites." [8] So, Paul was most probably a disciple of Shammai that taught a purging of sin after death. This fits 1 Cor 3:15 with an after death experience of God's punishment. After death, every Christian will receive recompense for what was done in the physical body, whether good or bad.

Finally, Chrysostom's use of σῴζω/σωθήσεται (will be saved/delivered) as "preserving" the sinner in the fire eternally (rather than experiencing annihilation) must be questioned. Not even one other NT use of σῴζω/σωθήσεται refers to a negative outcome. All refer to a deliverance from something negative unto something positive. The interpretation of "preserving" the Christian in the eternal fire of punishment does match Chrysostom's ascetic rigor, but it lacks NT support in his strained use of σῴζω/σωθήσεται (will be saved).

Therefore, the evidence favors understanding 1 Cor 3:15 as Paul's continuation of his training as a Pharisee—of being ultimately delivered from a purging trial through fire at God's judgment, not the interpretation of Chrysostom. As previously

---

[8] Louis Finkelstein, *Aktba: Scholar, Saint, and Martyr* (Cleveland, OH: Meridian Books, JP25 and Philadelphia, PA: Jewish Publication Society of America, 1962), 296. During the reign of Agrippa, Simeon ben Gamaliel (Hillel's great grandson) converted to the Shammaites (46). "Gamaliel's descent from Hillel, and the fact that after his removal from office he somewhat changed his policy have helped to conceal both from talmudic scholars and modern historians his definitively Shammaitic inclinations. But the record leaves no room for doubt on the subject." Finkelstein proceeds to list nine significant reasons Gamaliel was a Shammaite.] (304–6). He was a professor then Chancellor at the Jewish Theological Seminary (d.1991). https://archive.org/details/akibascholarsain0000fink/page/44/mode/2up?view=theater ; Accessed 19 May 2023.

stated, all major Christian groups teach a purifying experience prior to entering Paradise (the beatific vision, heaven).

But Protestant scholars like Thiselton argue against any punishment (by using nuances).[9]

> The parallels **will receive a reward** (v. 14 where λήμψεται is the future indicative of λαμβάνω) and **will suffer loss** (v. 15, ζημιωθήσεται), should be referred back to the inscription language of the building contract identified and discussed by J. Shanor (see above on 3:10).[75] There if necessary work (ἔργον) was delayed or inadequate, penalty clauses allowed for fines or loss of payment (ζαμίαι, ζαμιότω, allowing for an earlier and different regional dialect form in fourth-century-BC Arcadian Tegae). ζημιόω does not normally mean *to punish*, but *to deprive someone of something*. Only if this imagery is interpreted as point-for-point allegory to be decoded rather than as a broad image to make a forceful point can theoretical issues concerning possible "penalty" be transposed into some kind of postmortem doctrine.[76] (See also above on μισθός in 3:8 and on δοκιμάσει in 3:13.)

---

[9] Anthony C. Thiselton, *The First Epistle to the Corinthians: A Commentary on the Greek Text* (New International Greek Testament Commentary; Grand Rapids, MI: W.B. Eerdmans, 2000), 314. His citation 75 is "Cf. Shanor, 'Paul as Master Builder,' 461–71. The passive form carries a future middle meaning here." and 76 is "See J. Gnilka, *1 Kor. 3:10–15 ein Schriftzeugnis für das Fegfeuer?* (Düsseldorf: Triltsch, 1955)."

Note that Thiselton himself states "penalty clauses allowed for fines." This is receiving a penalty, not merely suffering the loss of something, or being deprived, or missing out on something. Thiselton ignores this aspect. Also, contra Thiselton, ζημιόω can normally mean *to punish*, as we discover when refuting another Protestant attempting to argue against punishment.

Ryrie claims, "The word *zemioo* in 1 Cor 3:15 carries no idea of suffering in the sense of physical or mental suffering. Its basic idea is loss in the sense of forfeiture of reward that could have been received."[10] Indeed, many Protestants claim 1 Cor 3 only refers to rewards or loss of rewards (since God no longer punishes sin). Ryrie cites Robertson and Plummer who prefer "mulcted of the reward." It is difficult to understand their preference (and Ryrie's) when the context of their very own proof text with *zemioo* (ἐπιζήμιον ζημιωθήσεται, LXX) in Exodus 21:22 is not about losing something that could have been gained (loss of reward), but a punishment of having to pay money for damages. I traced this "loss of reward" error back to Scofield (see Appendix B) and his followers, exposing their lack of any supporting scholarship. There is no valid reason to

---

[10] Charles Ryrie, *Basic Theology* (Chicago: Moody Press, 1986; repr. 1999), 598. [cites A.T. Robertson and Alfred Plummer, *A Critical and Exegetical Commentary on the First Epistle of St. Paul to the Corinthians* (Edinburgh: T. & T. Clark, 1914), 65.] This citation is quoted here: "ζημιωθήσεται. It does not much matter whether we regard this as indefinite, 'He shall suffer loss' (AV., RV.), detrimentum patietur (Vulg.), damnum faciet (Beza), or understand τον μισθόν from v. 14, 'He shall be mulcted of the expected reward.' In Exod. xxi. 22 we have ἐπιζήμιον ζημιωθήσεται. The αὐτός is in favour of the latter."

understand *zemioo* in any way other than "suffering loss" in the context of the next verse (3:16): "God will destroy that person."[11] This sounds like punishment. This also matches the meanings identified in BDAG as "**to experience the loss of someth., with implication of undergoing hardship or suffering**, *suffer damage/loss, forfeit, sustain injury*" and "**be punished**." (bold and italics original)[12] This does not sound like merely losing out on a reward. So, the former interpretations are biased, based on tradition.

Some persons will argue the analogy that only the works are burned, not the person who will be saved. But this ignores the text. "God will destroy him," not just the works. That Christian will be saved "yet as by fire." Actions speak louder than words or intentions. Our works often reveal who we are. Abraham was justified by works (James 2:21–24).[13] Not only our character but our works reveal our level of conformity to Christ.[14] Although Paul may be primarily thinking of church

---

[11] "Don't you know that you yourselves are God's temple and that God's Spirit lives in you? If anyone destroys God's temple, God will destroy him; for God's temple is sacred, and you are that temple." (NIV) Numerous pastors and priests have destroyed congregations and parishes yet received no punishment from God while on earth.

[12] BDAG, ζημιόω, 428.

[13] Although justified by his works (in the Jewish sense), this does not mean he was "saved" by his works in the modern Protestant understanding. See Wilson, "Reading James 2:20–21," 399–400.

[14] See Murray J. Harris, *The Second Epistle to the Corinthians: A Commentary on the Greek Text* (New International Greek Testament

leaders or the church corporate, that *every* person's work will undergo an evaluation through fire should be deduced from similar texts by Paul warning of judgment for all Christians (e.g., Rom 14:10–12; 2 Cor 5:10).

Schenk's commentary provides a more probable exegesis of 1 Cor 3:15. "One key to understanding these verses is to remember that although these Christians are carnal and off track they still have Christ as a foundation. What they have built will burn, but at a fundamental level are still a part of God's people."[15]

> The Corinthians were well acquainted with the idea of a judgment seat or *bēma*. Indeed, Paul himself stood before the *bēma* of Gallio while he was in Corinth (Acts 18:12; see map on p. 248). As in 1 Cor. 3:10–15, Paul reminds the Corinthians that they do not want to face God's wrath on the day when everyone's 'work will be shown for what it is' (1 Cor. 3:13)[16]

The scriptural pattern best correlates with understanding this

---

Commentary; Grand Rapids, MI; Milton Keynes, UK: W.B. Eerdmans Pub. Co.; Paternoster Press, 2005), 406–409: "Paul is implying that conduct will be judged as a whole, that 'it is character rather than separate acts that will be rewarded or punished,'[242] [cites Plummer,] we must insist that it is character as evidenced in separate acts, if not specific actions as reflective of character."

[15] Kenneth Schenck, *1 & 2 Corinthians: A Commentary for Bible Students* (Indianapolis, IN: Wesleyan Publishing House, 2006), 64.

[16] Schenck, *1 & 2 Corinthians*, 284.

text as God's Corinthian children facing the punishment of God for their sinful works (while still remaining his children in Christ).

God's Justice of Punishment in the Old Testament

Job—perhaps the oldest book in the Bible—references Job fearing God's punishment, thereby inciting righteous behavior. Just like human parents, God uses fear of punishment for disobedience as one method to motivate us to obedience.

> If I did despise the cause of my manservant or of my maidservant, when they contended with me;
>
> What then shall I do when God riseth up? and when he visiteth, what shall I answer him?
>
> Did not he that made me in the womb make him? and did not one fashion us in the womb?
>
> If I have withheld the poor from their desire, or have caused the eyes of the widow to fail;
>
> Or have eaten my morsel myself alone, and the fatherless hath not eaten thereof;
>
> (For from my youth he was brought up with me, as with a father, and I have guided her from my mother's womb;)
>
> If I have seen any perish for want of clothing, or any poor without covering;

If his loins have not blessed me, and if he were not warmed with the fleece of my sheep;

If I have lifted up my hand against the fatherless, when I saw my help in the gate:

Then let mine arm fall from my shoulder blade, and mine arm be broken from the bone.

For destruction from God was a terror to me, and by reason of his highness I could not endure. (Job 31:13–23, HCSB)

In the book of Job, Elihu exemplifies an erroneous direct retribution theodicy. This claims God always punishes the wicked and pays the righteous while they remain on earth.

He does not preserve the life of the wicked, But gives justice to the oppressed.

He does not withdraw His eyes from the righteous; But *they are* on the throne with kings,

For He has seated them forever, And they are exalted.

And if *they are* bound in fetters, Held in the cords of affliction,

Then He tells them their work and their transgressions—That they have acted defiantly.

He also opens their ear to instruction, And commands that they turn from iniquity.

If they obey and serve *Him,* They shall spend their days in prosperity, And their years in pleasures.

But if they do not obey, They shall perish by the sword, And they shall die without knowledge.

But the hypocrites in heart store up wrath; They do not cry for help when He binds them.

They die in youth, And their life *ends* among the perverted persons.

He delivers the poor in their affliction, And opens their ears in oppression. (Job 36:6–15, KJV)

The Lord rebukes Eliphaz and his friends for misrepresenting God (Job 42:7–9). Repeatedly in the Psalms, King David appropriately complains (contra Elihu in Job) that the wicked prosper in abundance on earth. There appears to be no punishment on earth for the evil ones as they persecute the righteous (Ps 10, 13, 17, etc.).[17] "Deliver my soul from the

---

[17] Ps 10:1–12, JUB "Why dost thou stand afar off, O LORD? *Why* dost thou hide *thyself* in times of trouble? The wicked in *his* pride persecutes the poor; let them be taken in the devices that they have imagined. For the wicked boasts of his heart's desire and blesses the covetous, *whom* the LORD abhors. The wicked, through the pride of his countenance, does not seek *after God:* God *is* not in all his thoughts. His ways are always grievous; thy judgments *are* far above out of his sight; *as for* all his enemies, he puffs at them. He has said in his heart, I shall not be moved, for *I shall* never *be* in adversity. His mouth is full of cursing and deceit and fraud: under his tongue *is* mischief and vanity. He sits in the lurking places of the villages: in the secret places he murders the innocent: his eyes are secretly set against the poor. He lies in wait secretly as a lion in his den: he lies in wait to catch the poor: he catches the poor when he draws him into his net. He crouches *and*

wicked by your sword, from men by your hand, O LORD, from men of the world whose portion is in this life. You fill their womb with treasure; they are satisfied with children, and they leave their abundance to their infants" (Ps 17:12b–14, ESV). "For I was envious of the arrogant when I saw the prosperity of the wicked. For they have no pangs until death; their bodies are fat and sleek. They are not in trouble as others are; they are not stricken like the rest of mankind." (Ps 73:3–5, ESV)

Here is the argument: If God is to remain truthful about justice, then the wicked who prosper on earth without negative consequences must be punished after death. This is not limited to those who we consider "wicked." King David requested, "Remove your stroke from me; I am spent by the hostility of your hand. When you discipline a man with rebukes for sin, you consume like a moth what is dear to him." (Ps 39:10–11, ESV) "You answered them, O LORD our God; You were to them God-Who-Forgives, Though You took vengeance on their deeds." (Ps 99:8, NKJV) Forgiveness does not erase temporal punishment. To answer injustice, God must punish the wickedness of his children in the next life.

God's Justice of Punishment in the New Testament

This theme of punishment is repeated in the New Testament.

---

hides himself, and many are those who fall under his power. He has said in his heart, God has forgotten; he hides his face; he will never see *it*. Arise, O LORD; O God, lift up thine hand; forget not the humble."

Numerous NT passages inform us of God's judgment upon his people. Unfortunately, many of these texts are assumed to apply only to unbelievers. Augustine was one of the earliest church fathers to relegate New Testament warning and punishment passages to unbelievers. He lived one-hundred years after Constantine had Christianized the Roman Empire by royal decree. The universal church (that had grown strong by withstanding persecution for centuries) had suddenly been invaded by pagans. Unfortunately, Augustine read the problems of his own generation back into the writings of the New Testament.

The early church was not a mixture of sheep and goats as Augustine anachronistically proclaimed.[18] Christians were being persecuted and martyred for confessing Christ. Were unbelievers frequenting those meetings so they could also suffer persecution? Unlikely. In fact, the only indication an unbeliever may have ever been in a meeting of the local church appears in 1 Cor 14:24. Historically, the epistles were written to believers in the local church, not a mixed audience. Caution must be exercised in anachronistically assigning punishment solely to unbelievers *a priori*, while ignoring the implications of warning passages to believers. When viewed from this perspective, many of the New Testament passages take on a meaning this

---

[18] Kenneth M. Wilson, "Reading James 2:18–20 with Anti-Donatist Eyes: Untangling Augustine's Exegetical Legacy," *Journal of Biblical Literature* 139.2 (2020): 389–410 at 405.

author believes more closely reflect their original intent.

Jesus warned in Luke 12:47–49 that punishment would come to those servants who did not obey.

> That servant who knows his master's will and does not get ready or does not do what his master wants will be beaten with many blows. But the one who does not know and does things deserving punishment will be beaten with few blows. From everyone who has been given much, much will be demanded; and from the one who has been entrusted with much, much more will be asked. (NIV84)

Whether one opines this refers to Israel as a nation, Jewish leaders, or Jesus' followers, the principle remains the same. The degree of punishment upon the master's disobedient servants will be according to their knowledge of the master's will. The word for beat (διχοτομήσει) refers to a *severe* physical act of cutting into two parts with a sword or saw.[19] Whether literal or figurative, this severe beating (or hacking in two) is more than merely missing out on something good.

The book of James addresses Christian brothers, using the term 'αδελφοί fifteen times.[20] Christians should fulfill the royal law by loving each other (2:8) since we will be judged by

---

[19] Gerhard Kittel, ed., *Theological Dictionary of the New Testament*, trans. by Geoffrey Bromiley, vol.2 (Grand Rapids, MI: Eerdmans, 2006), 225.

[20] These are 1:2, 16, 19; 2:1, 5, 14; 3:1, 10, 12 ; 4:11 ; 5:7, 9 , 10, 12, 19.

that law of liberty (2:12). The brother who does not show mercy will be judged without mercy (2:13). Brothers who are teachers will receive a more strict judgment for not acting upon their own teaching (3:1–2a). According to James 5:9, we should not complain about our fellow Christians. "Do not grumble [groan] against one another, brethren, lest you be condemned. Behold the Judge is standing at the door." Christians will most certainly be judged (κριθῆτε) by the Judge for this sin.[21] The judgment will occur at Christ's return (5:7–9), not life as we know it now.

One must wonder how a view of total absolution from future punishment fits with James' warning to his beloved brothers. Brothers who lack mercy, teachers who falter, and brothers who complain against fellow Christians all subject themselves to the Lord's *future* judgment upon his return. The warnings of James alert us to one of God's three significant motivations for godly living. James does not threaten his beloved brothers with hell, but with the Lord's judgment upon his own children at his return.

NT scriptures on God's punishment after death

Peter expresses the same concern in 1 Peter 4:17–18. "For the time has come for judgment to begin at the house of God; and if it begins with us first, what shall be the end of those who do

---

[21] The subjunctive verb in a ἵνα clause denotes purpose not merely a possibility. Daniel Wallace, *Greek Grammar Beyond the Basics* (Grand Rapids: Zondervan, 1996), 473–4.

not obey the gospel of God? Now 'If the righteous scarcely be saved, where will the ungodly and the sinner appear?'" (NKJV). Christians are not supposed to suffer as a murderer, thief, evildoer, or a busybody in other persons' matters, but only suffer as a Christian (1 Pet 5:15–16). Believers will be saved, but punished for sins such as those mentioned in the context. In contrast, those who mimic Christ by suffering faithfully for righteousness will be rewarded (cf., Matt 5:44–46).

Likewise, two passages in Hebrews warn of punishment for disobedience.

Heb 2:2–3a "For if the word spoken through angels proved steadfast, and every transgression and disobedience received a just reward, how shall we escape if we neglect so great a salvation." (NKJV)

Heb 10:26–29 For if we sin willfully after we have received the knowledge of the truth, there no longer remains a sacrifice for sins, but a certain fearful expectation of judgment and fiery indignation which will devour the adversaries…. Of how much worse punishment, do you suppose, will he be thought worthy who has trampled the Son of God under foot, counted the blood of the covenant by which he was sanctified a common thing, and insulted the Spirit of grace? (NKJV)

Hell or eternal damnation cannot be found in the book of

Hebrews. Nevertheless, most books and commentaries find eternal damnation in these warning passages.[22] The warnings in Hebrews do not mention eternal punishment (although earthly chastisement is explained in Heb 12:5–11). The warning of 12:28b rests between the promise of 12:28a and the fact of 12:29. "Since we are receiving a Kingdom that is unshakable, let us be thankful and please God by worshiping him with holy fear and awe. For our God is a devouring fire. Keep on loving each as brothers and sisters." (Heb 12:28–13:1, NLT). Brothers and sisters in Christ who are receiving the unshakeable kingdom (12:28) still need to fear God as a consuming fire. Why? Do these Christian brothers of promise still fear the possibility of hell? I suggest, "No."

Some commentaries interpret this as a motivational warning to persevere lest some persons prove themselves unregenerate by failing to persevere.[23] For them, a precarious

---

[22] Herbert W. Bateman, IV, ed., *Four Views on the Warning Passages in Hebrews* (Kregel Publications: Grand Rapids, Mich., 2007). William Lane, *Hebrews* in Word Biblical Commentary, Vol. 47B (Word Books: Dallas, Texas, 1991), 290–296. Charles Pfeiffer, *The Epistle to the Hebrews* in Everyman's Bible Commentary (Moody Bible Institute: Chicago, 1962), 87–88. However, see F.F. Bruce, *Commentary on the Epistle to the Hebrews* (Eerdmans Publishing Co.: Grand Rapids, Mich., 1963), 263. "These words have no doubt been used frequently as a warning to the ungodly of what lies in store for them unless they amend their ways; but their primary application is to the people of God."

[23] Ibid. But even "eternal salvation" (Heb 5:8–9) should mean eternal deliverance from enemies through obedient suffering in the context. Note that in the catena of Hebrews (1:1–13) all seven OT citations contain deliverance from enemies and inheriting the land in the original context.

balance of blessed covenant assurance and uncertain fear hold the Christian in a suspenseful tension.[24] Many authors correctly affirm that God's judgment is meant by, "God is a consuming fire."[25] Finding one who places this judgment upon the believer after death can be challenging. The force of the Greek word τιμωρίας contributes to this paucity since it appears only two other times in the NT, with Luke using the other two in reference to Paul's torture of believers (Acts 22:5, 26:11).[26] But according to Jeremiah, execution by stoning pales in comparison to starvation as a means of death (Lam 4:6, 9). Facing the holiness of God in person at his judgment seat—even as a believer covered in Christ's blood—would be more terrifying than physical death. We need not illegitimately presuppose eternal damnation. It is absent in this text. Christians can be and *should be* terrified of God's holiness and his future

---

Perseverance as a proof of being elect was invented by Augustine to explain why some baptized babies did not persevere in faith. See Kenneth Wilson, *The Foundation of Augustinian-Calvinism* (Regula Fidei Press, 2019).

[24] Arthur Pink, *An Exposition of Hebrews*, Baker Book House: Grand Rapids, MI; 2004), 1103.

[25] Paul Ellingsworth, *The Epistle to Hebrews* in The New International Greek Testament Commentary, I. Howard Marshall and Donald A. Hagner, eds. (Grand Rapids, MI: Eerdmans Publishing Co., 1993; reprint 2000), 692; "usually in Hebrews, as here, πῦρ denotes the activity of God, especially in judgment." Also, Harold W. Attridge, *The Epistle to Hebrews*, Helmet Koester, ed. (Philadelphia, PA: Fortress Press, 1989), 383; "The image of fire, here described as 'consuming'(καταναλίσκον),[83] is regularly associated with judgment and punishment,[84] as it was earlier in Hebrews (6:8)."

[26] The Protestant claim that God only disciplines his children in child training (from the Greek word παιδεύω, Heb 12: 5–10) is difficult to sustain. Killing a child creates difficulty in further training.

judgment upon us.

Paul echoes this warning to Christians in the epistle of Galatians.

> Brothers *and sisters,* even if a person is caught in any wrongdoing, you who are spiritual are to restore such a person in a spirit of gentleness; *each one* looking to yourself, so that you are not tempted as well. ... Do not be deceived, God is not mocked; for whatever a person sows, this he will also reap. For the one who sows to his own flesh will reap destruction from the flesh, but the one who sows to the Spirit will reap eternal life from the Spirit. Let's not become discouraged in doing good, for in due time we will reap, if we do not become weary." (Gal 6:1–8, NASB).

Eternal life is not merely a future in heaven, but expresses an intimate experiential knowledge of God in the present life. According to Jesus, "And this is eternal life, that they know you, the only true God, and Jesus Christ whom you have sent." (John 17:3, ESV) Eternal life is quality, not merely quantity. So Paul admonishes Christians to invest not in wrongdoing or fleshly pursuits but doing good in spiritual endeavors. The reaping of destruction (φθοράν, corruption) could be in this life (cf., 2 Pet 1:4) or in the next life (since the reaping [payment] for doing good remains in the future).[27] Again, few Christians seem to reap consequences for their sin in this life. The Apostle Paul emphasizes the future resurrection of the body (1 Cor 15:12–25), the final conquest of Christ's enemies (v.25), and admits "If we who are [abiding] in Christ have hoped only in this life [and this is all there is], then we are of all people most miserable *and* to be pitied. " (1 Cor 15:19, AMP). All are future.

Colossians 3:23–25

Colossians 3:23–25 warns, "Whatever your task, put yourselves into it, as done for the Lord and not for your masters, since you know that from the Lord you will receive the inheritance as your reward; you serve the Lord Christ. For the wrongdoer will be paid back for whatever wrong has been done, and there is no partiality" (NRSV). Paul contrasts a Christian receiving a bonus payment (ἀνταπόδοσιν) for service to the Lord versus a Christian who does wrong being paid back for that wrong (ἀδικῶν κομίσεται ὃ ἠδίκησεν, SBLGNT). When is it paid back? Because the payment for service is in the future (inheritance) then the payment for doing wrong should also be future. One Christian provides service to Christ while the other Christian does not serve. This might be compared to ballplayers on a team where some are on the bench. They drew no penalties

---

[27] 2 Pet 1:4 "God made great and marvelous promises, so his nature would become part of us. Then we could escape our evil desires and the corrupt influences of this world." (CEV)

or errors but were not on the field during the game. Only non-contextual assumptions (God does not punish Christians) force these Christians to be non-Christians or grossly immoral.

How we are paid back for the wrong done remains a mystery. Scripture does not reveal it. The phrase καὶ οὐκ ἔστιν προσωπολημψία (Col 3:25, SBLGNT), warns God is not partial. This matches Eph 6:9, "And masters, treat your slaves in the same way. Do not threaten them, since you know that he who is both their Master and yours is in heaven, and there is no favoritism with him." (NIV84). Again, the stern warning is to Christians regarding God who will punish them without partiality or favoritism.

According to 1 Thessalonians 4:3-6,

> For this is the will of God, your sanctification: that you should abstain from sexual immorality; that each of you should know how to possess his own vessel in sanctification and honor, not in passion of lust, like the Gentiles who do not know God; that no one should take advantage of and defraud his brother in this matter, because the Lord *is* the avenger of all such, as we also forewarned you and testified. For God did not call us to uncleanness, but in holiness. (NKJV)

In this text "the Lord is the avenger" for a Christian who defrauds his brother (or sister). The Greek word ἔκδικος means a punisher who brings justice in order to rectify a wrong. God will punish a Christian brother who was called in sanctification (set apart) but commits that sin of impurity. Few Christians are punished by God for their sins while on this earth. It must occur after death. Otherwise, God is neither truthful nor just.

2 Corinthians 5:10

"For we must all be made manifest before the judgment-seat of Christ; that each one may receive [κομίσηται] the things *done* in the body, according to what he hath done, whether *it be* good or bad." (ASV) Paul indicates that being well pleasing to God is the goal (5:9). However, the reason he is persuading men to good deeds concerns the terror of the Lord (5:11). Paul appears to be persuading Christians—such as the sinning Corinthians—to be reconciled to God (5:20, 6:1).

The Greek word κομίζω means to receive or repay.[28] Some authors view this as meaning only a loss of reward rather than receiving a punishment for the bad.[29] Yet, the text states that we will receive something for the bad, not that something will be withheld or a reward forfeited. Similarly, the word for bad (κακον) most commonly refers to moral issues.[30] The earlier Alexandrian and Coptic Greek texts contain the variant

---

[28] BDAG, 557, "to get back something that is one's own or owed to one" or "to come into possession of something or experience something."

[29] E.g., Charles Ryrie, *Basic Theology* (Chicago: Moody Press, 1986; repr. 1999), 598.

[30] BDAG, 501, "1. pert. to being socially or morally reprehensible, bad, evil."

φαῦλον. BDAG incorrectly interprets φαῦλον as referring to reward in 2 Cor 5:10.

> **2. pert. to being relatively inferior in quality, ordinary,** in ref. to the kinds of rewards that are offered in **2 Cor 5:10**. Yet, in this colloquially arranged sentence, the idea of the doing of good or bad (s. 1 above) certainly plays a part (The phrase τὰ φαῦλα, τὰ ἀγαθά [the bad, the good] [in] X., Symp. 4, 47 is formally but not conceptually sim. [similar] for X. [Xenophon] thinks of temporal chastisements by deities, whereas Paul of rewards intended for believers.)[31] [brackets added]

Here BDAG commits a theological presupposition in interpretation contrary to its own example ("thinks of temporal chastisements by deities"); and, without supporting evidence. The author somehow supposes that believers in Christ, after physical death, cannot be chastised by a deity. Therefore, Paul must be thinking differently. Yet, this appears to be the precise point of BDAG's own example (Xenophon's Symposium 4, 47) and Paul's example: believers will receive from God for the bad which they have done. Losing out on a reward is *not* receiving something. The text states one must *receive* something, not miss out on it. Why Paul's sober warning? Because Paul wants

---

[31] BDAG, p.1050 **φαῦλος** "μηδὲν ἔχων λέγειν περὶ ἡμῶν φαῦλον *if he has nothing bad to say about us* **Tit 2:8**." See also L. 1, 105 ἀγαθόν τε καὶ φαῦλον=a good and bad thing at the same time.

Christians to avoid the terror of the Lord: he persuades Christians (5:11) to please God by doing good works and avoiding bad works.

Jesus, warning his own disciples about hypocrisy, said, "For there is nothing covered that will not be revealed, nor hidden that will not be known. Therefore, whatever you have spoken in the dark will be heard in the light, and what you have spoken in the ear in inner rooms will be proclaimed on the housetops" (Luke 12:2–3). A private conference between the believer and Christ at his judgment seat seems difficult to imagine from these verses. Instead, a vast public display of our words and works ensues. That display includes the bad as well as the good. Jesus warns and challenges his disciples to use caution not only in normal conversation, but even in what they whisper. Everything we speak will be publicly exposed and judged by God.

In the same chapter, Peter asks Jesus if the warning about preparedness for the master's return was addressed to all people or to the disciples (12:41). Luke records that he was speaking to the disciples in 12:22ff when he says, "Do not fear little flock, for it your Father's good pleasure to give you the kingdom" (12:32). Jesus resumes speaking to the multitudes in 12:54 when he calls them hypocrites (12:56). Therefore, we expect Jesus to be addressing his disciples in 12:35–53. This concurs with verse 44: "Truly, I say to you that he will make him ruler over all that he has (*lit.*, all his possessions)." But the challenge appears in the next verse: "But if that servant says in his heart, 'My master is delaying his coming'" (12:45). The punishment of the servant includes being beaten with many stripes (v.47), being cut in two, and having his portion appointed with the unfaithful (v.46). Jesus does not say that the servant was an unbeliever, or that he will be appointed with the unbelievers in hell. Rather, Jesus will appoint that servant's portion/share/part (μέρος) with the unfaithful (ἀπίστων). The contrast highlights a faithful servant ruling over all of the master's possessions versus the unfaithful servant who does not rule but must share his portion with other unfaithful servants.

Both the previous specific warning to the disciples (12:2–3) and Luke's meticulous written communication of Jesus' intended audience as it changes (11:1,16,27,29,37,45,53; 12:13,22,54; 13:1) strengthen the probability that the answer to Peter's question was "to us (the disciples)." Both the promise of ruling as a payment/reward for faithful service and the warning of punishment for unfaithful actions were addressed to the disciples. Whether the beating is physical or figurative does not minimize the point that a punishment will ensue for disciples who are not faithful. If we assume *a priori* that believers will not be punished after death, this nullifies Jesus' warnings to his own disciples.

Protestant commentaries inevitably defend these NT passages against any idea of posthumous punishment. Here I have provided refutations for a few of them. For those persons desiring a more detailed exegetical rebuttal see Appendix A.

Conclusion

Both the OT and NT teach God's punishment of his children after they have been forgiven. This fact renders the Protestant doctrine untenable. If God punishes Christians on earth then there is no valid reason God cannot punish them after death. If God is not the avenger for his children abused by other Christians (1 Thess 4:6) then God is not truthful and God is unjust. If God does not punish those Christians while on earth then he must punish Christians after death.

Protestants refuse to see in scripture that Christians who are forgiven by Christ's blood (thereby preventing eternal separation from God) must still suffer God's punishment as his own children. The five-hundred year tradition of no culpability and total absolution remains so entrenched that even Protestant scholars find ways to avoid this inevitable conclusion. It seems God needed to write, "God will punish his children after death" for Protestants to accept this doctrine. Or, more likely, even then it would not be accepted. A side-step re-interpretation would triumph by tradition. The early church fathers held no such misguided tradition.

We now learn what the ancient Christian leaders (early church fathers) taught about God's punishment of the Christian.

Chapter 9

Early Church Fathers on Posthumous Purification of Christians

The writings of the earliest Christians about scripture are not scripture: they are not "God-breathed." Their opinions could be wrong. Yet, they provide us insight into how scripture was understood in matters of doctrine in early Christianity. Protestants often do not hold these Christian authors in the same high regard as the Roman Catholic and Orthodox churches. The *sola scriptura* (only scripture) of Protestants resists these ancient commentaries. Yet, the same Protestants frequently (and sometimes hypocritically) imbibe and quote their own modern commentaries and books when they interpret scripture.

Those persons who think historical theology to be unimportant are naïve, not recognizing that their own ideas on scripture originated from teachers who were taught by their teachers. I was not born on an isolated island when scripture suddenly washed ashore for me to read *de novo*. None of us were. Opinions of our prior teachers shape our thinking and interpretations, whether consciously or unconsciously.

Importantly, every ancient author writing on the topic of God punishing Christians expressed the same view—not one author dissented. Reading their understanding that God purifies his children after death prevents us from neglecting blind spots from our own interpretive biases.

Ancient Authors through 250 CE

Ignatius (ca.110 CE) was the earliest father to use the word βῆμα (Judgment Seat of Christ) as he referred to the punishment of believers.

> He who honors the bishop shall be honored by God, even as he that dishonors him shall be punished by God. For if he that rises up against kings is justly held worthy of punishment, inasmuch as he dissolves public order, of how much sorer punishment, suppose ye, shall he be thought worthy, who presumes to do anything without the bishop, thus both destroying the [Church's] unity, and throwing its order into confusion? (*To the Smyrnaeans*, 9)

The parallel precise wording with Hebrews 10:29 may surprise us since modern commentators frequently assign this scriptural passage to unbelievers. Ignatius applied the precise wording of the Hebrews 10 warning to believers within the church.

In his instructions to the church elders on forgiveness, Polycarp (ca.155) warns of the βῆμα. He advises Christians to serve God in reverential fear in view of God's future judgment.

> If then we entreat the Lord to forgive us, we ought also ourselves to forgive; for we are before the eyes

of our Lord and God, and 'we must all appear at the judgment-seat of Christ, and must every one give an account of himself.' Let us then serve Him in fear, and with all reverence, even as He Himself has commanded us. (*Epistle of Polycarp to the Philippians*, 6)

Justin Martyr (ca.157) wrote, "We have learned from the prophets and declare as the truth, that penalties and punishments and good rewards are given according to the quality of each man's action." (*First Apology* 43)

Clement of Alexandria (ca.190) discussed posthumous punishment of Christians in several of his writings.

For certain men have entered unawares, ungodly men, who had been of old ordained and predestined to the judgment of our God; not that they might become impious, but that, being now impious, they were ordained to judgment. "For the Lord God," he says, "who once delivered a people out of Egypt, afterward destroyed them that believed not"; that is, that **He might train them through punishment**. For they were indeed punished, and they perished on account of those that are saved, **until they turn to the Lord.** (*Commentary on the Epistle of Jude,* 4; bold mine)

Clement opined that fire purifies the Christian soul. "But we say that the fire sanctifies not flesh, but sinful souls; meaning not the all-devouring vulgar fire but that of wisdom, which pervades the soul passing through the fire." Daley concluded, "In this consistent interpretation of all punishment, including punishment after death, as purification rather than retribution, Clement can be considered the first Christian exponent of the doctrine of eschatological suffering; he thus paves the way for centuries of speculation and controversy on the subject of 'Purgatory' among Christian theologians." [1]

Tertullian (ca.205) wrote, "The faithful widow prays for the soul of her husband, and begs for him in the interim repose, and participation in the first resurrection, and offers prayers on the anniversary of his death." [2] (*On Monogamy*, De Monogamia 10)

Similar to Polycarp, Origen (ca.250) taught a judgment for the good and bad deeds of the Christian.

> For if 'we must all stand before the judgment-seat of
> Christ, that each one may receive the things done in
> the body, according to what he hath done, whether it
> be good or bad,' let each one with all his power do
> what he can so that he may not receive punishment
> for more evil things done in the body, even if he is
> going to receive back for all the wrongs which he has

---

[1] Brian E. Daley, *The Hope of the Early Church: A Handbook of Patristic Eschatology* (New York: Cambridge UP, 1991), 467.

[2] See also *Resurrection of the Body* (De Resurrectione Carnis, 43); *Exhortation to Chastity* (Exhortatio Castitatis 11); and *The Soldier's Crown* (De Corona Militis 3–4).

done; but it should be our ambition to procure the
reward for a greater number of good deeds....
(*Commentary on Matthew* II.12.30)

Origen explained, "I think that even after the resurrection from
the dead, we need to be resurrected by a sacrament that washes
us and cleanses [purges] us; because, no one is able to be
resurrected devoid of filthiness: I deny that anyone can find a
person who is presently devoid of all faults" (*Homily in Luke,*
14).[3] Origin expounded on the need for every Christian to be
purged from sin after death.

The future life is to be looked upon as one of progress
through discipline. "The Lord is a refiner's fire." It is
certain that the fire which is prepared for sinners
awaits us, and we shall go into that fire, wherein God
will try every man's work of what sort it is. .... Even
if it be a Paul or a Peter, he shall come into that fire,
but such are they of whom it is written, "Though thou
pass through the fire, the flame shall not scorch thee."
The holy and the just are cleansed, like Aaron and
Isaiah, with coals from off the altar. But sinners,
"among whom I count myself," must be purged with
another fire. This is not of the altar, it is not the

---

[3] My translation of Origin's *Homil. Lucam* "Ego puto, quod et post
resurrectionem ex mortuis indigeamus sacramento resugere eluente nos
atque purgante: nemo enim ansque sordibus resurgere poterit: neo ullam
posse animam reperiri quae universis statim vitiis careat." J.-P. Migne, vol.
13 *Origenes Opera Omnia* (1862), Homilia XIV (948), 1836.

Lord's, but is kindled by the sinner himself within his own heart. Its fuel is our own evil—the wood, the hay, the straw—sins graver or lighter, which we have built upon the foundation laid by Christ. (In Psalm 36, Homily 3.1)

Ancient Authors after 250 CE

Cyprian of Carthage (ca.253) contrasts the futures of different Christians.

> It is one thing to stand for pardon, another thing to attain to glory; it is one thing, when cast into prison, not to go out thence until one has paid the uttermost farthing; another thing at once to receive the wages of faith and courage. It is one thing, tortured by long suffering for sins, to be cleansed and long purged by fire; another to have purged all sins by suffering. It is one thing, in fine, to be in suspense till the sentence of God at the Day of Judgment; another to be at once crowned by the Lord (Letter 51[55]:20).

Lactantius (ca.315) in his *The Divine Institutes* testified of judgment with negative consequences for the righteous believers who have a plethora of sins or grievous sins.

> But when He shall have judged the righteous, He will also try them with fire. Then they whose sins shall exceed either in weight or in number, shall be scorched by the fire and burnt: but they whom full

justice and maturity of virtue has imbued will not perceive that fire; for they have something of God in themselves which repels and rejects the violence of the flame. (*The Divine Institutes*, VII.21)

Epiphanius of Salamis (ca.375) admonished,

And even though the prayer we offer for them {the dead} cannot root out all their faults—[how could it], since we {ourselves} often slip {stumble} in this world, {both} inadvertently and deliberately—it is still useful as an indication {reminder to us} of {the} something more perfect {for which we should strive}. For we commemorate both righteous and sinners. Though we pray for sinners, for God's mercy, and the righteous ...." (*Panarion* 75.8, Against Aerius)[4]

Ambrosiaster (ca.375) commented on 1 Cor 3:15.

To suffer loss is to endure punishment. For what person, when subjected to punishment, does not lose something thereby? The man himself will be saved, because his substance will not perish in the same way that his bad teaching will. The teaching is not essential to his being. Note that when Paul said that the man would be saved through fire he did not mean

---

[4] *The Panarion of Epiphanius of Salamis*, trans. Frank Williams (Leiden: Brill, 1994), 496. The bracket { } marks are mine.

that the man tested by the fire would escape burning on his own merit and be saved. What he meant was he will suffer punishments of fire and be saved only by being purged. Unlike complete unbelievers, he will not be tortured in eternal fire, and so to some extent it will be worth his while to have believed in Christ.[5]

Cyril of Jerusalem (ca.380) instructed the catechumens:

> Then we commemorate also those who have fallen asleep before us, first Patriarchs, Prophets, Apostles, Martyrs, that at their prayers and intercessions God would receive our petition. Then on behalf also of the Holy Fathers and Bishops who have fallen asleep before us, and in a word of all who in past years have fallen asleep among us, believing that it will be a very great benefit to the souls, for whom the supplication is put up, while that holy and most awful sacrifice is set forth. (*Catechetical Lectures* 23.9)[6]

Gregory of Nyssa (ca.380) discussed posthumous purging of sin in Christians.

---

[5] Ambrosiaster, *Ancient Christian Texts*, Commentaries on Romans and 1–2 Corinthians, ed. and trans. Gerald Bray (Downers Grove, IL: Intervarsity, 2009), 134.

[6] New Advent, "Fathers of the Church," https://www.newadvent.org/fathers/310123.htm ; Accessed 14 June 2023.

Anyone who has freely made a harmful choice instead of an expedient one has rejected both the good offered us and the honor befitting God. (Free will is itself divine). By its very nature free will rejects evil, a choice which divine wisdom has implanted in us in order that we may choose what we like. In this fashion man can taste the evils he has opted for and having learned by experience from his free will, man is again freely motivated to choose the blessedness of his original state. All the passion and irrational behavior which have weighed us down in this present life is now removed. Having been cleansed through prayer and wisdom, man returns [to his original blessedness] after the purifying fire has refined him. (*Concerning Those Who Have Died*, J54)[7]

But if man follows his irrational passions with the help of the skins belonging to irrational beasts, he will be advised in another way to choose the good after his departure from the body because he now knows how good differs from evil. He can only partake of the divinity unless [if] he has purged his soul of filth by the cleansing fire. (*Concerning Those Who Have Died*, J56)

---

[7] "Reflections on the Writings of Gregory of Nyssa," *On Those Who Have Died*, 23. https://lectio-divina.org/index.php/other-reflections/gregory-nyssa ; Accessed 12 June 2023.

Ambrose of Milan (ca.390) wrote concerning 1 Cor 3:15, "He...shall be saved, yet as by fire, and be thus purified; not like the unbelieving and wicked man, who shall be punished in everlasting fire."[8] Bishop Ambrose provides a glimpse into his reasoning for these prayers. "I have loved [Emperor Theodosius], and so I accompany him to the land of the living; and I will not abandon him until, by my tears and prayers, I shall lead the man wither his merits summon, unto the holy mountain of God, where there is eternal life" (*On the Death of Theodosius*, 37).[9]

John Chrysostom (ca.395) believed Christians would receive judgment for imposing Jewish traditions. He utilized verses on the βῆμα as a warning to Christians of future judgment.[10] Chrysostom stated, "Let us then give them aid and perform commemoration for them. For if the children of Job were purged by the sacrifice of their father [Job 1:5], why do you doubt that when we too offer for the departed, some consolation arises to them? ... Let us not then be weary in giving aid to the departed, both by offering on their behalf and obtaining prayers for them" (*Homilies on 1 Corinthians*, 41 [1 Cor 15:46]). He also spoke on assisting the deceased Christians.

---

[8] Ambrose, *Works*, edit. Paris 1661, vol. 3, p.351.

[9] Roy Deferrari, ed., *Funeral Orations by Saint Gregory Nazianzen and Saint Ambrose*, trans. Leo McCauley, John Sullivan, Martin McGuire, and Roy Deferrari (New York: Fathers of the Church,1953), 323.

[10] See Chrysostom, *Homily on Romans* 14:10 and *Homily on 2 Cor. 5:10*.

Weep for those who die in their wealth and who with all their wealth prepared no consolation for their own souls, who had the power to wash away their sins and did not will to do it. Let us weep for them, let us assist them [the deceased] to the extent of our ability, let us think of some assistance for them, small as it may be, yet let us somehow assist them. But how, and in what way? By praying for them and by entreating others to pray for them, by constantly giving alms to the poor on their behalf. Not in vain was it decreed by the apostles that in the awesome mysteries remembrance should be made of the departed. They knew that here there was much gain for them, much benefit. When the entire people stands with hands uplifted, a priestly assembly, and that awesome sacrificial Victim is laid out, how, when we are calling upon God, should we not succeed in their defense? But this is done for those who have departed in the faith, while even the catechumens are not reckoned as worthy of this consolation, but are deprived of every means of assistance except one. And what is that? We may give alms to the poor on their behalf. (*Homilies on Philippians*)

Jerome (ca.400) wrote, "If the man whose work is burnt and is to suffer the loss of his labour, while he himself is saved, yet not without proof of fire: it follows that if a man's work remains which he has built upon the foundation, he will be saved without probation by fire, and consequently a difference is established between one degree of salvation and another." (*Against Jovinianus* 2.22). He taught hierarchical places for the righteous (not equality in salvation). Jerome further concluded, "as we believe the torments of the devil and those wicked men who said in their hearts, 'There is no God,' to be eternal; so, in regard to those sinners, impious men and even Christians, whose works will be proved and purged by fire, we conclude that the sentence of the judge will be tempered by mercy." (*Commentary on Isaiah*, 65; cf., *Commentary on Amos* 4)

Augustine of Hippo when writing on the Psalms (ca.412–427) taught there would be separate fires for the believer and for the unbeliever.

> If they had built "gold and silver and precious stones," they would be secure from both fires; not only from that in which the wicked shall be punished forever, but likewise from that fire which purifies those who shall be saved by fire. But because it is said, "shall be saved," that fire is thought lightly of; though the suffering will be more grievous than anything man can undergo in this life. (*Expositions in the Psalms*, Ennaratio in Psalmum 38.2.3)

"Temporal punishments are suffered by some in this life only, by some after death, by some both here and hereafter, but all of them before that last and strictest judgment. But not all who suffer temporal punishments after death will come to eternal punishments, which are to follow after that judgment" (*City of God*, De civitate Dei 21.13) Augustine provides his analysis of 1 Cor 3:12–15.

> *O Lord, do not rebuke me in your wrath; nor chasten me in your hot anger* [Psalm 37:1]. Certain people are destined to be chastened by God's anger in the future, and rebuked in his wrath. It may be that not all those who are rebuked will be chastened as a result, but some at least will be saved through that chastening that is to come. This will certainly happen, because otherwise it would not be called a "chastening," but it will take place as though through fire. Others there will be who are rebuked, but not chastened, for Christ will certainly rebuke those to whom he is to say, or he will at all events rebuke those to whom He will say, "I was hungry and you did not feed me; I was thirsty and you gave me nothing to drink" (Matt 25:42) ... By pleading *Do not chasten me in your anger*, the psalmist asks, "Purify me in this life, and make me such that I will not need that chastening fire"; this prayer he makes with an eye to those who will be saved, but only as through fire. And why? Because here on earth they built on a foundation of wood or hay or straw. They ought to have built on gold, or silver, or precious stones [1 Cor 3:12] and then they would have been safe from both kinds of fire; not only the eternal fire which will torture the

impious for ever, but even that which will chastise those who are to be saved through it. Scripture says of the shoddy builder, *He himself will be saved indeed, though it be through fire* (1 Cor 3:15). Perhaps some people may trivialize this fire, because Scripture says, *He will be saved.* Yet even though it be for some the means of salvation, that fire will nevertheless be harder to bear than anything we can endure in this life. Think about it; how grievously the wicked have suffered, and can suffer, here. Yet for all that, they suffer no more grievously than good people do. (*Expositions in the Psalms*, Ennaratio in Psalmum 37.2)[11]

Writing on Gen 3:17–19, Augustine states, "The man who perhaps has not cultivated the land and has allowed it to be overrun with brambles has in this life the curse of his land on all his works, and after this life he will have either purgatorial fire or eternal punishment." (*On Genesis: A Refutation of the Manichees*, De Genesi contra Manicheos 2.20, 30) Augustine admonished praying for deceased Christians.

That's why, as the faithful know, Church custom has it that at the place where the names of the martyrs are recited at God's altar, we don't pray for them, while

[11] *The Works of Saint Augustine: A Translation for the 21st Century*, Expositions of the Psalms 33–50, III/16, ed. John Rotelle, trans. and notes Maria Boulding (Hyde Park, NY: New City Press, 2000), 147–8.

we do pray for the other departed brothers and sisters who are remembered there. It is insulting, I mean, to pray for martyrs, to whose prayers we ought rather to commend ourselves. They have tackled sin, after all, to the point of shedding their blood. To people on the other hand, who were still imperfect and yet partly justified, the apostle says in his letter to the Hebrews …. (*Sermon* 159.1)[12]

Conclusion

Therefore, numerous early church fathers taught a punishment of righteous believers in fire after death. None refuted such an idea.[13] The believers' experiences at Christ's βῆμα would not be merely observational, procedural, or to pass out rewards. The sense of these early Christian authors was that God's judgment was something to fear and could be personally traumatic. The righteous sacrifice of Christ did not spare Christians from answering God at the Judgment Seat of Christ for their works, both good and bad. The early church offered prayers and sacrifices for the Christian deceased. Protestant Christians may legitimately appeal to these earliest Christian leaders as additional support of a punishment of Christians after death. These ancient interpretations are just as valid as modern commentaries on scripture. Their unanimous consensus on the

---

[12] *Works of St. Augustine*, Sermons, III.5, 121.

[13] I read through these authors' works for my doctoral thesis at Oxford.

punishment of Christians after death should cause us to consider this possibility seriously. The early church fathers opposed the modern Protestant approach of assigning all punishment in Scripture to unbelievers.

Chapter 10

Is Postmortem Purification

Retributive or Restorative?

What is Retributive Justice and Restorative Justice?

Retributive justice includes the principle that morality demands a wrongdoer suffer punishment by a moral punisher in a proportional (limited) manner. God, as absolute good, morally requires retribution be served for all evil. In contrast, restorative justice focuses on repairing the harm done to the victim, either by restitution or reparations from the perpetrator in an attempt to help them assume responsibility for their actions and be rehabilitated. God, as absolute love, requires restitution for wrongs done to others, which includes the perpetrator repenting and seeking forgiveness.

God's Retributive Justice (Satisfaction)

God's justice in retributive punishment is impossible to deny as God deals with his people in the Old Testament. Obedience incurred blessing, yet disobedient sin resulted in punishment (Deut 30:15–19). God physically killed his own people due to their sin. The earth opened up to swallow sinners (Numbers 16:23–35), fire came down from heaven and torched sinners

(Lev 10: 1–3; Numb 16:35), enemies slaughtered God's people due to sin (Jer 39:6–7), God's punishment by famine became so severe that gentle mothers killed then ate their own babies (just as was prophesied, Deut 28:53–57; 2 Kings 6:28–9; cf., Ezek 5:10–13). Uzzah was assisting in the good deed of bringing the ark back on a cart when God struck him dead for touching the ark in violation of the law, despite Uzzah's good intention of protecting the ark from damage. (2 Sam 6:3–8)

How can physical death not be retributive? There is no redemptive value, or learning process, or sanctification involved when God kills persons due to their sin. Psalm 99:8 reveals the manner in which YHWH operates with his children. "O LORD our God, you answered them; you were a forgiving God to them, but an avenger of their wrongdoings."

Of course, some Protestant Christians reply, "That's Old Testament," implying God changed his divine nature requiring justice between the OT and NT. But we also find this severe divine retribution in the NT. Paul speaks of the Corinthian Christians dying physically as a result of their sin.

> Whoever, therefore, eats the bread or drinks the cup of the Lord in an unworthy manner will be answerable for the body and blood of the Lord. Examine yourselves, and only then eat of the bread and drink of the cup. For all who eat and drink without discerning the body eat and drink judgment against themselves. For this reason many of you are

weak and ill, and some have died. But if we judged
ourselves, we would not be judged. But when we are
judged by the Lord, we are disciplined so that we may
not be condemned along with the world. So then, my
brothers and sisters, when you come together to eat,
wait for one another. (1 Cor 11:27–33, NRSV)

According to Paul, these were "brothers and sisters" (11:33) in
Christ who suffered physical illness and even death as a result
of their sin. This is retributive punishment.

Other NT passages teach the same principal of
retribution. In Acts 5:1–11, Ananias and Saphira were killed by
God for lying.[1] Some teachers try to claim these are non-
Christians; but it is highly doubtful that Jewish non-Christians
would sign up to suffer persecution within a new sect and give
up financial resources (even if only part of the money).

Peter exhorts Christians to live holy lives in fear of
God's judgement of their deeds.

As obedient children, do not be conformed to the
passions of your former ignorance, but as he who
called you is holy, you also be holy in all your
conduct, since it is written, "You shall be holy, for I

---

[1] Meyers comments on Acts 5:3, "Ananias, according to his Christian
destination and ability (Jam 4:7; 1 Peter 5:9), ought not to have permitted
this, but should have allowed his heart to be filled with the Holy Spirit; hence
the question, διατί ἐπλήρωσεν κ.τ.λ." Heinrich, A.W. Meyer, *Meyer's New
Testament Commentary*, trans. Peter Christie; Frederick Crombie, rev. trans.
and ed. (Edinburgh: T & T Clark, 1880).

am holy." And if you call on him as Father who judges impartially according to each one's deeds, conduct yourselves with fear throughout the time of your exile (1 Pet 1:14–17; NIV).

The context demonstrates this "fear" is not the typical Protestant view of being in "awe of God" (i.e., there is no reason to fear him since we are justified by faith alone). Instead, the context demonstrates a serious concern that our lives exhibit holy conduct in anticipation of God's judgment for our deeds.[2]

Retributive punishment by God is a reality. My personal preference to view God as too loving for such punishment means nothing. In Chapter 8 we examined the many NT verses discussing God's judgment of Christians. God will judge every human, including Christians, for their deeds, both good and evil. We discovered this in 2 Cor 5:10. "For all of us must appear before the judgment seat of Christ, so that each one may receive suitable recompense for his conduct in the body, whether good or bad." (NCB)

Retribution is a punishment for committing a wrong. Although it is advantageous and preferable if the criminal is rehabilitated, the laws in our modern justice system require

---

[2] Cf., 2 Sam 6:7–9 "The anger of the Lord burned against Uzzah. God killed him there for his mistake. And he died there by the special box of God. David became angry because the Lord had gone against Uzzah. So that place is called Perez-uzzah to this day. David was afraid of the Lord that day, and he said, 'How can the special box of the Lord come to me?'" (NLT)

punishment for crimes. No restorative goal is required. But a prisoner with good behavior can make parole. With God, there is fortunately abundant evidence in scripture for a restorative aspect in discipline. However, one need not choose between one or the other. God can punish sin and simultaneously provide loving discipline for character development.

As anyone who is observant admits, the wicked do not always suffer retribution in this life. Job 21 even affirms the wicked *prosper* in this life—God's justice is not handed out while the wicked still live. King David voiced the same complaint. "The stupid man cannot know; the fool cannot understand this: that though the wicked sprout like grass and all evildoers flourish, they are doomed to destruction forever." (Ps 92:6–7) If the wrongs committed are not punished in this life, then they must be punished in the next life. Otherwise, a person does not reap what he sows; and, God is thereby mocked (Gal 6:7).

Thomas Aquinas, in support of purgatory, taught God required retributive punishment. In fact, the pain after death will be worse than any pain experienced while on earth.

> This purgation, of course, is made by punishments, just as in this life their purgation would have been completed by punishments which satisfy the debt; otherwise the negligent would be better off than the solicitous [meticulously obedient], if the punishment which they do not receive for their sins here need not

be undergone in the future. (*Summa contra Gentiles*,
4.91.6)[3]

In Purgatory there will be a twofold pain; one will be
the pain of loss, namely the delay of the divine vision,
and the pain of sense, namely punishment by
corporeal fire. **With regard to both the least pain
of Purgatory surpasses the greatest pain of this
life.** For the more a thing is desired the more painful
is its absence. And since after this life the holy souls
desire the Sovereign Good with the most intense
longing—both because their longing is not held back
by the weight of the body, and because, had there
been no obstacle, they would already have gained the
goal of enjoying the Sovereign Good—it follows that
they grieve exceedingly for their delay. Again, since
pain is not hurt, but the sense of hurt, the more
sensitive a thing is, the greater the pain caused by that
which hurts it: wherefore hurts inflicted on the more
sensible parts cause the greatest pain. And, because
all bodily sensation is from the soul, it follows of
necessity that the soul feels the greatest pain when a
hurt is inflicted on the soul itself. That the soul suffers
pain from the bodily fire is at present taken for
granted, for we shall treat of this matter further on
[*Cf. [5186] XP, Q [70], A [3]]. **Therefore it follows**

---

[3] Thomas Aquinas, *SCG*,
https://isidore.co/aquinas/ContraGentiles4.htm#91 ; Accessed 6 July 2023.

> **that the pain of Purgatory, both of loss and of sense, surpasses all the pains of this life.** (*Summa Theologica*, Appendix 1. qu 2. art1., bold added)[4]

When the apostle Paul states God will repay for the good and the bad which we did while in the body (2 Cor 5:10) then we should count on the fact that God will pay back our works in kind. Paying back is retributive justice.

Jurgie explains that at the moment of death the soul becomes perfectly holy, totally enraptured by God, and exudes pure love. "It has no means of bettering itself nor of progressing in virtue. That would be an impossibility after death and it must suffer for love the just punishment which its sins have merited."[5] As we have demonstrated from scriptures, God does not always remove the punishment when he forgives the sin. Retributive justice seems to explain this fact.

No Retributive Punishment Proposal

Travis considers the NT judgment passages on God's "vengeance" and "paying back" (arising from OT concepts) as not requiring a retributive meaning. "But in the context of his [Paul's] argument he makes them serve his conviction that the consequences of sin follow by inner necessity (under God's

---

[4] Thomas Aquinas, *ST*, https://drbo.org/summa/question/61301.htm. ; Accessed 6 July2023.

[5] Jurgie, *Purgatory*, 5.

control) rather than by acts of retribution imposed from outside."[6] Travis dismisses "judgment according to deeds" as not meaning Christians are really judged according to deeds. He concludes, "From these passages [Rom 2:1–11, 1 Cor 11:1, Gal 5:21, 1 Cor 6:9–11, Eph 5:5] it appears that for Paul deeds are not in themselves the criterion of judgment. Rather, they bear testimony to the depths of a person's character, and show whether their relation to God is fundamentally one of faith or unbelief." In my opinion, his personal theology demands interpretive gymnastics to dismiss what the text states.

It seems in Travis' theology all Christians will have bountiful good deeds and no Christian will be punished for bad deeds. That is not consistent with the biblical account. This Protestant error forces a misreading of scripture to conform to bad theology. In some Protestant circles, the conflation of faith and works—because good works are inevitable from God's perfect gift of faith (as in Gnosticism)—has created an antinomial dilemma: The biblical text does not really mean what it states. In fact for Travis, scripture actually means the exact opposite of what the text plainly states. In his view, "judgment according to works" really means we are *not* judged by works, only by faith. This is a case of special pleading due to tradition.

---

[6] Stephen Travis, *Christ and the Judgment of God: The Limits of Divine Retribution in New Testament Thought* (Milton Keynes, UK: Paternoster, 2008; repr. 2nd edn. Peabody, MA: Hendrickson), 84.

Restorative Justice (Sanctification)

Those few Protestants who have affirmed purgatory have historically held a restorative justice view wherein there is no suffering or punishment for sin. Walls discusses: 1) John Henry Newman's view of growth into perfection after death (Newman cites Phil 1:6), 2) Bernard's view that growth into perfection to enter heaven occurs as a natural sanctification process after death since faith alone does not sanctify, 3) Purtill's view of seeing our sin through the eyes of our victims which produces a total rejection of evil within us, and 4) Vander Laan's view of healing for the nations through the tree of life that means character growth through the Holy Spirit.[7] Walls notes that the natural consequences of our sin can cause pain without punishment *per se*. "Such profitable pain that is the natural result of absorbing truth that clashes with our selfish attitudes and other sinful dispositions should not be objectional."[8] The restorative model of sanctification carries with it a natural pain of suffering without inflicting further punitive damages. This was also the view of C.S. Lewis.

Composite Retributive and Restorative Justice

Protestants (and many Catholics) will avoid the retributive justice model (satisfaction) due to the historically widespread

---

[7] Walls, *Purgatory*, 82–7.

[8] Walls, *Purgatory*, 88.

and serious abuses created by it. But is the abuse of a truth sufficient reason to reject the truth itself? Aquinas taught the human will must be recalibrated to perfection with God's will—this is a voluntary conforming of human desires, not merely from acts of sin, but even in the inclinations to sin.

> So, man cannot be brought to this end unless he be united with God by the conformation of his will. And this is the proper effect of love, for "it is proper to friends to approve and disapprove the same things, and to be delighted in and to be pained by the same things." Hence, by sanctifying grace man is established as a lover of God, since man is directed by it to the end that has been shared with him by God. (*SCG* 3.151.3)[9]

For Aquinas, God only utilizes punishment when repentance has not totally transformed the person. "The punishment has the quality of satisfaction." (*ST*, Ia IIae, 87, 6) The more we sin the more layers of glue harden our hearts and wills. Because God's divine image within us includes our free wills, this requires our voluntary peeling of these layers of sin from the will. Aquinas merges the retributive justice with restorative justice. Is there any requirement to choose between the two?

The wrath of a holy God against sin is not a popular topic

---

[9] Aquinas, *SCG* 3.151.3, https://isidore.co/aquinas/ContraGentiles3b.htm#151; Accessed 5 July 2023.

in modern Christianity. Years ago, R.C. Sproul stopped at a book booth where I was working. I had the opportunity to compliment Him on his book, *The Holiness of God*. He told me that it went out of print faster than any other book he had written. Popular Christianity wants to hear only about the love of God, not the wrath of God. Yet the OT is filled with descriptions of God's wrath against sin among his people, resulting in severe punishments. The NT repeats this.

Romans 1:18 tells us, "For the wrath of God is revealed from heaven against all ungodliness and unrighteousness of people who suppress the truth by their unrighteousness." (NET) In Rev 6:16 we read, "and they said to the mountains and the rocks, 'Fall on us and hide us from the sight of Him who sits on the throne, and from the wrath of the Lamb.'" (NASB) Similarly Rev 19:15 states, "and out of his mouth doth proceed a sharp sword, that with it he may smite the nations, and he shall rule them with a rod of iron, and he doth tread the press of the wine of the wrath and the anger of God the Almighty." (YLT) Peter warns us, "But now you must be holy in everything you do, just as God who chose you is holy. For the Scriptures say, 'You must be holy because I am holy.'" (1 Pet 1:15–16, NLT) The imputed righteousness of Christ does not substitute for obeying God. God does not merely prefer righteous behavior, he demands it. "Imputed righteousness" must become actual righteousness before we are able to live forever intimately with a holy God.

False Dilemma/Disjunction

As we demonstrated from the early church fathers, the earliest writings about purgatory contained elements of punishment for the Christian in order to satisfy the justice of God. The suffering was due to God's punitive action against sin. In those same early writings we found instances where the continuing process of transformation into the character of Christ was paramount. The Christian suffered the natural consequences of a choice to become more like Christ through purging of sinful thinking and attitudes within the person's being. Both the retributive punishment satisfying God's justice and the sanctifying model simultaneously co-existed to explain suffering after death.

A soul who begins the restorative process may then see God more clearly and develop more desire to be holy for the purpose of achieving greater intimacy with God. The voluntary suffering of purgation becomes a small price to pay to achieve that goal. Similarly, the soul receiving the due payment for disobedience voluntarily suffers punishment from the Father in order to be restored to intimacy. The punishment itself is not desired but becomes the only pathway to greater intimacy.

In his holy justice, God punishes sin in his children. He warned of this punishment for those who disobeyed. This is a matter of truthfulness to God's own testimony in scripture. Dismissing posthumous punishment impugns God's warnings in scripture. It affronts God's holiness. It rejects God's justice. In contrast, if we go to the other extreme by teaching only punishment, then we caricature God by omitting his love. Our Father in heaven desires to lovingly embrace his children who have been perfected through the purging of all possibility of sin.

Conclusion

Over the millennia the pendulum has swung from the pure retributive model (with Christians experiencing terrible torments for hundreds of years) to the other extreme of a pure sanctification model (no retributive punishment of suffering or pain). We are under no obligation to choose between these two models. The earliest Christians and Thomas Aquinas accepted both as true. Perhaps they understood that God's holiness and justice require retributive satisfaction while in his love he provides restorative sanctification for his children. This balance answers injustice.

Chapter 11
Modern Protestant Advocates
of Posthumous Purification

Protestants have generally rejected the concept of purgatory. Yet there are modern theologians who support the idea of a posthumous purgation of sins in Christians. We have already read the thoughts of C.S. Lewis on this subject in support of an unpleasant purging of Christians after death. We now explore the ideas of other more modern Protestants.

Protestant Advocates

Wolfhart Pannenberg (a famous German Protestant theologian, 1928–2014) was critical of the concept of purgatory as a distinct, temporally extended intermediate state. However, he affirmed purgation as an aspect of judgment.

> The judgment that is put in Christ's hands is no longer destruction but a fire of purging and cleansing. […] It involves the completing of penitence, but only as a moment in integration into the new life in

fellowship with Jesus Christ. Thus the fire of
judgment is purifying, not destructive fire.[1]

He develops this view in a discussion of the ideas of Joseph
Ratzinger on a non-locative purgatory and concludes: "There is
thus no more reason for the Reformation opposition."

The American theologian Donald Bloesch (1928–2010)
opined, "It is my contention that a change of heart can still
happen on the other side of death."[2] This follows the nineteenth
century theologians K. F. A. Kahnis and Hans Martensen. Both
defended the view that a Christian's conformation to Christ after
death would be not be instantaneous.[3] "Both objected that a total
transformation at death did violence to the inherently
developmental nature of the self. Such a transformation would
be a violent 'act of magic' [*Zauberschlag*], Kahnis argued."[4]

Kittel confirms the biblical concept of Christians being
judged on the last day.

---

[1] Wolfhart Pannenberg, *Systematic Theology, Volume 3.*, trans. Geoffrey
W. Bromiley (Grand Rapids, MI: Eerdmans, 1998), 619.

[2] Donald Bloesch, *The Last Things: Resurrection, Judgment, Glory*
(Downers Grove, IL: InterVarsity Press, 2005), 146.

[3] Karl F. A. Kahnis, *System der lutherischen Dogmatik*, vol. 3 of *Die
lutherische Dogmatik historischgenetisch dargestellt* (Leipzig: Dörffling
und Franke, 1868), 554; Hans Martensen, *Christian Dogmatics: A
Compendium of the Doctrines of Christianity*, trans. William Urwick
(Edinburgh: T. & T. Clark, 1892), 458-459.

[4] https://www.usccb.org/committees/ecumenical-interreligious-
affairs/hope-eternal-life , (section 201); Accessed 23 June 2023.

All men without exception must come before God's judgment, including Christians, 2 C.5:10. The suggestion that this concept of judgment is purely dialectical, applying only in controversy with the Jews, is without foundation, for Christians themselves are to be judged, 2 C.5:10. … Paul is sure that believers will be saved in the last judgment, R.8:31-39. This applies even to the incestuous man, 1 C.5:5. Believers are justified. But he does not ground this confidence on the moral renewal which is associated with justification or which follows on the possession of the Spirit. He grounds it on Christ alone, R. 5:9,10; 8:33f. For this reason He can expect salvation even for those whose work will not stand in the last judgment, 1C.3:15. [5]

Furthermore, Kittel's footnote explains, "The doctrine of judgment by works is the constant presupposition of the doctrine of justification by faith. Without it, the latter loses its seriousness and depth."[6]

Louis Berkhof (a Reformed theologian, 1873–1957) also suggested there may be two different aspects to justification and judgment.

---

[5] Kittel, 938.

[6] Ibid., footnote 68.

For all those who appear in judgment entrance to, or
exclusion from, heaven, will depend on the question,
whether they are clothed in the righteousness of Jesus
Christ. But there will be different degrees, both of the
bliss of heaven and of the punishment of hell. And
those degrees will be determined by what is done in
the flesh, Matt. 11:22,24; Luke 12:47,48; 20:47; Dan.
12:3; II Cor 9-6 [sic, 9:6].[7]

Dodson, citing Heb 10:28–29, taught the punishment of
the Christian at Christ's judgment would be "sorer punishment
than physical death."[8] This follows Augustine and Aquinas.

Panton opined:

Present chastisement—even bodily, as Miriam struck
with leprosy by God's own hand (Num. xii.10), or
Church members afflicted and cut off for sin (1 Cor.
xi.30)—all acknowledge; but most assume that all
chastisement is sharply confined to this life. *The
Judgment Seat is thereby shorn of all judicial
function, and made totally unreal.* ... If the
backslider, even the worst, is instantaneously and
miraculously cleansed and perfected at death, and by
the act of death, there would neither be need for the
prolonged process of sanctification through a lifetime

---

[7] Berkhof, 733.

[8] Kenneth Dodson, *The Prize of the Up-Calling* (Grand Rapids, MI:
Baker, 1969), 84.

of suffering, nor justice to those countless sufferers who have achieved holiness through agony. [...] It is the resurrection of an old and (one had thought) obsolete assumption that all curses are for the Jew, and all blessings are for the Church.[9] (italics original)

Johnson concluded "Perhaps the most neglected aspect of the Judgment Seat of Christ is that having to do with punishment. ... Although the discipline administered at the Judgment Seat of Christ must of necessity take on a form different from that experienced in this life, the reality of such a loss and its severity must not be overlooked."[10]

Lutzer writes on the Judgment Seat of Christ regarding resolution of wrongs. "The judgment seat of Christ will be the place where God will satisfy our craving to have masks torn away, lies exposed, and reality prevail. The wrongdoers will finally admit the truth, and the victims will be vindicated; forgiveness among believers will be both given and accepted. Only then will justice prevail."[11]

Benware concluded Christians will be judged with negative consequences.

---

[9] D. M. Panton, *The Judgment Seat of Christ* (Hayesville, NC: Schoettle Publishing, 1984), 59 footnote 1, and 69.

[10] Carl Johnson, *The Account Which We Must Give: Studies on the Judgment Seat of Christ* (Beckley, WV: np, 1989), 100.

[11] Erwin Lutzer, *Your Eternal Reward: Triumph and Tears at the Judgment Sat of Christ* (Chicago: Moody Press, 1998), 67.

The point is that if Christ's work on the cross does not keep a believer from experiencing negative disciplines from God in this life, what prohibits there from being negative disciplines from Christ at the judgment seat? It would seem that there is nothing to keep this from being true. It is obvious that justified people still have to deal with their sins and not to do so always brings negative consequences. Beyond this logical deduction, several portions of scripture directly indicate that negatives will be part of the judgment seat. Sin apparently is a factor in Christ's evaluation.[12]

The Problem of Protestant Conflation

The conflation of faith and works in Protestant circles—while still claiming to teach "faith alone"—continues to amaze me. Travis opines that justification is merely a provisional acquittal based upon future performance in faith and good works.

Justification is not an irreversible verdict which renders the final judgment unnecessary. It is a provisional, anticipatory verdict of acquittal, given in response to faith, and it will be confirmed at the final judgment, except in the case of those who have ceased to exercise faith and show this by their lives. It is not so much that they are condemned for evil

---

[12] Paul Benware, *The Believer's Payday* (Chattanooga, TN: AMG Publishers, 2002), 91–2.

deeds, as that they condemn themselves by repudiating the grace of God which alone can save them.[13]

Once again, every person must either receive an A+ or an F based upon works. Travis claims a denial of grace and salvific faith is the cause of God's judgment. There is no middle ground where Christians are actually judged for their evil deeds prior to spending eternity with God. The conflation of faith (as God's unilateral gift) combined with good works (inevitably accomplished by God) in the Christian thereby determines the interpretation of every passage. Alan Stanley, writing in an Evangelical Theological Society Monograph Series, comes to the same conclusion. "That is, if works are present one can expect to spend eternity with God in heaven; if works are absent, one can expect to spend eternity without God in hell."[14] For these Protestants, the Reformation cry of *sola fide*, faith alone, is a corpse propped up, attempting to make it look respectable.[15]

---

[13] Travis, *Christ and the Judgment of God,* 158.

[14] Alan P. Stanley, *Did Jesus Teach Salvation by Works?: The Role of Works in Salvation in the Synoptic Gospels* 4th edn. (Eugene, OR: Pickwick Publications, 2006), 2–3.

[15] Despite over five-hundred years of tradition, the Augustinian-Calvinist theology of modern Reformation theology has suffered a serious credibility issue with the exposure of Augustine's novel syncretism of his prior pagan ideas with Christianity in 412 CE when fighting the Pelagians. See Kenneth Wilson, *Augustine's Conversion from Traditional Free Choice to "Non-free Free Will": A Comprehensive Methodology,* Studien Und Texte Zu Antike Und Christentum 111 (Tübingen: Mohr Siebeck, 2018) and Kenneth Wilson, "Chapter 6: Calvinism is Augustinianism," in David Allen and Steve Lemke,

Walls on Purgatory

Jerry Walls (a Wesleyan philosopher) has written a book as a
Protestant supporting purgatory. *Purgatory: The Logic of Total
Transformation* was published by Oxford University Press in
2012.[16] Although Walls is a Protestant, most Wesleyans are
similar to Roman Catholics in understanding justification as a
process intimately connected to sanctification. Methodists do
not emphasize the Christian as being "declared righteous by
God through faith" in forensic justification so much as being
sanctified (made righteous) through faith.[17]

Walls enters a critical discussion with other
philosophers and theologians on the necessity of maintaining
personal identity and character transformation that requires a
process over time, rather than it being instantaneous. Walls cites
David Brown's thought experiment.[18] I will paraphrase it. What
would you think if you awakened from sleep with an identical
person staring at you with all of your memories, yet this person
is morally perfect? I would probably question whether this

---

eds. *Calvinism: A Biblical and Theological Critique* (Nashville, TN: B & H
Publishing, 2022), 213–238.

[16] I recommend this book for those persons who are interested in a more
philosophical approach to the question of postmortem transformation.

[17] See Jerry Walls and Joseph Dongell, *Why I am Not a Calvinist*
(Downers Grove, IL: InterVarsity, 2004) versus Robert Peterson and
Michael Williams, *Why I Am Not an Arminian* (Downers Grove, IL:
InterVarsity, 2004).

[18] Walls, *Purgatory*, 114–5. He cites David Brown, "No Heaven without
Purgatory," *Religious Studies* 21 (1985): 451–2.

radically different moral person is really me. However, if you or I underwent a gradual transformation process of moral improvement in thoughts and attitudes, we would not doubt that this person was indeed our true self. Continuity must exist between the past and present to maintain personal identity.

Furthermore, Ratzinger considers that our personal identity is only forged through accepting or refusing love in relationships with other humans, and especially with God.[19] A person in the process of being perfected in love would experience guilt over the harm done to others while on earth. This guilt would not be legal (requiring forgiveness), but rather a natural suffering from me finally experiencing unresolved guilt due to me having caused "broken and damaged relationships."[20] This requires a process, as Walls describes it:

> They must own the hurt and the broken and damaged relationships, they must acknowledge the role their actions have played in causing the hurt and damage. And they must be prepared to change their attitudes and actions to restore those broken relationships in light of the truth they have come to see. Again, seeing and owning this truth arguably takes time, and cannot happen by fiat, not even by divine fiat.[21]

---

[19] Ratzinger, *Eschatology*, 183–4.

[20] Walls, *Purgatory*, 117.

[21] Walls, *Purgatory*, 121.

Bernard has argued that if God requires progressive
sanctification in this life by our free choice as such a sufficient
good that he does not instantaneously purify us in this life, then
neither will God immediately purify us in the next life.[22] Walls
demonstrates that free choice is required for genuine moral
transformation: Time is essential for free choices to be made.[23]

Conclusion

It appears the Protestant Reformation cry of "faith alone"
against the Roman Catholic Church is less than accurate today
(perhaps even dishonest?). Because most Protestants reject a
posthumous punishment of Christians, Protestants are caught in
a quagmire of semantic maneuvering wherein good works are
the primary criterion for entrance to heaven. The extreme of
either hell for bad behavior or heaven for good behavior are
determinative, while faith has been ejected from center stage to
backstage. Is this baptized philosophy instead of Christianity?

The embracement at face value of the biblical account
of posthumous punishment for Christians would solve this
dilemma. Because there are some modern Protestants who
endorse a punishment of Christians after death, this does not
prove it exists. However, it does prove this theology of

---

[22] Justin Bernard, "Purgatory and the Dilemma of Sanctification," *Faith
and Philosophy* 26 (2009): 311–27 at 318–25. This entails a variant on the
evidential problem of evil. (Walls, *Purgatory*, 121)

[23] Walls, *Purgatory*, 122.

posthumous punishment is compatible with Protestant theology.

I find the arguments convincing for retention of self-identity through a process of progressive moral purification rather than an instantaneous total transformation into perfection. If instantaneously perfected, then I would not recognize myself (and my wife would certainly not recognize me!). God values free choice. Free choices require time.

In the next chapter we discuss the implications of a punishment for Christians after death.

Chapter 12

Implications of a Postmortem
Judgment of Christians

The majority of Protestants think all Christians after death will be ushered immediately into the joy of God's presence. Joy will abound and only joy. After death, the Christian will never suffer consequences for sins of lying, jealousy, anger, premarital sex, adultery, gossip, or greed (1 Cor 5:9–13; Gal 5:16–21). But these are not merely wrong actions. These sins represent a wrong heart that has not been conformed to the image of Christ. Does that essential heart transformation occur instantaneously upon death or does it continue in a process of transformation?

Is Transformation Instantaneous or Progressive after Death?

Walls astutely asks, "If God could perfect us unilaterally without our help why does He not do it right now rather than having us continue to suffer evil?"[1] Yes, God could do so unilaterally, but has chosen to allow his creation freedom of

---

[1] Jerry Walls, *Purgatory: The Logic of Total Transformation* (Oxford: Oxford University Press, 2012), 81. The concept is here and is derived from Bernard; https://www.youtube.com/watch?v=BDgBmMMfams : "HBU: CS Lewis on Why Our Souls Demand Purgatory"; Accessed 21 June 2023.

choice. As we behold God we desire to become more like God. That cannot be accomplished completely while we reside in mere physical bodies. We will require glorified bodies with super-charged DNA.

Aquinas logically opined that a punishment after death must occur for the justice of God to be satisfied. Because, if Christians could escape the consequences for their sins on earth *and* escape them in the afterlife then we would all be better off being negligent in paying our debts. No advantage ensues from being "solicitous."[2] If no penalty is ever assessed, the Christian could live as if there is no God.

The Protestant Inconsistency on Faith and Works

For Protestants, the believer faces two extremes. In the first scenario, he believes unto immediate permanent justification and inevitably fulfills a life of good deeds. If he perseveres in faith and works, then he enters heaven. This proves he was elect (Reformed theology) or that he worked out his own salvation without falling from grace (Arminian theology). The result becomes eternal bliss without having to answer to God or victims for any evil or sin committed while on earth. So, had Hitler converted to Christ on his death-bed there would be no

---

[2] Thomas Aquinas, *Summa Contra Gentiles* 4.91.6. Solicitous means meticulous concern for another person. One could argue that the damaged personal character that will require future painful purification would be a motivation for current holiness.

consequences for murdering millions of people. In the second scenario, the believer fails to produce sufficient good works. This either proves that he was a fake Christian hypocrite and not one of the elect (Reformed theology), or that he fell from grace and lost his justification/sanctification (Arminian theology). Either view results in eternal damnation.

These two extremes seem to place Protestants in the uncomfortable position of worshipping a God who knows no degrees of faithfulness to Christ. Each professed believer either receives a perfect A+ for the class with no negative marks or else fails the class with an F. There are no grades between the two extremes. This is an extreme pass-fail theology. Expressed in other terms, either the sinful infraction receives complete acquittal with no consequences or else it receives the death penalty. Despite the claim to faith alone, works ultimately determine the eternal destinies of most Protestant evangelicals.

In fact, Schreiner boldly pronounces, "If the works aren't present, the person will be damned. That's a criterion!"[3] Of course, Calvinists claim God performs those good works within the elect Christian as the inevitable fruit of God-implanted faith. But good works issuing from God (not ourselves) is exactly what the Catholics taught during the Protestant Reformation. Cardinal Bellarmine (1542–1621)

---

[3] Thomas Schreiner, "Response to James D.G. Dunn," in Alan Stanley, ed., *The Role of Works at the Final Judgment* (Grand Rapids: Zondervan, 2013), 154.

wrote:

> "Work out our own salvation with fear and
> trembling." [Phil 2:12] There man is called his own
> redeemer and savior, but no injury is done to Christ
> on that account, the whole strength of our works and
> satisfaction depends upon the blood of Christ, and if
> we redeem sins, or work out our salvation, we do it
> by a gift of his spirit to us, or rather the very spirit of
> Christ works these things in us, just as nothing
> detracts from God which will be done through
> secondary causes.[4]

So Calvinists teach the very same defense as Roman Catholics
who they criticize. Both the Calvinists and the Catholics require
good works to enter heaven. *Sola fide* (faith alone) falters,
stripped of its meaning. As R.C. Sproul wrote,[5]

> Roman Catholic View: Faith+Works=>Justification
>
> Reformation View: Faith=>Justification+Works
>
> The difference in the *order* of these terms in the two
> equations, however, points to the radical difference
> between the two positions. In the Roman formula

---

[4] Robert Bellarmine, *On Purgatory*, trans. Ryan Grant (Post Falls, ID: Mediatrix Press, 2017), 121.

[5] R.C. Sproul, *Faith Alone: The Evangelical Doctrine of Justification* (Grand Rapids, MI: Baker Books, 1995), 156, with Figure 8.1 which he borrowed from Gerstner.

works are a necessary precondition *for* justification.

In the Reformed view works are a necessary fruit *of* justification. (italics original)

Catholics are more forthright that works are required. Calvinists, like Sproul, insert works within the definition of faith which God gives the person for justification. Sproul cites John Calvin, "Christ, therefore, justifies no man without sanctifying him."[6] But therefore, in reality, there is no "radical difference between the two positions." Both Catholics and Calvinists require good works and sanctification to enter heaven. The only difference is semantics.

Contra Sproul, here is the radical difference: The Catholic who believed upon Christ, but lacks enough good works and sanctification, can still enter heaven after being purged postmortem. The Calvinist lacking enough good works and sanctification goes to hell. This person was never a Christian, because the Calvinist "Sovereign God" (cf., the Gnostic god) always gives his elect both the gift of faith and perseverance. This Christianized Stoic view of the "Sovereign God" was derived by Calvin from Augustine's later revised theology.[7] Faith in tradition may be required to maintain this

---

[6] John Calvin, *Institutes* 3.16.1.

[7] See Kenneth Wilson, "Augustine of Hippo's Tenuous Tension between Stoic Providence and Christian Free Will," *Studia Patristica* 119 (2021): 153–168; Kenneth Wilson, "Chapter 6: Calvinism is Augustinianism," in *Calvinism: A Biblical and Theological Critique*, eds. David Allen and Steve Lemke. (Nashville, TN: B & H Publishing, 2021).

theology.

In contrast, Roman Catholics view good works as a continuum with corresponding punishment or rewards. Believers may have genuine faith yet lack sufficient good works, requiring more conformity to Christ in sanctification after death. These persons are not doomed to hell; instead, they are sufficiently punished for their evil after death and continue in progressive sanctification after death. Consistent with reality and scripture, varying degrees of sanctification unto godliness are recognized.

Motivations for Obedience

The Scriptures provide us with three motivations for obedience—punishment, reward, and love. In both the Old and New Testaments, punishment serves as a primary reason to obey God's commandments. Moses, the Prophets, and the Apostles all appeal to God's sure punishment upon his children as a legitimate reason to obey him. Reward and blessing are promised to those who obey. The blessings and cursings of Deuteronomy 28 typify these contrasting motivations for obedience. Blessings result, "if you diligently obey the voice of the Lord your God to observe carefully all of his commandments." (Deut 28:1) Cursings result, "if you do not obey the voice of the Lord your God to observe carefully all his commandments and his statutes." (Deut 28:15)

Although Jesus and the Apostles speak of both payment

and punishment, the higher motivation for obedience becomes love. It can be found in the Old Testament, but becomes prominent in the New Testament as Jesus perfectly expresses this motivation of love of God. Although this author would prefer to claim such maturity that love has become my sole motivation, both the fear of punishment and the promise of reward continue to influence my level of obedience. God is wise in providing his own children all three motivations for obedience.

When Protestants remove God's motivation of punishment through a peculiar view of total absolution from all future punishment, we remove one of God's prescribed motivations. This is neither wise nor safe. We do not need to accept the medieval Roman Catholic doctrine of purgatory in order to reclaim this doctrine of postmortem punishment.

The medieval Roman Catholic doctrine of purgatory included intricately prescribed lengths of absence from God's presence for various sins solely in retributive punishment. The believer need not be afraid of absence from our Holy God. Instead, we should be terrified of standing in his holy presence with our innate sinfulness. Although Christ permanently removed our sins that separated us eternally from God, as God's children we still answer for sins committed for reward or punishment. "Our God is a consuming fire" (Heb 12:28–29) applies to believers. The analogy of 1 Corinthians 3:12–15 describes the believers' experience before God's holiness. The more dross (wood, hay, and stubble) we have acquired, the greater the heat of the conflagration. If gold, silver, and precious stones comprise most of our works, the fire of God's holiness will not burn so hot. Even if our sin burns away in a fraction of a second, the intensity of God's holiness which purifies us will be extreme. As believers in Christ, we fear (for a short time) the Lord's presence (James 5:9)—not his absence. Only when our love has been perfected do we no longer fear (1 John 4:18). The fire may or may not be literal, but the fiery experience will be literal.

God does not always forgive sin to remit the consequences. "The LORD of Heaven's Armies told me this: 'Certainly this sin will not be forgiven as long as you live,' says the Sovereign LORD of Heaven's Armies." (Isa 22:14, NET) God pays each person for their deeds, good or bad. "But I, the LORD, look into a person's heart and test the mind. So I can decide what each one deserves; I can give each one the right payment for what he does." (Jer 17:10, NCV). Paul repeated this concept in Romans 2:5–8.

> But by your hard and impenitent heart you are storing up wrath for yourself on the day of wrath, when God's righteous judgment will be revealed. For he will repay according to each one's deeds: to those who by patiently doing good seek for glory and honor and immortality, he will give eternal life; while for those who are self-seeking and who obey not the truth

but wickedness, there will be wrath and fury. (NRSV)

Note that eternal life is granted to the righteous Christians while "wrath and fury" (not eternal death or Hell) will be poured out on those Christians who are self-absorbed and wicked. A lexical study of wrath in both the OT and NT demonstrates wrath refers to God's reaction to sin. It does not demand or imply hell.

Case Scenarios

The following case studies are true accounts. Most Christians— regardless of their affiliation—will understand the difficulties that occur if God does not punish these persons after death.

Scenario 1

A pastor announces that he is leaving his wife, but claims there is no other woman involved. His best friend and music leader comes to me for advice. I advised him that the pastor is most likely lying: the pastor is obtaining his sexual fulfillment from another woman. Four months later it becomes known the pastor is indeed committing adultery. The pastor divorces his wife, leaves the church, and starts a new church in an adjacent city. The pastor's best friend and music leader had survived the death of a child from cancer with his faith and ministry intact. However, this betrayal was so severe that he never entered a church again. It has been over twenty years.

Jesus warned his disciples that they should watch

themselves so they do not cause another person to sin. (Luke 17:1–3) Being thrown into the sea with a large concrete block around your neck seems like punishment. This is likely not literal but depicts an even worse future severity. Is there some type of severe punishment after death, or is there zero punishment for this Christian pastor's sin that caused another Christian (who still believes in Christ) to fall away from the body of Christ?

Scenario 2

A priest in a local parish was arrested for multiple counts of childhood sexual abuse. After the trial he spent ten years in prison for his crimes. Numerous children have been permanently scarred both emotionally and physically as result of his sin. Some of these victims (now adults) no longer want anything to do with the Church. Families were torn apart and the local parish suffered after the conviction and incarceration. This priest caused more than "one of these little ones to stumble." Would it be better from him to wear a millstone necklace into the depths of the sea? Is this hyperbole, or does this pastor enter the beatific vision only after being punished for his egregious sin that severely damaged God's other children?

Scenario 3

The head of the mafia in a prior Russian country hears about forgiveness and salvation through Jesus Christ. He becomes a

Christian, marries a Christian woman, then relocates across the globe to another country for protection. He continues in faith and charity for another twenty years. Does God hold him responsible for his many murders committed while leading the mafia? Will he be punished for this? Or, does his baptism and forgiveness erase all consequences?

Would a genuine, heart-felt deathbed conversion really absolve tyrants like Stalin, Hitler, Pol Pot, Mao Zedong, etc. of all punishment for committing genocide or mass murder by the millions? That would be a travesty of justice. God will punish.

Scenario 4

A Christian woman was sexually abused as a child by her father (who was a pastor). When she became a very attractive young woman, she set out to seduce as many pastors as possible. In a large city, she would attend a church for one year then systematically slowly seduce the pastor. She would confide in the pastor that her husband was a homosexual; therefore she was not having her sexual desires met. She successfully seduced six pastors into adultery in one metropolis over eight years. Six pastors were removed from ministry as a result of her sinful enticements. Does she plead the blood of Christ so that there is no punishment for her sin? Or, must she undergo punishment for this deliberate sin prior to entering heaven? Does her abusive father bear consequences of his sin that contributed to the devastation for so many Christian leaders and churches? Or, does the father suffer no consequences for the domino effect of his sin that destroyed so many lives?

Scenario 5

A married Christian man divorced his wife of twenty-five years and has had an intimate relationship for five years with a woman who is still married to another man. These two claim they are married and advertise themselves as married. (Common-law divorce does not exist.) When his blood brother calls out his sin of adultery, the brother in adultery says, "Don't judge me for my sin, because the Bible says God will judge you more than me for being judgmental."

A different Christian couple is struggling and receives marriage counseling. The husband is concerned about his two very young children spending time with the wife's family without him present. There are numerous indications that child sexual abuse may be in the family. The wife and her parents see no problem with the very sinful behaviors in the wife's two sisters and their children. The husband, as a follower of Christ, refuses to divorce his wife. The wife complains her husband hates her family. The wife quits counseling, stops attending church, and files for divorce without biblical cause. When sent a text of concern by the compassionate female marriage counselor, the wife fired back, "Do not judge me."

This is a common refrain from Christians in sin. These Christians have missed 1 Cor 11: 31–32. "For if we would judge ourselves, we should not be judged. But when we are judged, we are chastened of the Lord, that we should not be condemned with the world." (KJV) Also, "But now I have written unto you not to associate with anyone calling himself a brother if he is a fornicator or covetous or an idolater or a railer or a drunkard or an extortioner; with such a one do not even eat. For why shall I judge those that are without? Do ye not judge those that are within? But those that are without, God shall judge. Therefore, put away from among yourselves that wicked person." (1 Cor 5: 11–13, JUB) Modern Christians are willfully ignorant about God's requirement for holiness within his church.

Jesus made a profound impression upon his disciples teaching against divorce. It was so profound that the disciples uttered a critical statement in response to Jesus' teaching on divorce. In Matthew 19:9–11, we read,

> And I say to you, whoever divorces his wife, except for immorality, and marries another woman commits adultery." The disciples said to Him, "If the relationship of the man with his wife is like this, it is better not to marry." But He said to them, "Not all men *can* accept this statement...."

Malachi calls divorce "treachery." "God hates divorce" says the prophet. (Mal 2:14–16) Our modern culture does not seem to understand the seriousness of divorce about which Jesus spoke. They will understand on judgment day. "Marriage is to be held in honor among all, and the marriage bed is to be undefiled; for fornicators and adulterers God will judge." (Hebrews 13:4, NASB95)

Over half of adult Protestants have been divorced. At the risk of offending them, I am compelled to repeat those words of Jesus. Judgment day is coming for those who file for divorce. When committing this serious sin that "God hates," tell your excuses to the Judge. He will ask why you caused your spouse to commit adultery. May the Lord have mercy on you.

Scenario 6

For this final scenario, we discuss a public figure who most Christians will recognize. Ravi Zacharias (1946–2020) spent forty years in ministry worldwide as a highly effective teacher and apologist for Christianity. After his death, Ravi Zacharias International Ministries hired the law firm of Matin and Miller to investigate numerous claims of sexual misconduct by Zacharias. The investigative team of prior federal law enforcement officials concluded that Zacharias had masturbated hundreds of times in front of various women (especially massage therapists) and received hundreds of texts of nude women in their twenties. He propositioned women for sex.

Many Christians claimed Zacharias was not a genuine Christian, but only a sexual predator and a fraud. Certainly "genuine Christians" cannot act at this level of depravity and immorality. Or, can they? Anyone who has spent a few decades in Christian leadership can tell you that Christians can be just as sinful as any other people. What Zacharias did was evil and hurt God's children. His hypocrisy insulted and shamed the name of Christ. But we must not deny the good Zacharias did for Christ and Christianity. So is Zacharias in hell, or in heaven (without consequences because he believed in Christ)? I suggest neither option is true. Both are extreme. God balances his purifying judgment and mercy.

Comments

We have already noted that many Christians will claim the persons in these scenarios were not genuine Christians. We have elsewhere demonstrated that this theology is bankrupt, based upon extreme assumptions. Others will claim these Christians committed mortal sins that prevent them from ever achieving the beatific vision. However, King David—a man after God's own heart—committed the sins of adultery and murder. Is he in hell (even if a milder degree)? Or, after death, will David be appropriately punished for those sins through suffering as he is conformed to Christ's image? Does a Christian who dies prior to confession and penance of a mortal sin really suffer eternal hell? Or, does that Christian suffer temporary punishments from God in purgation prior to entering eternal bliss?

Posthumous punishment vindicates the holiness and justice of God while simultaneously providing grace for his children. This theology best explains the Scriptures. It also explains reality. Protestants may retain justification by "faith alone" as the only requirement for entrance into God's family. After entering God's family, works are then judged for payment or punishment as God's children. God's children must be purged of sin's effects after death to spend eternity with God.

Must we dread meeting Christ after death?

Protestants will still react with disbelief at the idea of God punishing us. The joyous anticipation of being with our loving Christ has now been changed into a fearful expectation of punishment from a God of justice. This is especially true for those Christians who have committed adultery, murder, premarital sex, robbery, divorce, etc. But, I do not see dread as the inevitable consequence of a posthumous punishment.

We should remember that all of us are sinners. None of us are without sin that requires God's punishment. Those who commit "big" sins (mortal sins) may be surprised to see persons who are prideful, covetous, gossips, angry, cheaters, immoral, or causing division in Christ's body receive similar punishment (1 Cor 5:11; Gal 5:19–21). God will judge justly. The most important clarification on punishment is that we will not be chained for years being tortured by a God who must extract vengeance.

First, there is no time frame provided. We have no idea whether God will punish for hundreds of years or a few seconds. But, we can surmise that the severity of punishment (if not the length) will be proportional to the offenses, failures, and required character conformation needed. A good earthly father does not punish the children (who he loves) any longer than necessary to match the wrongdoing. We know that our Father God's manner of divine interaction far exceeds earthly fathers. "You parents—if your children ask for a loaf of bread, do you give them a stone instead? Or if they ask for a fish, do you give them a snake? Of course not! So if you sinful people know how to give good gifts to your children, how much more will your heavenly Father give good gifts to those who ask him. (Matt 7:9–11, NLT) "Since we respected our earthly fathers who disciplined us, shouldn't we submit even more to the discipline of the Father of our spirits, and live forever? For our earthly fathers disciplined us for a few years, doing the best they knew how. But God's discipline is always good for us, so that we might share in his holiness." (Heb 12:9–10, NLT)

Furthermore, our heavenly Father is compassionate.

> The Lord passed in front of him [Moses] proclaiming, "The Lord, the Lord, a compassionate and gracious God, slow to anger and abounding in steadfast love and fidelity, who shows mercy to thousands. He forgives iniquity and transgression and sin, but will by no means forgive the iniquity of the fathers, visiting it upon their sons and their sons' sons, to the third and fourth generation." (Exodus 34:6–7, NCB)

When King David was being punished by God for his sin, David trusted in God's compassionate mercy.

> The Lord told Gad, David's prophet, "Go, tell David, 'This is what the Lord says: "I am offering you three forms of judgment from which to choose. Pick one of them."' Gad went to David and told him, "This is what the Lord says: 'Pick one of these: three years of famine, or three months being chased by your enemies and struck down by their swords, or three days being struck down by the Lord, during which a plague will invade the land and the angel of the Lord will destroy throughout Israel's territory.' Now, decide what I should tell the one who sent me." David said to Gad, "I am very upset! I prefer to be attacked by the Lord, for his mercy is very great; I do not want to be attacked by men!" (1 Chr 21:9–13, NET)

David knew God. David understood God punishes sin, yet gives mercy to those whom he loves. This should be our mindset as we consider God's punishment of us.

An analogy might be helpful. A father finds his child in blatant disobedience as the family is entering the car to depart on their two week vacation full of fun and excitement. The loving father does not ban the child from the vacation. Instead, he sits the child down and explains why punishment is necessary prior to taking this fun trip. The father punishes the child for a short time then lovingly embraces his child, saying, "You are still my child. I love you. Now let's go have some fun." Justice and mercy are balanced.

This is the Father God who we serve. Scripture makes abundantly clear both the holy justice and faithful love of God. After prophesying terrible disaster upon Israel, Isaiah writes, "Therefore, the LORD is waiting to show you mercy, and is rising up to show you compassion, for the LORD is a just God. All who wait patiently for Him are happy." (Isa 30:18, CSB) There is no reason for us to hyperfocus on the punishment with dread and consternation. Instead, we should focus on the eternal joy of being intimately loved by God. The painful memory of the short period of punishment will eventually wane with God's perpetual embrace of love. The purging of our sinful selves allows us to be even more intimate with God. Our joy will be inexpressible. Like the young child being punished by his father prior to vacation, we should focus on the eternal joy, not the temporary pain. "Fear God and keep his commandments; for that is the whole duty of everyone." (Eccl 12:13, NRSV) Our obedience will minimize the pain by keeping the "fire" smaller. Fear God—but don't be paranoid.

Finally, God promised special honors for those who serve well. Even Jonathan Edwards (1703–1758), the famous Protestant Puritan preacher of "Sinners in the Hands of an Angry God" taught degrees of honor in the afterlife based upon

Christian service.[8] Since all are sinners and yet many serve Christ, we should expect punishment for our wrongs then payment (rewards) for our service. Even persons like Ravi Zacharias can be rewarded for the good and then punished severely for the bad that was done while in the body. Only God knows what that will entail, but it will be just.

Sin diminishes our eternal intimacy with God and our position assisting Christ reigning in his eternal kingdom. The consequences of our sin are eternal. Obedience matters.

We are now ready for our conclusion.

---

[8] Jonathan Edwards, "The Portion of the Righteous," December, 1740 on Romans 2:10, *"But glory, honor, and peace, to every man that worketh good."* "The glory of the saints above will be in some proportion to their eminency in holiness and good works here. Christ will reward all according to their works. He that gained ten pounds was made ruler over ten cities, and he that gained five pounds over five cities. 'He that soweth sparingly, shall reap sparingly; and he that soweth bountifully shall reap also bountifully.' And the apostle Paul tells us that, as one star differs from another star in glory, so also it shall be in the resurrection of the dead. Christ tells us that he who gives a cup of cold water unto a disciple in the name of a disciple, shall in no wise lose his reward. But this could not be true, if a person should have no greater reward for doing many good works than if he did but few. It will be no damp to the happiness of those who have lower degrees of happiness and glory, that there are others advanced in glory above them. For all shall be perfectly happy, every one shall be perfectly satisfied. Every vessel that is cast into this ocean of happiness is full, though there are some vessels far larger than others."

Conclusion

As we surveyed the beliefs about posthumous punishment, we discovered the ancient Jews, early Roman Catholic, and Orthodox Christians all taught a purification of persons prior to eternal bliss (entering paradise or heaven, the beatific vision, or intimacy with the Almighty through deification). Only the Protestants in the sixteenth century rejected a period of personal transformation, and this was in reaction to the Roman Catholic abuses of indulgences for purgatory. Modern scholarly and popular teachings in Judaism and Catholicism have remained similar to the earliest concepts. God pays (rewards) and punishes his children after death.

I have outlined my agreements and offered my challenges to the various belief systems. An argument has been made for a temporary posthumous punishment of Christians who will spend eternity with their Lord. The historical and biblical reasons for this doctrine have been presented.

Ancient Judaism

Judaism taught that there was place where sin was purged prior to entering Paradise. The location and amount of time spent in Gehenna (not hell) varied with each sect. Saul the Pharisee probably adhered to the teaching of Rabbi Shammai, the most strict sect. After his conversion, Paul did not alter this teaching, but he did alter other popular teachings of Judaism. Numerous epistles by Paul teach on this judgement of the Christian after death. Jesus Christ boldly denounced (then corrected) many popular teachings of the Pharisees. Jesus never corrected their teaching that after death God would temporarily punish sinners prior to entering Paradise.

The Roman Catholic Church

The Roman Catholic doctrine of a temporary purging of sin in expiatory suffering has both biblical and historical support. Numerous scriptural texts warn of God's judgment upon his children. That judgment can include physical death, in addition to some type of suffering after death (of unknown quality or quantity).

The practices of prayers for the dead and indulgences have historical support and tradition. Indulgences for the dead and atonement (through a relative's prayers or good deeds) lacks definitive evidence as an approved practice in scripture. This ancient tradition is unlikely to change.

The Orthodox Church

The Eastern Orthodox Church emphasizes continual conformity to the character of God throughout eternity. There is logical reasoning supporting this doctrine. The Orthodox Christians teach a corporate nature of the Church in contrast to the individualistic approach of the West.

A process of purification persisting after death stands as a foundational pillar of Orthodoxy. In contrast to earlier Orthodox teachings, the modern Orthodox Church does not teach that individual suffering exists as part of this process. Certainly no location of "purgatory" exists. But, neither does an explanation exist for how God deals with deliberate sin in his children. Is God mocked because the sinning Christian does not receive any punishment for disobedience? "God is love" (1 John 4:8). But do we caricature God if we emphasize love but exclude his loving punishment (Rev 3:19)?

The justice of God in punishing his children emerges prominently from the pages of both the OT and the NT. Slaughter by enemies, starvation (so that women eat their own children), slavery, and divine sentences of immediate death occur. In the NT, God punishes by expulsion from the congregation (1 Cor 5:9–13), physical death (Acts 5, 1 Cor 11:27–31, Jas 5:19–20, 1 John 5:16–17), and other disciplinary measures (Heb 12:5–11).[1] Even a loving father knows he must

---

[1] I find it puzzling that most Christian commentaries dismiss the physical life in the strongly Jewish epistle of James in 5:19–20. See Rabbi Simon Glustrom, "Saving a Life (Pikuach Nefesh)" at My Jewish Learning: "The preservation of human life takes precedence over all the other commandments in Judaism. The emphasizes this principle by citing the verse from Leviticus [18:5]: "You shall therefore keep my statutes …which if a man do, *he shall live by them.*" The rabbis add: "*That he shall live by them,* and not that he shall die by them." (Babylonian Talmud, Yoma 85b) When life is involved, all Sabbath laws may be suspended to safeguard the health of the individual, the principle being *pikkuah nefesh doheh Shabbat*–

sometimes cause pain in his children to conform them to his desired character.

Protestants

The medieval doctrine of purgatory was legitimately rejected by Protestants in the Reformation. No scriptural basis exists for this elaborate theory. However, ejecting Roman Catholic purgatory from Protestant doctrine inadvertently ejected the biblical doctrine of punishment of the believer after death. The resultant Protestant view of total absolution from any punishment after forensic justification cannot be found in the Scriptures. Despite legitimate arguments against the abuses regarding purgatory, the Reformation rejection of posthumous punishment was reactionary and unfounded. To this day, a misunderstanding and caricaturizing of the Roman Catholic doctrine of purgatory persists. Not much progress has been made since John Calvin penned his reactionary analysis five-hundred years ago.

This leaves Protestants without a coherent method of dealing with Christians who do not overcome all sin in their lives. This would be all—all Christians continue to sin and fall short of the glory of God (Rom 3: 23; 1 John 1:9 and 2:1).[2] The

---

[rescuing a] life in danger takes precedence over the Sabbath." https://www.myjewishlearning.com/article/saving-a-life-pikuach-nefesh/   ; Accessed 16 May 2023. See Appendix A.

[2] Calvinists must attribute Paul's arguments in Rom 7:14–25 to his pre-Christian person (following Augustine). This is despite Jerome making it clear that this is the Christian experience, because it is impossible for a non-

Calvinists must claim these sinners were never Christians. The Arminians must claim those Christians lost their salvation, falling from grace. In both of these groups a Christian must receive either a grade of A+ or F (heaven or hell) based on works. What happens to the majority of Christians who are Bs, Cs, and even Ds? Hell bound. Only the indoctrination of tradition can make this theology seem reasonable. Both of these Protestant groups are unable to admit their own personal sinfulness and depravity for fear of not being a "genuine Christian" or "falling from grace."[3] A person would be better off as a Roman Catholic than a Protestant under these impossible criteria.

The Reformation battle over forensic justification marginalized or dismembered warning passages directed to believers. The doctrine of the Christian assurance in Christ's sacrificial sufficiency extended beyond biblical limits. This erroneous doctrine exceeded the legitimate provision of forensic justification: Christ's sacrifice delivers only from the penalty of eternal damnation. Yet the Reformers automatically excluded *a priori* any future judgment by God upon his children in this life or the next. This imbalance omitted a critical motivation God

---

Christian to delight in God in his inner being (7:22). The ὢν πρῶτός εἰμι ἐγώ (1 Tim 1:15) is unlikely to be an historical present, since it would be the only one in the NT using εἰμι ἐγώ. Paul recognized the depths of his sinfulness as he grew closer to intimacy with his Holy God.

[3] The Calvinist doctrinal TULIP dedication to Gnostic-Manichaean total depravity (inability) inherited through Augustine's error has dire consequences.

designed for his children found throughout the Scriptures. That motivation is that disobedience of a child would result in God's punishment of that child—in the present life and/or after death.

The NT passages concerning conditional forgiveness from God and his temporal judgment upon believers seriously challenge any Protestant theory of total absolution from punishment. Numerous NT passages directed to believers warn them of God's judgment. Paul's epistles, the Jewish epistles, and the Gospels all confirm a future judgment upon Christians. We must use caution in anachronistically assigning these warning passages to non-Christians.

The appeal by some authors to the judgment seat of Christ as being solely for reward does not withstand scrutiny. It lacks a factual basis. In fact, this idea was founded upon erroneous assumptions. (See Appendix B) Protestant authors such as C.S. Lewis, Kittel, and Berkhof leave room for a doctrine of Christians undergoing a serious judgment based upon works, both good and bad.

The Early Church Fathers on Judgment

The early church fathers wrote extensively on a postmortem judgment of Christians for their works, including payment and punishment prior to eternal intimacy with God. Their writings do not support the medieval Roman Catholic view of purgatory, but they do provide evidence that the early church believed in an actual judgment and punishment of the Christian based upon works. Far from losing the doctrine of grace, the fathers viewed God's grace as providing sanctifying opportunity for believers.[4] Judgment of the deceased Christian resulted in an eternal reward (payment for service, not heaven) or temporal punishment (not hell).[5]

God's Judgment Answers Injustice

We have seen that God's court may be compared to modern legal courts. A person can be acquitted in criminal court, yet suffer damages in civil or family court for the same crime or sin. This is no way negates the cross of Christ. Both the OT and NT demonstrate that God punishes his children while on earth. Therefore, the Protestant argument that the cross erases all future punishment is invalid.

A doctrine of punishment for a believer's evil works allows for a theodicy against the complaints of agnostics who can otherwise impugn God's justice. A person's evil works even prior to regeneration may be legitimately judged and punished as long as it does not result in eternal damnation. A believer's

---

[4] Thomas F. Torrance, *The Doctrine of Grace in the Apostolic Fathers* (Oliver and Boyd LTD: Edinburgh, 1948; reprint, Wipf and Stock Publishers: Eugene, Oregon, 1996).

[5] I distinguish between temporal punishment (active) and temporal consequences (passive). Temporal punishment, by definition, has an end point. But consequences may be eternal in nature. The only eternal punishment is eternal separation from God. But my sin can have the eternal consequence of less intimacy with God with less payment/reward if I failed to diligently pursue godliness into Christ-likeness. The temporal punishment for my sin will end but the consequence can be eternal.

works after regeneration may also be justly punished without detracting from Christ's all-sufficient sacrifice. God is not mocked since every person reaps what he or she sows. Sanctification of the believer is not "all or nothing" but can be righteously judged and due recompense received.

Rather than (as advertised in *sola fide*) eliminating good works in justification salvation, the Calvinist view demands good works of sanctification before assigning eternal destinies, just like Catholicism. In reality, the eternal destinies of heaven and hell are based upon good works, not faith alone. Works are hidden within the definition of faith (unilaterally infused by God), because those good works are also allegedly unilaterally divinely bestowed.

This was Calvin's error derived from Augustine, who borrowed it from Gnostics, Manichaeans, and Neoplatonists. Therefore, for any unbiased observer, this particular Protestant view is no different than the Roman Catholic view requiring good works. For these Protestants, good works are covert— hidden within their redefinition of faith—rather than the overt Roman Catholic requirement.

Finally, the fear of the Lord encourages believers in Christ to live godly and holy lives. A biblical motivation for godly living emerges in the expectation of future punishment for evil deeds. Pastors need not constantly threaten erring members with hell for their unrighteousness. Those persons who believe in Christ are not subsequently eternally damned due to their sin. Contra mere human judges who would damn God's children for "continual sin," God looks on the heart of faith for adoption. Works are judged by God within his family. Even those who believe in eternal security (heaven regardless of subsequent behavior) finally have something with which to motivate believers in gross moral sin. A day of punishment is coming: the Judge stands at the door (James 5:9). Actions have consequences—God is not mocked (Gal 5:7).

The goal of Christianity is not "reaching heaven." As C.S. Lewis stated, the goal is that "Every Christian is to become a little Christ."[6] Posthumous punishment encourages that goal. Posthumous punishment does not conflict with grace. Why? Because, God's grace does not stop with forgiveness to reach heaven. Grace transforms us into Christ-likeness as God sanctifies us and purifies us from our sin.

Specific Punishments

One of the deficiencies of this study concerns the lack of specifics in scripture regarding God's punishment. We are not informed as to the nature, length, guidelines, or specific criteria God will use in punishing his children. But why should we demand that God be specific? What if I tell my child, "You had better not do that or Daddy will punish you."? The child does not need specifics. The general warning of punishment is

---

[6] C.S. Lewis, *Mere Christianity* (San Francisco: Harper San Francisco, 2001), 177.

sufficient. The particular punishment depends on numerous factors. Similarly, God warns us that our behaviors and attitudes that are inappropriate for those bearing the name of Christ will incur punishment.

The biblical evidence and the early church fathers' writings concerning scripture indicate that "forensic justification" does not absolve the Christian of all future punishment. We must be cautious in elaborating on specifics of that punishment. Otherwise, we fall into the same error as the medieval Roman Catholic Church.

Jurgie taught that the principal pain of purgatory is the frustrated overwhelming desire to experience God fully; but, that cannot be accomplished until the soul has been perfected in love.[7] A patient experiencing momentary pain from the doctor can still be joyous knowing it will cure the deadly cancer. Sin is the cancer that pervades our souls, even after we die. The sacrifice of Christ erased the guilt separating us from God. However, the sin still indwelling our beings (our being having been damaged by prior sins committed) requires the purifying fire of God after death.

Justice as Retributive Satisfaction versus Restorative Sanctification

The history of posthumous punishment begins with a balanced view. God requires a punishment for sin to satisfy his holy

---

[7] Jurgie, *Purgatory*, 47.

justice and simultaneously demands progressive sanctification to eradicate sin prior to living in God's presence. The Middle Ages virtually excluded the sanctification model to highlight the punitive satisfaction model, even to the point of Christians being tormented by devils in purgatory. Modern Catholicism has largely swung the pendulum to the sanctification model, downplaying any punitive justice. The Orthodox Church concurs with the progressive process of deification but teaches this does not require any pain or suffering. No punishment exists for the ill sinner who is in need of treatment.

Modern theologians seem to have dismissed the early centuries wherein both punitive satisfaction and restorative sanctification were balanced. One need not be forced to decide between the two. This dual model satisfies the justice of a holy God while magnifying the love and mercy of God who desires every human to be restored to him in perfection. Both the OT and NT contain numerous examples of God forgiving his children then punishing them. But the Father then gently places those children in his arms to lovingly embrace them for eternity.

Sin and Confession

We have learned that just as the legal system has two judgments of criminal court and civil court, Christians have been acquitted in criminal court by Christ himself. However, the civil family court may then extract separate damages for disobedience. Both retributive punishment and restorative sanctification can occur simultaneously. But does confession erase this punishment?

There is no evidence that confession of sin and even repentance *guarantees* we will avoid God's civil family punishment. King David confessed and repented, yet God in his justice punished David for the effect those sins had on others. Nevertheless, God in his mercy spared David's life contrary to the legal requirement of the law. Contrary to the popular opinion of many Protestants, confessing sin (1 John 1:9) does not erase the consequences at God's judgment of the Christian. James 2:13 seems to provide the way to lessen the severity of the judgement. The giving of alms (helping the poor with physical needs, James 2:13–16) as practiced by the Jews and early Christians appears to be the primary way to lessen suffering for our sins at the judgment seat of Christ (cf., Jas 3:1, 5:9).[8] Therefore, the best course is preventative—obedience.

Final Thoughts

Protestants should admit and abandon their unbiblical tradition that denies God's punishment after death. God did not change his child discipline model between the OT and the NT. "My son, do not despise the LORD's discipline or be weary of his reproof, for the LORD reproves him whom he loves, as a father the son in whom he delights." (Proverbs 3:11–12, ESV) "And

---

[8] See Appendix A for my discussion on James 2, and Luke 6:27–36 for other ways Jesus taught we could demonstrate mercy to others and thereby encourage God's mercy upon us as sinners.

you have forgotten that word of encouragement that addresses you as sons: 'My son, do not make light of the Lord's discipline, and do not lose heart when he rebukes you, because the Lord disciplines those he loves, and he punishes everyone he accepts as a son.'" (Hebrews 12:5–6, NIV) The OT and NT are in exact agreement. God punishes his children for disobedience.

"For we must all appear before the judgment seat of Christ, so that each may be repaid for what he has done in the body, whether good or evil. Therefore, since we know the fear of the Lord, we try to persuade people [immoral Corinthian Christians]" (2 Cor 5:10–11, CSB) ... We implore you on Christ's behalf: Be reconciled to God. God made him who had no sin to be sin for us, so that in him we **might become** the righteousness of God." (2 Cor 5:20–21, NIV, bold added).[9] This righteousness of God is not imputed, but requires ongoing sanctifying grace for conformation to Christ-likeness.

"Moses said to the people, 'Do not be afraid; for God has come only to test you and to put the fear of him upon you so that you do not sin.'" (Exod 20:20, NRSV) The fear of God produces obedience to avoid sin and its punishment. "The end of the matter; all has been heard. Fear God, and keep his commandments; for that is the whole duty of everyone. For God will bring every deed into judgment, including every secret thing, whether good or evil." (Eccl 12:13–14, NRSVCE) I

---

[9] Some individuals attempt to use first, second, third, and zero class conditionals to avoid this conclusion but without justification.

suspect even a mere nano-second in the presence of Holy God as he purifies us from our sin as a consuming fire (Heb 12:28–29) may seem like an eternity of suffering.

Jesus himself told the church, "As many as I love, I rebuke and chasten." (Rev 3:19, NKJV) The Greek meanings indicate a punishment for the purpose of correcting ungodly behavior and instructing in good behavior.[10] In my opinion, we have two generations of Americans in which the majority of men and women have never known unconditional love from a godly father who punishes in love in order to produce godliness. This is another reason why Protestants have trouble accepting God's punishment as a reality. We have such a severe deficit of intimate godly love that we only want to hear about God's love. But love without punishment is not godly love. In fact, it is not love at all: because, so-called "love" without punishment is detrimental to the soul and to other persons.[11]

We never found a scripture verse that states, "God punishes Christians after death." Yet, neither did we find a verse that states, "The Trinity consists of Father, Son, and Holy

---

[10] ἐγὼ ὅσους ἐὰν φιλῶ ἐλέγχω καὶ παιδεύω· (SBLGNT); ἐλέγχω **1. to scrutinize or examine carefully, *bring to light, expose, set forth*... 2. to bring a pers. to the point of recognizing wrongdoing, *convict, convince* someone of someth., *point someth. out to someone*... 3. to express strong disapproval of someone's action, *reprove, correct*** (BDAG, 315)*;* "παιδεύω ... **2. to assist in the development of a person's ability to make appropriate choices, *practice discipline*.**" ... *a. correct, give guidance* (LXX) τινά *(to) someone* .... b. *discipline* w. punishment α. mostly of divine discipline (BDAG, 749). Bold and italics are original.

[11] King David fell into this error with his son Absalom.

Spirit." Through comparing and combining various passages we may deduce the Trinitarian doctrine. The same holds true for God recompensing his children in posthumous punishment. The warnings are there—unless they are evacuated by tradition.

This does not mean we must be consumed with dread at meeting Jesus Christ. Our God is a loving and merciful Father, full of compassion for his children. His justice in punishment will be balanced with his mercy and love. Our temporary pain will end with an eternity of joy in intimacy with our Creator. Punishment is not our future focus. But, punishment must be acknowledged.

It was not a Roman Catholic, but the Protestant theologian Forsythe who wrote that Calvin inadvertently threw out the baby with the bathwater. It is time to rescue Calvin's baby from the bathwater sewage. I suggest that the denial of God's punishment of his children after death is a deadly fiction of Satan, which nullifies the Scriptures, inflicts unbearable contempt upon God's justice, and overturns and destroys our faith. This denial dangerously seduces us with a lie that tolerates and even encourages immorality among Christians, especially Protestants. It robs Christians of one of God's three motivations for obedience unto godliness. Teachers who deny God's punishment will endure the angst of suffering brothers and sisters in Christ who they falsely taught there would be no more consequences for their sins. God will judge those teachers more severely (James 3:1).

The principle of purgatory balances the mercy of God with the justice of God. The holy justice of God demands we give an accounting for our lives and for sin before him as God's children. The Epistle of James warns fellow Christians, "For judgment will be merciless to one who has shown no mercy; mercy triumphs over judgment. What use is it, my brethren, if someone says he has faith but he has no works? Can that faith save him?" (Jas 2:13–14, NASB95) Faith alone cannot save a Christian at the Judgment Seat of Christ where our works are judged for payment or punishment as God's children. (Jas 3:1) Paul agrees: "Since we have these promises, beloved, let us cleanse ourselves from every defilement of body and spirit, bringing holiness to completion in the fear of God." (2 Cor 7:1, ESV)

The evidence has been presented. Scripture shows us that even after forgiveness God's children do indeed suffer God's punishment while on earth. So, it is time to answer one of the most critical questions we will ever be asked. It is time for us to render a verdict:

Does God, as our Father, purge us of our sin and punish us for our sin after we die?

If so, this should motivate us to pursue holiness and godliness now, striving to become holy and godly like Christ. God will inevitably transform his children of faith into holy persons like himself. This is the concept of purification and purgation of sin, starting now and continuing after death. This is the principle of purgatory.

> Since all these things are to be dissolved in this way,
> what sort of persons ought you to be in leading lives
> of holiness and godliness, waiting for and hastening
> the coming of the day of God, because of which the
> heavens will be set ablaze and dissolved, and the
> elements will melt with fire? But, in accordance with
> his promise, we wait for new heavens and a new
> earth, where righteousness is at home. Therefore,
> beloved, while you are waiting for these things, strive
> to be found by him at peace, without spot or blemish.
> (2 Pet 3:11–14, NRSV)

Appendix A
Critique of Protestants' Scholarly Exegetical Claims

This Appendix A will be more technical than the prior chapters in order to explain how Protestants arrive at their conclusions. It will not be exhaustive but will primarily choose the works of leading Protestant scholars to provide their principles of interpretation. Specific NT texts will be evaluated in order of their NT appearances. All Greek texts are cited as SBLGNT.

Matthew 6:15

ἐὰν δὲ μὴ ἀφῆτε τοῖς ἀνθρώποις, οὐδὲ ὁ πατὴρ ὑμῶν ἀφήσει τὰ παραπτώματα ὑμῶν.

The force of this passage involves forgiving others, without which God will not forgive the unforgiving sinner. Allison and Davies come to the correct conclusion.

> By placing the negatives (3, 4) after the positives (1, 2), the evangelist shows that for him the stress lies on the warning of judgment rather than on the promise of forgiveness (cf. 7.24–7). ... The right of the eschatological community to utter the Lord's Prayer depends, as does the efficacy of the prayer, upon communal reconciliation. Hence the Lord's Prayer

must be prayed by a church whose members have forgiven one another. (As Stendhal (v), p. 83, n. 20 observes, this interpretation of 6:14–15 implies that , despite the use of ἀνθρώποις, the ὀφειλέται in the Lord's Prayer are thought of primarily as members in the Christian community.)[1]

Despite accurately identifying Matthew's emphasis as being on God's judgment (not forgiveness), these authors are completely silent on how members of the Christian community are to be judged by God (who will not forgive those Christians). How can that be possible for God not to forgive his children? This question is not even asked.

R. T. France is more forthright.

Like the debtor of 18:23-25, one of the recipients of grace turns out not to meet the expectations on which the continuation of that salvation depends. So here also, if the forgiveness of sins which is achieved through the saving death of Jesus (26:28) is not matched by an appropriately forgiving attitude on the disciple's part, it cannot be presumed upon. ... there is certainly a clear difference of perspective on what the forgiveness of sins involves, though the parable of 20:1-15 will make it clear that Matthew has no room for a crudely mechanical view of salvation

---

[1] Dale Allison, Jr. and W. D. Davies, *The Gospel According to St. Matthew*, ICC, vol. 1 (Edinburgh: T&T Clark, 1988), 616–7.

earned in proportion to human effort. ... Hard as it may be for human nature, there is to be no limit to disciples' willingness to forgive those who offend them.[2]

According to France, one cannot presume upon personal salvation unless you forgive others (as you have been forgiven). For France, the alleged salvation by faith alone (*sola fide*) has the additional work of "forgiving others" attached as a requirement for this salvation.

Luke 12:47–48

ἐκεῖνος δὲ ὁ δοῦλος ὁ γνοὺς τὸ θέλημα τοῦ κυρίου αὐτοῦ καὶ μὴ ἑτοιμάσας ἢ ποιήσας πρὸς τὸ θέλημα αὐτοῦ δαρήσεται πολλάς· ὁ δὲ μὴ γνοὺς ποιήσας δὲ ἄξια πληγῶν δαρήσεται ὀλίγας. παντὶ δὲ ᾧ ἐδόθη πολύ, πολὺ ζητηθήσεται παρ' αὐτοῦ, καὶ ᾧ παρέθεντο πολύ, περισσότερον αἰτήσουσιν αὐτόν.

Bock claims the "unfaithful servant" translation should be "unbelieving" servant due to the degree of punishment.

> The action of the unfaithful servant is severely judged upon the master's return. Ἄπιστος (*apistos*) usually means "faithless," but in contrast to the faithful steward in 12:42, and in light of the severe nature of the punishment, it should be rendered to mean "unbelieving." ... God's smiting the servant

---

[2] R. T. France, *The Gospel of Matthew*, NICNT (Grand Rapids, MI: Eerdmans, 2007), 253.

depicts punishment of the most severe type, but it is figurative, despite the opinion of some that it is literal (Plummer 1896:332; Creed 1930:177). A figurative sense emerges from the next line, which shows that the servant is still able to be placed among another group of people.[3]

Being severely punished then placed among other "unbelieving" servants and hypocrites only requires them to be "unbelieving" as a result of Bock's theological bias. Contra Bock, faithful servants are rewarded and unfaithful/faithless (his admitted usual translation) servants are punished—some very severely. This is consistent with God's severe punishment of Israel and Judah. God sent such terrible starvation that women were eating their own babies (Lam 4:8). That sounds like severe punishment. Bock's bias against Christian punishment is evident.

Romans 14:10–12

Σὺ δὲ τί κρίνεις τὸν ἀδελφόν σου; ἢ καὶ σὺ τί ἐξουθενεῖς τὸν ἀδελφόν σου; πάντες γὰρ παραστησόμεθα τῷ βήματι τοῦ θεοῦ, γέγραπται γάρ· Ζῶ ἐγώ, λέγει κύριος, ὅτι ἐμοὶ κάμψει πᾶν γόνυ, καὶ πᾶσα γλῶσσα ἐξομολογήσεται τῷ θεῷ. ἄρα ἕκαστος ἡμῶν περὶ ἑαυτοῦ λόγον δώσει.

Douglas Moo also dismisses any judgment on Christians.

---

[3] Darrell Bock, *Luke 9:51–24:53*, ECNT (Grand Rapids, MI: Baker Academic, 1996), 1182.

Paul may be warning the believers that they stand in danger of suffering God's judgment for their sinful criticism of one another. But, in light of vv. 7-9, we think it more likely that he is reminding them that it is God, and not other Christians, to whom each believer is answerable. In "judging" and "despising" others, therefore, they are arrogating to themselves a prerogative that is God's only. He will pronounce his judgment over every believer's status and actions on that day when 'each will receive good or evil according to the things he or she has done in the body (2 Cor. 5:10).[4]

Moo dismisses any judgment on Christians by using a sidestep of restating what this text and other texts plainly state: God is the sole judge. Moo then must admit every believer "will receive good and evil," but Moo is silent about this judgment by God on the Christian after death.

Cranfield remarks, "The remembrance that all Christians will have to stand before the judgment seat of God is a powerful dissuasive from all sitting in judgment on one's fellows."[5] That sentence is the totality of Cranfield's comments explicating this verse, yet he discusses the textual variant of judgment seat of God versus judgment seat of Christ. Why is it

---

[4] Douglas Moo, *The Epistle to the Romans*, NICNT (Grand Rapids, MI: Eerdmans, 1996), 846–7.

[5] C. E. B. Cranfield, *Romans*, ICC, vol.2 (Edinburgh: T&T Clark, 1975), 709.

dissuasive? Does God actually punish or is this mere hyperbole?

Thomas Schreiner writes similarly, "All believers will stand before God's judgment seat. The verb παραστησόμεθα (*parastēsometha*, we shall stand) is a technical term for standing before a judge (Acts 27:24; Pol. Phil. 6.2; cf. BAGD 628; MM 494–95)."[6] Schreiner spends the remainder of the discussion on the judgment seat of God versus Christ's seat without ever explaining how a Christian can possibly be judged by God.

Leon Morris claims, "A reason is introduced by *For*,[34] but it is not clear whether the warning against judging others is because those who judge will themselves face judgment in due course (cf. Matt. 7:1; Luke 6:37) or whether Paul means that the brother who is the object of this 'judgment' will in due course be judged by God (not by his fellows)."[7] So Morris (along with others) continues to resist the doctrine that Christians will be judged by God for sin.

Jewett states, "The phrase λόγον δίδωμι ("give account") is a technical expression from the administrative realm of accounting for one's actions as a subordinate, handing in the account books for audit, and so on. ... As in 14:10c, the emphasis here is that none can escape accountability to God."[8]

---

[6] Thomas Schreiner, *Romans*, BECNT (Grand Rapids, MI: Baker Academic, 1998), 722.

[7] Leon Morris, *The Epistle to the Romans*, PNTC (Grand Rapids, MI: Eerdmans, 1988), 483.

[8] Robert Jewett, *Romans: A Commentary*, Hermeneia (Minneapolis, MN: Augsburg Fortress, 2007), 852.

"The verb παρίστημι (place, stand before) is a legal technical term for appearing before a judge.[212]"[9] Jewett sees these persons as belonging to the "'spiritual brotherhood' of believers," "not a mere acquaintance but a brother in Christ.[204]"[10]

Thielman concurs with Jewett that τῷ βήματι τοῦ θεοῦ is a judicial bench for judgment. Like Jewett, he merely asserts all Christians will stand before God's tribunal without any explanation of the consequences at that tribunal or what judgment is to be rendered.

> The expression 'to stand before the tribunal' (παριστᾶν τῷ βήματι) was a common way of describing the appearance of a Roman subject before a magistrate to account for some behavior. Josephus, for example, uses it to describe the leaders of Jerusalem presenting themselves before the procurator Gessius Florus to account for a public insult that a few rabble-rousers had given to the procurator on his arrival in the city (Josephus, *J.W.* 2.301). Paul's point, then, is that since all believers will eventually have to explain to Christ how they have lived out their faith (cf., 2 Cor 5:10), human judgments in the present usurp his authority.[11]

---

[9] Jewett, *Romans*, 850. His footnote 212 is from BDAG, 628.

[10] Jewett, *Romans*, 850. His footnote 204 is from Morris, 483.

[11] Frank Thielman, *Romans*, ECNT (Grand Rapids, MI: Zondervan Academic, 2018), 634.

My response? I doubt that Christ needs us to explain how our faith was or was not lived out. So in Thielman, judgment of the believer for unrighteousness or sin is conspicuously absent.

Longenecker renders these persons non-Christians calling them "so-called Christ followers" (following the NIV84 and NASB95 theological bias "so-called brothers" in 1 Cor 5:11).[12]

> **14:11–12** In 14:11 Paul asserts that what he has just proclaimed in his declaration "We will all stand before God's judgment seat!"—as well as, implicitly, what he writes in the present passage about the arrogant judgments of so-called Christ followers against other professing Christ followers—is directly "in line" with the pronouncement of God expressed much earlier through the prophet Isaiah to the people of Israel in Isa 45:23. ... And so in this final statement of his guidelines of 14:1–12, Paul gives the following warning to the Christians in Rome, as well as to all believers in Jesus today: "Each of us will give an account of ourselves to God" (ἕκαστος ἡμῶν περὶ ἑαυτοῦ λόγον δώσει τῷ θεῷ).[13]

---

[12] The Greek τις ἀδελφὸς ὀνομαζόμενος is better rendered "named" or "called" a brother as we find this use throughout the NT. E.g., Luke 6:14, "He named Peter," Eph 3:15 "receives its name," etc. Only bias renders it "so-called brother" claiming no "genuine Christian" would sin like this.

[13] Richard Longenecker, *The Epistle to the Romans: A Commentary on the Greek Text*, NIGCT, ed. I. Howard Marshall and Donald Hagner (Grand Rapids, MI: Eerdmans, 2016), 994–1005.

For Longenecker, Christians must only "give an account," because only non-Christians actually receive a judgment for evil. Apparently (for Longenecker), no consequences ensue for Christians. Silence persists about this "warning to the Christians in Rome" of standing at God's tribunal to receive for the good and the bad (cf., 2 Cor 5:10).[14]

1 Corinthians 3:14–15

εἴ τινος τὸ ἔργον μενεῖ ὃ ἐποικοδόμησεν, μισθὸν λήμψεται· εἴ τινος τὸ ἔργον κατακαήσεται, ζημιωθήσεται, αὐτὸς δὲ σωθήσεται, οὕτως δὲ ὡς διὰ πυρός.

Gordon Fee typifies the Protestant approach to this text. Protestants claim this text is about the church corporate, not individual Christians being judged within the church. So, it has nothing to do with God's actual judgment of Christians. It is merely a metaphor.

> This sentence is often seen as expressing a purifying element to the judgment, and has served as the NT support for the concept of purgatory.[45] But that is to miss Paul by a wide margin. This is a metaphor, pure and simple, …. Thus, Paul is not so much making a

[14] For examples of how the early church fathers taught this passage see J. Patout Burns, Jr., trans. and ed., *Romans* in The Church's Bible, Robert L. Wilkin, gen. ed. (Grand Rapids, MI: Eerdmans, 2012), 344–47, esp. 345: "Christ … looks into the heart and conscience of each one, displays the hidden and reveals the concealed, so that he may bestow praise on good acts and exact the punishments which the evil [acts] deserve. This divine judgment is still in the future."

soteriological statement as warning his Christian friends. He obviously, as elsewhere (e.g., 6: 11) sees them as within the context of the faith; salvation after all is by grace, not by one's works. ... But their current behavior is so seriously aberrant that he must warn them yet once more (in vv. 16-17), this time in the strongest terms yet: those who persist in these activities and attitudes are in fact in eternal danger. This text has singular relevance to the contemporary church. It is neither a challenge to the individual believer to build his or her life on the foundation of Christ, nor is it grist for theological debate.[15]

Fee tries to have it both ways. It is not a "soteriological statement," yet "those who persist in these activities and attitudes are in fact in eternal danger." That sounds soteriological to me. Fee is illogical and inconsistent. In fact, "eternal danger" sounds far worse than undergoing God's judgment as his child. So, Fee can find "eternal danger" in this "metaphorical" passage but he cannot find judgment of the Christian after death.

We exposed Thiselton's neglect of his own primary source on punishment or fines in Chapter 8. This line of thinking continues as he denies anything resembling purgatory by appealing to metaphor (although none of his examples match

---

[15] Gordon Fee, *The First Epistle to the Corinthians,* NICNT, 2nd edn. (Grand Rapids, MI: Eerdmans, 2014), 144–5.

this one in 1 Cor 3).

> It is far more likely that the phrase had become a
> metaphor like "brand plucked from the burning"
> (Amos 4:11), comparable to "saved by the skin of
> one's teeth."[78] One of the standard detailed
> commentaries on Amos interprets 4:11 as "being
> rescued at the last moment. The expression was a
> proverbial one" (cf. Zech 3:2).[79] J. Weiss also points
> to a range of Greek literature (e.g., Euripides) and
> Latin texts (e.g., Livy) for similar proverbial
> parallels.[80]... Witherington explicitly observes,
> "This cannot be a reference to purgatory since Paul
> is referring to what happens on the judgment day ...
> after the return of Christ .... He is not referring to
> what happens to a person after death and before the
> final judgment .... 'As through fire' is a metaphor for
> escaping ... by the skin of one's teeth."
> [Witherington, *Conflict and Community*, 134] [16]

But note that in Amos 4:11(a) the literal fire overthrew and
destroyed Sodom and Gomorrah. The brand plucked from the
fire was in a literal fire—it was a *burning* stick. The fire
analogy, even if proverbial, is there for a reason. The Christian

---

[16] Anthony Thiselton, *The First Epistle to the Corinthians*, NIGTC
(Grand Rapids, MI: Eerdmans, 2000), 315.

readers in Corinth are the burning stick of Amos.[17] Fire signifies judgment: "worship God acceptably with reverence and awe, for our God is a consuming fire." (Heb 12:28–29)

2 Corinthians 5:10

τοὺς γὰρ πάντας ἡμᾶς φανερωθῆναι δεῖ ἔμπροσθεν τοῦ βήματος τοῦ Χριστοῦ, ἵνα κομίσηται ἕκαστος τὰ διὰ τοῦ σώματος πρὸς ἃ ἔπραξεν, εἴτε ἀγαθὸν εἴτε φαῦλον.

Lenski provides the typical Protestant dichotomy between good works of Christians and bad works of unbelievers. "The one is the fruit of a life of faith that was marked and beautiful by trust in Christ and thus revealed to all eyes who it was that produced this 'good.' The other is the product of a condition where faith was absent and reveals the unbeliever as what he truly was."[18] Lenski seems to believe Christians only have good works and non-Christians only have bad works. Really?

Barnett defends the tribunal background of this passage where Paul had stood four years earlier in Corinth. "The imagery used here for the future moment of eschatological revelation is that of the forensic process whereby the Roman governor sat on his tribunal[145] to hear accusation and defense of an accused person standing before him. If he judged the accused

---

[17] Amos 4:11, "'I overthrew some of you as I overthrew Sodom and Gomorrah. You were like a burning stick snatched from the fire, yet you have not returned to me,' declares the LORD." (NIV)

[18] R.C.H. Lenski, *The Interpretation of St. Paul's First and Second Epistles to the Corinthians* (Minneapolis, MN: Augsburg, 1963), 1016.

guilty, the governor would order immediate punishment." [19] After rejecting Sander's suggestion that believers are "kept in" salvation by their works, Barnett expresses the standard party line.

> A more consistent explanation would be that believers do not experience condemnation at Christ's tribunal (see Romans 5:16, 18; 8:1) but rather *evaluation* with a view to the Master's commendation given or withheld (1 Cor 3:10-15; 4:5; cf. Luke 12:42-48). Perhaps, too, they will receive back within themselves elements of what they had practiced in the body (so 5:10), as eternal reminders that they had been saved through God's mercy, and not by their own efforts. Those "outside Christ" face the sinners' judgment; on the other hand, those "in Christ" face this judgment bench as saints. [20]

Barnett has no explanation for how his "saints" in Corinth (who he somehow distinguishes from "sinners") are to receive for the evil done while in the body. Do his "saints" not sin or do any evil in the body? Per the usual exegetical maneuvering that nullifies the text, Christians are not judged for the evil done in the body.

Murray Harris astutely clarifies that the tribunal

---

[19] Paul Barnett, *The Second Epistle to the Corinthians*, NICNT (Grand Rapids, MI: Eerdmans, 1997), 275.

[20] Barnett, *2 Corinthians*, 276–7.

concerns works, not eternal destinies.

> In the middle voice, κομίζω ("bring") means "get for
> oneself," "get back," "receive back," what one owns
> or is owed or deserves. ... The recompense received
> comes from Christ, for it is his tribunal. A
> comparison of Col. 3:25 with Col. 3:24 (cf. Eph. 6:8)
> suggests that in 2 Cor. 5:10 "So that each may receive
> back the things (performed through the body)" means
> "so that each may receive recompense[232] from the
> Lord for things (performed through the body)." ...
> ἀγαθὸν and φαῦλον should be construed with their
> immediate antecedent ἃ ἔπραξεν, not with the more
> remote κομίσηται ... τὰ. If so, these adjectives do not
> represent two possible verdicts (commendation-
> condemnation) or two types of recompense (reward-
> punishment), but two kinds of action (good-bad). ...
> The personal character of the retributive process and
> the fact that the recompense might be received for
> good as well as for bad actions prove that, in Paul's
> thought, the notions of recompense and reward are
> not incompatible. Reward may be recompense for
> good; the "suffering of loss" (ζημιωθήσεται, 1 Cor.
> 3:15), the forfeiture of reward or privilege, may be
> part of the requital for evil. ... Since the tribunal of
> Christ is concerned with the assessment of works, not
> the determination of destiny,[250] it will be apparent
> that the Pauline concepts of justification on the basis
> of faith and recompense in accordance with works

may be complementary.²⁵¹ Not status but reward is
determined …. The fear inspired by this expectation
(v.11) doubtless intensified Paul's ambition that his
life should meet with Christ's approval both during
life and at the βῆμα (v. 9).²¹

So Harris views the "suffer loss" as mere deprivation, not
punishment, despite the fact that the text states one must receive
for the bad. His "immediate antecedent" move does not resolve
the issue. The Christian will be recompensed (paid back) for
what good or bad was done in the body. He will be paid back
for the good and paid back for the bad. Furthermore, Paul uses
the same κομίζω in Col 3:25 where antecedents cannot cause
confusion: ὁ γὰρ ἀδικῶν κομίσεται ὃ ἠδίκησεν (SBLGNT),
"The one doing wrong will be repaid for the wrong." Harris'
anti-judgment bias unduly influences his promising exegesis.

Victor Furnish clarifies the nature of this judgment.

It is the final judgment of all *believers* that is in view
here, not a universal judgment (see NOTES), and the
issue is not salvation or damnation (as in 2:14; Rom
2:5–11, etc.) but whether as a Christian, one has been
committed to the Lord (Mattern 1966:157) (italics
original) … Nothing specific is said about rewards or
punishments, or what those might entail. The

---

²¹ Murray Harris, *The Second Epistle to the Corinthians*, NIGTC (Grand
Rapids, MI: Eerdmans, 2005), 407–9.

emphasis falls on one's present accountability (cf.
Mattern 1966:158).[22]

I agree that the judgment of Christians is not for salvation or
damnation. But I am confused as to how the judgment emphasis
must fall on "one's present accountability." Does this mean God
only punishes or disciplines his children while they are on earth?
How can this be when the corresponding reward of the
inheritance is clearly future in Col 3:24–25? Is this not highly
selective exegesis?

Galatians 6:6–8

μὴ πλανᾶσθε, θεὸς οὐ μυκτηρίζεται· ὃ γὰρ ἐὰν σπείρῃ
ἄνθρωπος, τοῦτο καὶ θερίσει· ὅτι ὁ σπείρων εἰς τὴν σάρκα
ἑαυτοῦ ἐκ τῆς σαρκὸς θερίσει φθοράν, ὁ δὲ σπείρων εἰς τὸ
πνεῦμα ἐκ τοῦ πνεύματος θερίσει ζωὴν αἰώνιον.

Longenecker writes that for Christians who sow to the flesh
"destruction is their final end."

> Paul's emphasis in the use of this maxim seems to be
> twofold: (1) that there is a direct correlation between
> sowing and reaping, which is how God has
> established matters; and (2) that the onus rests on the
> person (ἄνθρωπος) himself as to whether life
> eventuates in blessing or judgment, for God is not a
> deity who reverses his laws or can be tricked into

---

[22] Victor Furnish, *II Corinthians*, AYB (Garden City, NY: Doubleday,
1984), 304–5.

believing something to be so when it is not. Thus, generally the maxim supports the proverb: "God is not mocked" by mankind's attempts to ignore the cause-and-effect relationships of justice or to trick God into bestowing blessings instead of judgment. ... What Paul seems to have in mind here in speaking about sowing to the flesh are the libertine tendencies of his Galatian converts that he has alluded to earlier in this section: quarrelsomeness (5:15, 26), conceit (5:26), envy (5:26), living aloof from the needs of others (6:1-2; perhaps also 6:6), and pride (6:3-4). Such things not only reflect a misuse of Christian freedom (cf. 5:13) but also have disastrous results both personally and corporately, for "destruction" is their final end.[23]

He does not describe what this destruction might be. Is hell the necessary equivalent? Is hell the "final end" of those judged Christians? We are left wondering why the only punishment option is hell. "Destruction" does not mean "hell."

Colossians 3:24–25

εἰδότες ὅτι ἀπὸ κυρίου ἀπολήμψεσθε τὴν ἀνταπόδοσιν τῆς κληρονομίας· τῷ κυρίῳ Χριστῷ δουλεύετε· ὁ γὰρ ἀδικῶν κομίσεται ὃ ἠδίκησεν, καὶ οὐκ ἔστιν προσωπολημψία.

---

[23] Richard Longenecker, *Galatians*, WBC 41 (Nashville, TN: Thomas Nelson, 1990), 673–7.

O'Brien discusses whether the judgment will be on slaves or masters but spends minimal space explaining how disobedient Christians (slaves, masters, or others) receive judgment. [24]

> The ethical injunctions are set within the context of rewards and punishment in verses 24 and 25, and the judgment on disobedience is as sure as the reward for faithfulness. While the Bible generally, and Paul in particular, make it plain that salvation is according to grace, judgment is always according to works, good or bad, for believer and unbeliever alike. So to Christians the apostle writes, 'For we must all appear before the judgment seat of Christ, that each one may receive what is due (ἵνα κομίσηται) the same verb as in Col 3:25) to him for the things done while in the body, whether good or bad' (2 Cor 5:10; cf. Rom 14:10–12; 1 Cor 3:12–15; 4:4, 5). Bruce, 295, comments [O'Brien's own quotation of Bruce]:

> > It may seem difficult to understand how one who by grace is blessed with God's salvation in Christ may yet before the divine tribunal "receive again the wrong that he has done." But it is in accordance with the teaching of Scripture throughout that judgment "should begin at the house of God"; and even if the

---

[24] Peter O'Brien, *Colossians, Philemon*, Word Biblical Commentary, vol. 44 (Nashville, TN: Thomas Nelson, 1982), 231.

tribunal be a domestic one, for members of
the family of God, it is none the less a solemn
reality.[25]

I concur with F. F. Bruce quoted above. If one rejects
posthumous punishment of the Christian then, yes, "It may seem
difficult to understand." In fact, I suggest it is impossible to
understand this passage without posthumous punishment of
God's children.

James Dunn recognizes the tension between salvation by
grace and judgment by works.

So JB/NJB are justified in translating "Anyone who
does wrong will be repaid in kind." The force of this
warning or reassurance is twofold: it encouraged
harshly treated slaves that their masters could not
escape due judgment, in the final judgment if not in
this life, and it earned the slaves themselves to
maintain their own high standard of integrity as far as
possible. The teaching is not antithetical to the
Pauline doctrine of justification by faith, but echoes
Paul's own earlier teaching (Rom. 2:6-11; 1 Cor.
3:13-15; 2 Cor. 5:10).[26]

---

[25] F. F. Bruce, 295, in *The Epistles to the Colossians, to Philemon, and to the Ephesians* as cited within O'Brien's text. The full citation is provided under Bruce's own commentary on the following pages.

[26] James Dunn, *The Epistles to the Colossians and to Philemon*, NIGTC (Grand Rapids, MI: Eerdmans, 1996), 258.

Dunn does not explain how Christian slave owners (e.g.,
Philemon) might be judged or "repaid in kind." If this "teaching
is not antithetical," how does Dunn explain Christians being
repaid for their wrongs? He does not take the biblical step that
God punishes his children.

Bruce was cited above by O'Brien but his comments
deserve further elaboration.

> It is uncertain why the emphasis here should be on
> requital for the wrongdoer. It has been suggested that
> there was unrest at the time among the salves in
> Colossae, so that a warning was thought necessary;
> but there is no substantial evidence for this. The
> judgment on disobedience is as certain as the reward
> for faithfulness. While salvation in the Bible is
> according to grace, judgment is according to works,
> whether good or bad, for believers as for unbelievers.
> It is probably implied that, while the sowing is now,
> the reaping is hereafter—before the tribunal of Christ
> (as in 2 Cor. 5:10). It may be difficult to understand
> how one who by grace is blessed with God's
> salvation in Christ will nevertheless be requited for
> wrongdoing before the divine tribunal, but it is in
> accordance with biblical teaching that judgment
> should "begin with the household of God" (1 Pet.
> 4:17), and even if the tribunal is a domestic one, for

members of the family of God, it is by no means to
be contemplated lightly.[27]

Bruce accurately point out that salvation is by grace and
judgment is based on works. There is a very good reason Dunn,
Bruce, and other Protestant scholars find it "difficult to
understand how one who is blessed with God's salvation in
Christ will nevertheless be requited for wrongdoing before the
divine tribunal." When Calvin's anti-Catholic mantra of "no
judgment" becomes biblical tradition then this text is indeed
"difficult to understand." In fact, no explanation can be
forthcoming. There is no way to reconcile all of the problem
texts created by dismissing posthumous punishment of the
Christian. Creative gymnastics (or silence) must be exercised.

1 Thessalonians 4:5–6

τὸ μὴ ὑπερβαίνειν καὶ πλεονεκτεῖν ἐν τῷ πράγματι τὸν ἀδελφὸν
αὐτοῦ, διότι ἔκδικος κύριος περὶ πάντων τούτων, καθὼς καὶ
προείπαμεν ὑμῖν καὶ διεμαρτυράμεθα

Wanamaker highlights the intense judgment of God upon
Christians who sexually abuse their spiritual siblings.

> διότι in v. 6b is causal and indicates that what follows
> is the reason that a follower of Christ must not wrong
> a fellow believer in the matter of sexual conduct,

---

[27] F.F. Bruce, *The Epistles to the Colossians, to Philemon, and to the Ephesians*, NICNT (Grand Rapids, MI: Eerdmans, 1984), 169–170.

though περὶ πάντων τούτων ("concerning all things")
shows that the instructions in vv. 3b-5 fall under the
sanction as well. The actual sanction that Paul
employs is the most powerful one available to him.
He threatens his readers with the fact that the Lord is
an avenger or punisher (ἔκδικος κύριος) in all the
matters just mentioned by him. The language is
drawn from the OT (see esp. Ps. 94:1, which Paul
may be quoting). But he probably has in mind here
an apocalyptic image of the Lord Jesus as the coming
avenger or agent of God's wrath who will inflict
severe punishment on wrongdoers who violate the
demands of the gospel.[28]

I concur with Wanamaker. But how does this "severe
punishment" correspond with the fact that Christians cannot be
punished by God after death? The explanation appears to be
missing. Are non-Christians the only "wrong-doers"?

Surprisingly, Williams admits Christians can be judged
by God after death:

The only other instance of this word in the NT
concerns the civil magistrates in Romans 13:4. It
would appear, then, that Paul envisions a trial in
which Jesus is the judge (cf. Acts 10:42; 17:31; 1
Cor. 4:5; 2 Thess. 1:8). His thought is probably of the

---

[28] Charles Wanamaker, *The Epistles to the Thessalonians*, NIGTC
(Grand Rapids, MI: Eerdmans, 1990), 156.

Parousia, although the NT, and indeed Paul himself, is not unfamiliar with the idea of divine judgment taking place even now (cf. John 3:18; Rom. 1:24, 26, 28). And this judgment will take account of, among other things, sexual immorality.

Earlier, the missionaries warned the Thessalonians about this. Christians, no less than others will be judged, although in their case the judgment will not be a matter of life and death. As far as that is concerned, they have already been acquitted of the "capital offense" of sin; that is, they are already justified. But they will still be called to give an account of themselves as Christians ....[29]

Williams dares not utter the word "punishment," but his understanding of the severity of the trial of judgment is evident. Christians need only "give an account." No punishment exists.

In contrast, Frame *does* use "punishment." "First he [Paul] appeals, as he had done before when he was with them, to the sanction of the judgment when Christ will punish all these sins of the flesh (v.[6b]). Next, he reminds them that God's call had a moral end in view, holiness (v.[7])."[30]

Hogg and Vine similarly teach that God judges his

---

[29] David Williams, *1 and 2 Thessalonians*, NICB (Peabody, MA: Hendrickson, 1992), 74.

[30] James Frame, *The Epistles of St. Paul to the Thessalonians*, ICC (New York: Scribner's Sons, 1912), 153.

children with punishment. "The Apostle reminds his readers that the God who loved them and called them in grace, is none the less the God of recompenses, Who will surely requite every deflection from his laws, Jer. 51.56, as well as reward all faithful obedience to them, for not the heathen but the Christian is in view throughout the passage."[31] This is a rare but refreshing admission.

Hebrews 10: 29–31

πόσῳ δοκεῖτε χείρονος ἀξιωθήσεται τιμωρίας ὁ τὸν υἱὸν τοῦ θεοῦ καταπατήσας, καὶ τὸ αἷμα τῆς διαθήκης κοινὸν ἡγησάμενος ἐν ᾧ ἡγιάσθη, καὶ τὸ πνεῦμα τῆς χάριτος ἐνυβρίσας. οἴδαμεν γὰρ τὸν εἰπόντα· Ἐμοὶ ἐκδίκησις, ἐγὼ ἀνταποδώσω· καὶ πάλιν· Κρινεῖ κύριος τὸν λαὸν αὐτοῦ. φοβερὸν τὸ ἐμπεσεῖν εἰς χεῖρας θεοῦ ζῶντος.

Lane highlights McCown's claim regarding the author's switch from "for if *we* deliberately persist in sin …. How much sorer punishment do *you* suppose will he deserve?"[32] But the *you* is merely questioning fellow believers as to the degree of punishment deserved, not stating "you sinned and we did not." Lane claims, "Nothing less than a complete rejection of the Christian faith satisfies the descriptive clauses in which the effects of the offense are sketched." (294) He speaks of the

---

[31] C.F. Hogg and W. E. Vine, *The Epistles to the Thessalonians* (Grand Rapids, MI: Kregel, 1959), 119.

[32] William Lane, *Hebrews*, WBC, vol. 47B (Dallas, TX: Word, 1991), 293.

"magnitude of the sin of apostasy and the of impending judgment from which there is no escape" but neglects to answer what the consequences are for these Christians who have apostatized. How are they punished in judgment? Hell? How does this align with "God will judge his people"?

F.F. Bruce warns,

> Our author has a deep conviction of the awesome holiness of the divine majesty. "It is fearful thing to fall into the hands of the living God." These words have no doubt been used frequently as a warning to the ungodly of what lies in store for them unless they amend their ways; but their primary application is to the people of God.[33]

Bruce does not explain how or when God will punish his people.

Ellingworth writes, "The objects of fear are probably connected (cf. on death and judgment), and in each case something more negative than reverence is implied." [34] Ellingworth alludes to the typical Protestant understanding of fearing God by downgrading it to a reverential awe. The OT and NT speak otherwise. Fearing God is obeying God to avoid his punishment. (Eccl 12:13–14; Heb 12:28–29) Ellingworth does not address the fate of these persons.

---

[33] F.F. Bruce, *Commentary on the Epistle to the Hebrews*, NICNT (Grand Rapids, MI: Eerdmans, 1964), 263.

[34] Paul Ellingworth, *The Epistle to the Hebrews*, NIGTC (Grand Rapids, MI: Eerdmans, 1993), 543.

Attridge explains that, "In both of its occurrences in the Old Testament, the 'judgment' refers to the justice or vindication that Yahweh will render on behalf of his people. Here the people are warned that they will stand under judgment."[35]

Schreiner states:

> We should also note that the author speaks of the blood "by which" the readers were "sanctified" (ἡγιάσθη). Here is powerful evidence that those addressed are truly believers, confirming what was argued in 6:4–5, for Jesus' blood sanctifies and sets them apart (cf. 13:12 and 2:11). Jesus by his once-for-all offering "perfected forever those who are sanctified" (10:14)[36]

But Schreiner then writes,

> The words "his people" should not be read to say that God's people will not face final judgment even if they depart from him since they are "his people." Those who depart show that they were only God's people phenomenologically, i.e., in appearance only. Of course, the writer isn't saying that the readers have fallen away. The passage consists of a *warning*.

---

[35] Harold Attridge, *The Epistle to the Hebrews*, Hermeneia (Philadelphia, PA: Fortress Press, 1989), 296.

[36] Thomas Schreiner, *Commentary on Hebrews*, BTCP (Nashville, TN: B & H Publishing, 2015), 327–8.

The readers must not fall away as Israel did. (italics
original)

His theology (Calvinist) thereby follows McKnight's strained
designation of [pseudo-genuine] Christians who fall away from
the faith as merely—"phenomenological believers."[37] These
fake believers gave every evidence of being Christians until
they fell away. All genuine Augustinian–Calvinists teach a
"genuine" Christian must inevitably persevere due to
Augustine's invention of a second gift of grace after infant
baptism.[38] Therefore, in this theological system, "genuine"
Christians need not worry about fearing any judgment from
God.

James 5:19–20

Ἀδελφοί μου, ἐάν τις ἐν ὑμῖν πλανηθῇ ἀπὸ τῆς ἀληθείας καὶ
ἐπιστρέψῃ τις αὐτόν, γινωσκέτω ὅτι ὁ ἐπιστρέψας ἁμαρτωλὸν
ἐκ πλάνης ὁδοῦ αὐτοῦ σώσει ψυχὴν αὐτοῦ ἐκ θανάτου καὶ
καλύψει πλῆθος ἁμαρτιῶν.

---

[37] Scot McKnight, "The Warning Passages of Hebrews: A Formal
Analysis and Theological Conclusions," *Trinity Journal* 13:1 (Spring
1992), 23.

[38] Kenneth Wilson, *Augustine's Conversion*, 189, 304–6. Augustine had
to explain how some infants who received the Holy Spirit at water baptism
did not continue in the faith as adults. He misinterpreted Phil 1:6 to read God
guarantees perseverance through a second gift of grace (stronger than the
Holy Spirit). But see David Black, *Linguistics for Students of New Testament
Greek*, 2nd edn. (Grand Rapids, MI: Baker Books, 1995), 177–8. Cf. Phil
4:10–20 where the good work of financial support for the ministry (4:15,
ἐκοινώνησεν) matches Phil 1:5–6 (κοινωνία, fellowship in the gospel).
Eternal life or perseverance must be (inappropriately) read into the text.

Peter Davids thinks the subjective "tone" of the epistle is
decisive for eternal death in this passage.

> The concept of saving a soul from death is clear
> enough, for death is plainly the final result of sin,
> usually thought of as eternal death or the last
> judgment (Dt. 30:19, Jb. 8:13; Pss. 1:6; 2:12; Pr.
> 2:18; 12:28; 14:12; Je. 23:12; Jude 23; 2 Esd. 7:48;
> Syr. Bar. 85:13; Did. 1; Test Abr. 10; cf. W.
> Schmithals, *DNTT* I, 430–44). That sin can result in
> physical death is also clear (1 Cor 15:30, as well as
> many of the above OT examples) and this may be
> part of James' meaning (as in 5:14–16), but the tone
> appears to go beyond physical death and recognize
> death as an eschatological entity, at least when one
> dies in sin (cf. 1:15). It is the soul, i.e. the whole
> person, (cf. comment on 1:21; Moule, 185; C.
> Brown, DNTT III, 676–689), which is liable to death.
> It is probable that one should read "his soul" (ψυχὴν
> αὐτοῦ with ℵ A P 33 it. Vg), not simply "a soul"
> (ψυχὴν with K ψ) or "a soul from death itself "
> (ψυχὴν ἐκ θανάτου αὐτοῦ with **p**[74] B), partly because
> of the weight of the witnesses and partly because it
> explains both the other variants. [...] He does not
> discuss sins simply to moralize or condemn. He
> discusses sin to point out the erring community
> members the results of their behavior and to bring

them to repentance. He hopes to save them from damnation and procure forgiveness for their sins. [39]

Davids admits that his eight OT citations allegedly representing "eternal death or the last judgment" and "damnation" may refer to physical death. I concur, with the critical caveat that *only* physical death, not eternal death, is found in these OT passages. Despite this evidence for physical death, Davids subjectively assumes 1:15 refers to eternal death, when the OT (and especially the wisdom literature) repeatedly warn that sin leads to physical death. "Whoever is steadfast in righteousness will live, but whoever pursues evil will die" (Prov 11:19, NRSV).

In Ezek 3:20–21, ψυχὴ is paralleled with ζωῇ where the righteous one who falls into sin repents due to Ezekiel's warning and thereby saves his physical life. The references to delivering (saving) the physical life by repentance appear throughout the book of Ezekiel (13:18–22, 14:20, 17:17), and are especially repeated in 18:3–32 (32, τὴν ψυχὴν αὐτοῦ ἐφύλαξεν, LXX). Both Ezekiel 33:5 (τὴν ψυχὴν αὐτοῦ ἐξείλατο) and 33:9 (σὺ τὴν ψυχὴν σαυτοῦ ἐξήρησαι, LXX) speak of saving the life from physical death. "'Tell them: As I live'—the declaration of the Lord GOD—'I take no pleasure in the death of the wicked, but rather that the wicked person should turn from his way and live.'" Ezekiel 33:11 follows: "'Repent, repent of your evil

---

[39] Peter Davids, *The Epistle of James*, NIGTC (Grand Rapids, MI: Eerdmans, 1982), 199–201.

ways! Why will you die, house of Israel?'" (HCSB).[40]

> Though I say to the righteous that he shall surely live,
> yet if he trusts in his righteousness and does injustice,
> none of his righteous deeds shall be remembered, but
> in his injustice that he has done he shall die. Again,
> though I say to the wicked, 'You shall surely die,' yet
> if he turns from his sin and does what is just and right,
> if the wicked restores the pledge, gives back what he
> has taken by robbery, and walks in the statutes of life,
> not doing injustice, he shall surely live; he shall not
> die. None of the sins that he has committed shall be
> remembered against him. He has done what is just
> and right; he shall surely live. Yet your people say,
> 'The way of the Lord is not just,' when it is their own
> way that is not just. When the righteous turns from
> his righteousness and does injustice, he shall die for
> it. And when the wicked turns from his wickedness
> (ἀποστρέψῃ ἀπὸ τῆς ἁμαρτίας αὐτοῦ) and does what
> is just and right, he shall live by this. Yet you say,
> 'The way of the Lord is not just.' O house of Israel, I
> will judge each of you according to his ways." (Ezek
> 33:13–21, ESV).

Ezekiel is the obvious OT source of James 5:19–20. Physical
life and physical death are the topics.

---

[40] Ezek 33:11 SBLGNT τὸ ἀποστρέψαι τὸν ἀσεβῆ ἀπὸ τῆς ὁδοῦ αὐτοῦ
καὶ ζῆν αὐτόν. ἀποστροφῇ ἀποστρέψατε ἀπὸ τῆς ὁδοῦ ὑμῶν, καὶ ἵνα τί
ἀποθνήσκετε, οἶκος Ισραηλ;

Davids' only other explanation for his choice of "eternal death" is that the "tone" of the epistle is "eschatological" and so it must refer to eternal death. As a result of his reading, if a Christian falls into a sinful lifestyle, the text must mean the Christian who had believed must now be saved from eternal damnation. Is eternal damnation the result of sin in the Christian who has believed in Jesus Christ? The same problem surfaces. When there is no posthumous punishment for the sinning believer, then God must either be mocked (a person does not reap what he sows); or, there is only one other "eschatological" alternative—that sinning "soul" goes to hell.

Ralph Martin reasons,

> ...that a soul (ψυχή used here in the theological sense of the "eternal soul" as in 1:21; Moule, *Idiom Book*, 185) has been saved from death (see Note d). The connotation of death here is that of eternal consequence rather than only physical demise (Deut. 30:19; Job 8:13; Pss 1:6; 2:12; Prov 2:18; 12:28; 14:12; 15:10; 4 Ezra 7:48; 2 Apoc. Br. 85:13; and especially in this letter 1:15; cf. Volz, *Die Eschatologie der jüdischen Gemeinde*, 306; Michaelis, TDNT 5:48–65). ... An exegetical

questions is: who is saved from eternal death and
whose sins are covered?[41]

However, there is nothing in the context of James 1:21 to
necessitate Martin's "eternal soul." His reference to Moule does
not explain why Jas 1:21 must mean eternal soul. Moule's entire
argument is that it means the person himself, not an eternal soul.
"It is difficult to decide when the word becomes more
significant than this: in some passages it clearly does so; e.g. in
I Peter. ii. 11, 25, James. i. 21, v. 20;[1] but in others it is clear
that the soul would be a far too theological rendering."[42]

In footnote 1, as proof for his scarce "eternal soul" idea
in Jas 1:21, Moule references de Witt Burton (*Peter and James*).
This reference is quoted as relevant to this discussion.

Ψυχή in I Peter is noteworthy because of its distinctly
religious sense and its futuristic aspect. The ψυχή is
the soul as the seat of religion (2:11, 25), capable of
existence after death, and its salvation is to be
revealed in the last time (1: 5, 9; 4:19). Cf. the similar
use in Jas. 1:21; 5:20. This usage has apparently had
more influence than any other in the New Testament

---

[41] Ralph Martin, *James*, Word Biblical Commentary, vol. 48 (Grand
Rapids, MI: Zondervan, 1988), 220.

[42] C.F.D. Moule, *Idiom Book of the N.T. Greek*, 2nd edn. (Cambridge:
Cambridge University Press, 1979), 185.

in fixing the meaning of the word 'soul' in modern religious terminology.[43]

Therefore, neither Moule nor de Witt Burton offer any objective support for their opinions. Yes, indeed, "this usage has apparently had more influence than any other in the New Testament in fixing the meaning of the word 'soul' in modern religious terminology." But this is an incorrect meaning.

Allison's commentary provides the critical Jewish background of James 5:19–20. [44] He outlines the striking parallels between this text and Ezekiel 34 in the LXX. "We have seen that Ezek 34 supplies part of the background to James' conclusion. So too does Ezekiel's famous refrain, according to which God does not wish the death of sinners but rather waits so that they might 'turn and live.'"[45] Yes, these all refer to physical death, as we previously demonstrated. Turning from sin prevents the punishment of physical death and God allows that sinner to live physically.

Nevertheless, Allison cites BDAG for support that the soul is "the seat and center of life that transcends the earthly." As a result, he decides,

---

[43] Ernest de Witt Burton, *Spirit, Soul, and Flesh* (Chicago: University of Chicago Press,1918), 204.

[44] In my opinion, this is the best commentary on *James* in the English language.

[45] Dale Allison, Jr., *James*, ICT (London: Bloomsbury T&T Clark, 2013), 784.

'Death' is not simply physical death but the spiritual death of the individual, that is, alienation from God in the world to come; cf. 1:15, where sin is also the origin of death. The "second death" of Revelation is analogous. [310] James 3:6 has already implied that post-mortem alienation is experienced in Gehenna, a place of fire, and 5:3 has reinforced that expectation. Note the future tense, σώσει: salvation will be won at the end.[46]

Allison's footnote 310 is revealing: "The LXX appears never to use θάνατος of an other-worldly fate." That is precisely my point. The NT usually adds "eternal death" or "eternal life" for a reason. In the NT, the standard Jewish physical death and life must be clarified when referring to the eternal. James 3:6 simply states the tongue is set on fire by hell. Nothing is said about alienation from God. Do we not all have difficulty controlling our tongues? "But no human being can tame the tongue." (Jas 3:8a, ESV) Neither does James 5:3 say anything about alienation from God. Wealthy Christians who defraud the poor in order to hoard treasure will have that money eat their flesh like fire. Why is this hell?

Why (in this very Jewish epistle) is this not rather the Jewish concept of a temporary Gehenna where purification must occur? Protestants reflexively assign persons to hell rather

---

[46] Allison, *James*, 786.

than God's severe posthumous judgment. Perhaps a better exegesis in context is that the Christian who helps turn the erring brother or sister in Christ from the wrong path will save that person from physical death and covers (hides) the multitude of sins that would have been committed on that wrong path. (cf., Amos 5:1–15) This is the Christian community responding in love and unity.

In fact, Johnson has correctly identified the meaning of "will cover a multitude of sins." "But it seems to me that the entire thrust of James' composition demands that we take this to mean that such correction will prevent a multitude of sins in the future, both the sins that the erring member might otherwise commit and the sin of the community that continues to fail in its speaking of truth to that erring brother."[47] Therefore, according to both *James* and *Ezekiel,* God punishes his own children.

James 2:17–18 (2:14–3:1)

Ἀλλ' ἐρεῖ τις·Σὺ πίστιν ἔχεις κἀγὼ ἔργα ἔχω. δεῖξόν μοι τὴν πίστιν σου χωρὶς τῶν ἔργων, κἀγώ σοι δείξω ἐκ τῶν ἔργων μου τὴν πίστιν. σὺ πιστεύεις ὅτι εἷς ἐστιν ὁ θεός; καλῶς ποιεῖς·καὶ τὰ δαιμόνια πιστεύουσιν καὶ φρίσσουσιν. θέλεις δὲ γνῶναι, ὦ ἄνθρωπε κενέ, ὅτι ἡ πίστις χωρὶς τῶν ἔργων ἀργή ἐστιν;

I have placed this text after 5:19–20 in order to explain "faith cannot save" only after discussing saving the ψυχή (delivering

---

[47] Luke Timothy Johnson, *The Letter of James*, AYB 37A (New York: Doubleday, 1995), 345–6.

the life). Virtually all Protestant commentaries assume this passage teaches eschatological salvation from hell with "true faith" versus "false faith." Why?—because Protestants claim Christians cannot be punished by God after death. So, there is nothing to fear standing before God. In my opinion, this is why the James 2:17–18 passage has been so difficult to understand.

Allison offers twelve interpretations, then candidly admits, "Not one of these explanations satisfy, and as this commentator is unable to offer anything better in their place. . .. If every interpretation seems dubious, it is best to defend none."[48] Dibelius opposed Augustine's two types of faith and the adding of the demonstrative, arguing that "this faith" or inventing a "false or alleged faith" is outside the scope of James's argument: it should not be asserted.[49] Commentaries unanimously claim Jas 2:19 is sarcastic in the sense of "Good for you" (καλῶς ποιεῖτε) but never offer any proof, or even one other example in the ancient literature.[50] The reason is that not even one exists. Instead, it means, "You do good [works]. Even Catholic commentaries wrongly assume with Protestants— good works prove "true" faith.[51]

---

[48] Allison, *James*, 441–58.

[49] Dibelius, *James*, 154.

[50] E.g., Johnson, *James*, 241; James Adamson, *The Epistle of James*, NICNT (Grand Rapids: Eerdmans, 1976), 125.

[51] E.g., Kelly Anderson and Daniel Keating, *James, First, Second, and Third John,* Catholic Commentary on Sacred Scripture, eds. Peter Williamson and Mary Healy (Grand Rapids: Baker Academic, 2017), 59. N.B. the Augustinian, "works demonstrate true faith."

My article in the *Journal of Biblical Literature* explained how Augustine's polemical use of this passage against the Donatists created an erroneous distinction between true faith (Catholics) versus false faith (demons and Donatists).[52] This *Epistle of James* is addressed to Christians, with fifteen references to "brothers" and "beloved brothers." These sinning brothers are in danger of being judged by God with physical death for their sin, and then after death receiving punishment at the judgment seat of Christ.

"For he will have judgment without mercy who has shown no mercy." (2:13, NKJV). "Not many of you should become teachers, my fellow believers, because you know that we who teach will be judged more strictly." (3:1, NIV) The intervening verses address *what* God will judge. The works of Christians will be judged. Since works are being judged, faith alone cannot save (deliver) that Christian from God's judgment upon their evil works. Arriving with faith without good works at God's judgment of Christians is like arriving to compete in a tennis match with a paddle ball racquet—useless. You will be beaten badly.

The *specific* works are caring for the poor and needy (2:14–16). The context of James 2 is the poor. James mentions the poor six times in the first two chapters. Judaism and early

[52] Kenneth M. Wilson, "Reading James 2:18–20 with Anti-Donatist Eyes: Untangling Augustine's Exegetical Legacy," *Journal of Biblical Literature* 139.2 (2020): 389–410.

Christianity diligently taught giving alms to the poor. The judgment is in the future and is for Christians, as is evident in 5:7. James warns Christians not to grumble against one another since the Judge is standing at the door ready to return for judgment upon Christians.[53] God will judge Christians based upon their good and bad works to determine payment (reward) and punishment. This will determine their hierarchy in God's eternal kingdom, not whether they go to heaven or hell.

The greatest obstacle is "demons believe" (2:19) being interpreted as "false faith." Because Augustine did not know the Greek language, he read the Latin translation that omitted the Greek interlocutor markers. These markers demonstrate that the interlocutor—not James—uttered these (untrue) words "demons believe." It is not possible for demons to have faith; instead, they know (*oida*) without any doubt. Purely spiritual beings see God directly, as explained by C.S. Lewis regarding demons and by Thomas Aquinas regarding angels.[54] Faith cannot exist when there exists a direct spiritual vision of God. The interlocutor's false argument is explained in detail in my

---

[53] The forthcoming judgment in 2:13 and 3:1 match 5:7 where the Judge returns to judge his people. This is a judgment outside of our current physical existence. Paul explained that flesh and blood cannot inherit the kingdom of God and that living persons will somehow be transformed in their bodies. (1 Cor 15:50–55; 1 Thess 4:13–18) Whether we term this postmortem or post-transformational, the warning of an eschatological judgment for sin remains.

[54] Thomas Aquinas, *Summa Theologica* II.2.1.4 and C.S. Lewis, *Screwtape Letters* (London: The Centenary Press, 1942; repr., New York: Bantam, 1982), 11.

JBL article. This passage does not teach a "true faith" versus "false faith." It teaches Christians will be judged for their works, both good and bad. God will reward us for the good works and punish us for the evil works.

My conclusion is that this very common theology within Judaism, the NT, and the early church supporting punishment of Christians after death has been ignored and rejected. The Protestant rejection of posthumous punishment renders this passage incomprehensible. [55] This entire epistle stresses the Jewish *halakha* of righteous living to avoid both earthly and posthumous punishment as God's people (Jewish Christians).

1 Peter 4:15

μὴ γάρ τις ὑμῶν πασχέτω ὡς φονεὺς ἢ κλέπτης ἢ κακοποιὸς ἢ ὡς ἀλλοτριεπίσκοπος

Achtemeier draws the conclusion that Christians can indeed commit serious crimes in sin.

---

[55] Jeffrey Dale attempted a rejoinder to my article: Jeffrey M. Dale, "Demonic Faith and Demonic Wisdom in James: A Response to Kenneth M. Wilson," *JBL* 141.1 (2022): 177–195. He repeats the usual arguments without refuting my significant historical and exegetical arguments, while misrepresenting my position (his pejorative "oversimplifies" when I use "typically"). His only contribution was *Herm.* Mand. 9.11 [39.11] attempting to validate the typical reading of James. However, *Shepherd of Hermas* utilizes *James*'s words with different meanings. Not only does Hermas claim faith is from God, Hermas also claims being δίψυχος originates from the devil. James does not state this, or even imply it. Hermas follows a Gnostic pattern of exegesis. Dale failed to refute any of my major arguments.

> Yet the regular inclusion of three of these words in
> lists of vices, often directed specifically to the readers
> in the Christian community, along with the presence
> of an imperative that clearly implies one is to avoid
> suffering because one does such things, indicate they
> are probably to be taken at face value, indicating
> actual deeds. One ought not to allow a romanticizing
> of the early church to blind one to the realities of
> those communities.[56]

Achtemeier recognizes the reality of sinning Christians. What happens to these Christians who suffer as evildoers for serious crimes? Do they receive posthumous punishment then spend eternity with God, or do they go to hell? If Protestants teach there is no posthumous punishment, then they must go to hell.

2 Peter 1:10–11

διὸ μᾶλλον, ἀδελφοί, σπουδάσατε βεβαίαν ὑμῶν τὴν κλῆσιν καὶ ἐκλογὴν ποιεῖσθαι· ταῦτα γὰρ ποιοῦντες οὐ μὴ πταίσητέ ποτε· οὕτως γὰρ πλουσίως ἐπιχορηγηθήσεται ὑμῖν ἡ εἴσοδος εἰς τὴν αἰώνιον βασιλείαν τοῦ κυρίου ἡμῶν καὶ σωτῆρος Ἰησοῦ Χριστοῦ.

Moo, who defends his Calvinist paradigm in this text, sees no significant difference between a welcome into the kingdom versus a "rich" or "abundant" (πλουσίως) welcome into the

---

[56] Paul Achtemeier, *1 Peter*, Herm. (Minneapolis, MN: Augsburg Fortress, 1996), 311.

kingdom. This forces him to write,

> As a Calvinist, I would add that those whom God has truly chosen will always, because of his Spirit, so respond to God and thus confirm their election and get to heaven. In faithfulness to Scripture, we face here what some call an "antinomy": truths that are not contradictory but which we cannot neatly reconcile either. God chooses us and ensures that we get to heaven. We need to choose God and live godly lives so that we can reach heaven.[57]

This problem is not Moo's "antinomy" but a contradiction. These are blatant contradictions of his opposing ideas of faith alone and yet "we need to choose God and live godly lives so that we can reach heaven." His "cannot be neatly reconciled" is a litotes. This is not a mere "antinomy." In contrast, I understand the biblical author to encourage a rich/abundant welcome or entrance into the kingdom. How? By becoming more like Christ in virtues (vv. 3–9, extra payment/honor for service, as Jesus and the Apostles taught). This avoids contradiction and antinomy. Protestants consistently twist and distort scripture to mean "get to heaven." Everything is pigeon-holed into the heaven versus hell categories, mistakenly thinking heaven is the goal. The NT teaches conformation into Christ-likeness is the goal; and, that God rewards diligence in this pursuit.

---

[57] Douglas Moo, *2 Peter, Jude*, NIVAC (Zondervan, 1997), 60.

Moo repeats this pattern in 2 Peter 2:17–22. He ultimately decides the "they" must be the immediate antecedent (false teachers) and not those Christians "who have just escaped from those who live in error" (2:18, NRSV). For Moo, this means the false teachers go to the "terrible judgment awaiting them." This eschatological judgment must be hell for non-Christians since posthumous punishment of God's children cannot occur (for a Calvinist).[58] I appreciate Moo's academic honesty when he admits he cannot explain how those false teachers, "who gave every evidence of being Christians," were doomed for hell, yet had actually "escaped the defilements [corruption] of the world through the [full experiential] knowledge [ἐπιγνώσει] of our Lord and Savior Jesus Christ." (2:20, NRSV) Moo ultimately concludes, "the false teachers of 2 Peter 2:20–22 are not really genuine Christians. I admit that this is not the most natural reading of the text…. I must honestly admit that I am not finally satisfied with this conclusion…."[59]

Perhaps they are "genuine Christians" but not "really genuine Christians"? No, I think the answer lies in the fact that the end being worse than the beginning is not the eternal destiny (hell) of those who actually escaped the world's corruption. Rather, their later immoral condition here on earth is worse than before they became Christians.

---

[58] Moo, *2 Peter, Jude*, 140–159.

[59] Moo, *2 Peter, Jude*, 155.

But because Moo's Augustinian-Calvinist God (a type of Stoic-Manichaean-Neoplatonic god) gives the perfect gift of faith (non-human divine faith) unilaterally, that faith *must* persevere without fail.[60] Moo's theology forces him to conclude (contrary to his own admitted natural reading) these are not "really genuine Christians," and therefore "they" go to hell. This inconsistency is the result of Protestants rejecting God's punishment of his children for disobedience after death.

Bauckham follows the typical Protestant conclusion, "2:18–20, which deals with apostasy from Christianity." He does this by associating it with Matt 12:45.[61] His citation of and comments on *Herm. Sim.* 9:17:5–18:2 fail to detail the critical distinction between ἐπιγνώσει (full experiential knowledge) and γνώσει (knowledge). The ἐπι intensifies the meaning.[62] Three

---

[60] See Wilson, *Augustine's Conversion*; and Chapter 5 in *Critiquing Calvinism; and "Augustine of Hippo's Tenuous Tension between Stoic Providence and Christian Free Will," Studia Patristica 119 (2021): 153–168.* Stoicism, Manichaeism, and Neoplatonism taught Divine Unilateral Predetermination of Eternal Destines (DUPED) which the early church fathers unanimously refuted for three centuries. Augustine reverted to his earlier adherence to these three pagan philosophies in 412 CE by ascribing dictatorial micromanagement to a "Sovereign God" with humans being devoid of free choice (except to sin; Stoic "non-free free will").

[61] Richard Bauckham, *2 Peter and Jude*, WBC 50 (Grand Rapids, MI: Thomas Nelson, 1983), 277.

[62] Four Greek lexicons see ἐπι as "full knowledge," "fuller knowledge," complete knowledge, or "*expert knowledge*." See *Liddell and Scott's Greek English Lexicon* (Oxford: Clarendon Pres, 1891), 249; G.W.H. Lampe, ed. *A Patristic Greek Lexicon* (Oxford: Clarendon Press, 1961; repr. 2008), 519; T. Muraoka, *A Greek-English Lexicon of the Septuagint* (Leuven: Peters, 2009), 270: "2. *expert knowledge*"; BDAG, 369: "with the prep. making its

prior times this epistle uses ἐπιγνώσει cognates referring to
Christians (1:2,3,8). [63] The alleged parallel to the demon
possessed man is invalid. That man never had an ἐπιγνώσει of
godliness sufficient to escape the world's corruption as did the
persons in 2 Peter 2:20–22. This full knowledge of the Lord
resulted in them walking in Christ morally ("having known the
way of righteousness" ἐπεγνωκέναι τὴν ὁδὸν τῆς δικαιοσύνης).
Nevertheless, Bauckham astutely concludes:

> Because moral apostasy involves sinning with full
> knowledge of God's moral demands and spurning the
> grace which is available through Christ for holy
> living, its culpability is much greater than that of the
> sins committed in ignorance during a person's pre-
> Christian life. … the apostate does not simply return
> to his pre-Christian condition, but enters a worse
> state, in danger of more severe judgment.[64]

Bauckham correctly views these persons' moral conditions as
being worse than their pre-Christian conditions. Therefore, they
are "in danger of a more severe judgment." But since Protestants
do not allow God to punish Christians after death, these people
must go to hell. This invalid thinking matches Bauckham's

---

influence felt, *know exactly, completely, through and through.*" This is in
contrast to Kittel's TDNT which claims no distinction (I. 704). Italics are all
original.

[63] Cf., 1:5, 2:20, 3:3, and 3:17–18 that use merely γνῶσις cognates.

[64] Bauckham, *2 Peter and Jude*, 281.

message of the false teachers: "freedom from fear of eschatological judgment will have been the fundamental freedom." [65] This remains true today for most Protestants. Because Protestants have no fear of punishment by God they are deceived into libertine freedom.

1 John 5:16–17

ἐάν τις ἴδῃ τὸν ἀδελφὸν αὐτοῦ ἁμαρτάνοντα ἁμαρτίαν μὴ πρὸς θάνατον, αἰτήσει, καὶ δώσει αὐτῷ ζωήν, τοῖς ἁμαρτάνουσιν μὴ πρὸς θάνατον. ἔστιν ἁμαρτία πρὸς θάνατον·οὐ περὶ ἐκείνης λέγω ἵνα ἐρωτήσῃ. πᾶσα ἀδικία ἁμαρτία ἐστίν, καὶ ἔστιν ἁμαρτία οὐ πρὸς θάνατον.

Marshall follows the scholarly bandwagon that death is eternal. "Sin that leads to death is deliberate refusal to believe in Jesus Christ, to follow God's commands, and to love one's brothers."[66] Kruse points out the one and only other time this phrase "not unto death" is used in the NT. This is used by Jesus referring to the illness of Lazarus not ending in physical death. Yet, Kruse writes,

> His sickness was not *pros thanaton* in the sense that the ultimate outcome was not physical death because Jesus restored him to life. However, when speaking about 'sin that leads to death' the author does not

[65] Ibid, 275.

[66] I. Howard Marshall, *The Epistles of John*, NICNT (Grand Rapids, MI: Eerdmans, 1978), 248.

> have physical death in mind, for all sinners are
> susceptible to physical death because of sin. What he
> has in mind is spiritual death, that failure to
> experience eternal life which is the privilege of those
> who believe in the Son of God.[67]

Despite the obvious reference of Jesus to physical death, Kruse concludes John's meaning is not physical death but spiritual death. But contra Kruse, Lazarus *did die* physically from his illness, then Christ resurrected him. Yes, all persons, including Christians, do die physically. But Kruse imports a modern Protestant heaven/hell mindset into Jewish theology and scripture. This epistle was written to readers who already possess eternal life ("little children" who have "overcome the evil one"). The punishment of physical death is well attested in both the OT and NT. Once again, Protestants consistently assign all punishment to eternal hell.

Conclusion

These examples are hardly exhaustive. However, they reveal that Protestant scholars will not consider that Christians might be seriously punished by God after death. Therefore, the warning passages (although written to Christians) must be arbitrarily reassigned to unbelievers due to theological presuppositions. Rarely, some scholars will admit these

---

[67] Kruse, Colin G. *The Letters of John, 2nd edn.,* PNTC (Grand Rapids, MI: Eerdmans, 2020), 192.

warnings are written to believers (usually as "motivational warnings" by God to help believers persevere, lest they prove themselves to be unbelievers), yet remain silent when the scripture speaks of punishment of those believers as Christians. Meanwhile, scripture repeatedly reveals that God punishes his children: sin has permanent consequences.

> And the Levites who went far from Me, when Israel went astray, who strayed away from Me after their idols, they shall bear their iniquity. Yet they shall be ministers in My sanctuary, *as* gatekeepers of the house and ministers of the house; they shall slay the burnt offering and the sacrifice for the people, and they shall stand before them to minister to them. Because they ministered to them before their idols and caused the house of Israel to fall into iniquity, therefore I have raised My hand in an oath against them," says the Lord GOD, "that they shall bear their iniquity. And they shall not come near Me to minister to Me as priest, nor come near any of My holy things, nor into the Most Holy *Place;* but they shall bear their shame and their abominations which they have committed. Nevertheless I will make them keep charge of the temple, for all its work, and for all that has to be done in it. (Ezek 44:10–14, NKJV)

God restores his punished children by his grace to usefulness, but the consequences of their sin can remain.

There is often no distinction made when railing against a medieval Catholic "purgatory" versus more modern concepts of posthumous punishment (see Chapter 2). The reticence of Protestant scholars to take the scripture at face value when God judges his own people (e.g., 1 Pet 4:17, "judgment to begin with the household of God") can be explained by the impenetrable barrier of pure tradition. John Calvin's mantra against purgatory and "no Christian punishment" remains alive and vibrant, controls exegetical decisions, and prohibits any discussion of Christian punishment after death by God. Again, I suggest it is time to recover the baby that was thrown out with the bathwater. Posthumous punishment of Christians is valid biblical theology.

Appendix B

The Judgment Seat of Christ

as Reward Only

Some Christians claim the βήμα (Judgment Seat) of Christ exists solely for rewards or loss of rewards for Christians, instead of being an actual judgment seat. This is a tiny minority view found only in a few conservative evangelical circles. This is the reason it appears in an Appendix rather than in the body of the book.

Origin of the "Rewards Only" Error

The first misuse of the Judgment Seat of Christ as a "reward only" seat (of which I am aware) was by C. I. Scofield in his 1909 *Scofield Reference Bible* regarding 2 Cor 5:10. "The result is 'reward' or 'loss' (of the reward), 'but he himself shall be saved'."[1] Citations for support are absent. Scofield pastored churches in Dallas, Texas and Dwight L. Moody's (of Moody Bible Institute) church in Massachusetts. His questionable character and fraudulent credentials have been exposed, including divorcing his wife, abandoning his two young

---

[1] Cyrus I. Scofield, *The Scofield Reference Bible* (New York: Oxford University Press, 1909; rev. 1917), 1233.

daughters, and stealing from his mother-in-law.[2] His Doctor of Divinity title appears to have been an honorary degree for marketing purposes from the University of Oxford Press.[3] Scofield's claim that the Judgment Seat of Christ in 2 Cor 5:10 was only for reward or loss of reward was baseless (and possibly a convenient self-deception).

In 1936, Sale-Harrison taught that only Christians appear at the Judgment Seat of Christ while only unbelievers appear at the Great White Throne judgment.[4] He assumed all judicial proceedings must deal with salvation from hell: "the Judgment Seat of Christ cannot suggest condemnation […] It is not a judicial bench. It is not to ascertain whether one's salvation is secure."[5] He erroneously claimed the *bema* was an Olympic games term:

> It [*bema*] really means a "raised platform." … In the Grecian games in Athens, the old Arena contained a raised platform on which the president (or umpire) of the Arena sat. From here, he watched over all the

---

[2] Joseph Cranfield, *The Incredible Scofield and His Book* (Vallecito, CA: Ross House Books, 1988; Chalcedon/Ross House Books, 2nd edn., 2005).

[3] This book was the first to sell a million copies for Oxford University Press.

[4] Leonard Sale-Harrison, The Judgment Seat of Christ: An Incentive and a Warning (New York: Sale-Harrison Publications, 1938), 5. This error is repeated on page 71. Leonard Sale-Harrison was a bible teacher and evangelist from New Zealand and Australia, who graduated from Wheaton College in 1937, and died in 1955 at the age of 80.

[5] Sale-Harrison, *Judgment Seat*, 5, 7.

contestants; and here he rewarded all the winners. It was called the "bema" or, "the reward seat." It was never used as a judicial bench. Therefore, the Judgment Seat of Christ is a reward seat and not a judicial bench." (Sale-Harrison, 8–9)

These comments are false. His book on the judgment seat makes numerous unsubstantiated claims without ever citing references. His primary example for his view of the Judgment Seat of Christ uses Australian judges examining sheep in a contest for prizes. He writes,

Chastisement has to do with this life, and not the Judgment Seat of Christ. Chastisement is for the purpose of discipline and not for condemnation; also, all need for disciplinary measures is [*sic*] over when we leave this earthly pilgrimage. It must be borne in mind that all sins that were pardoned when we came to Christ are wiped out as iniquities; for God sees them through the finished work of Calvary. (Sale-Harrison, 36–37)

Sale-Harrison claims "It does not examine my life prior to my new birth in Christ, for that is all changed through the finished work *of* Christ" (Sale-Harrison, 38). After citing 1 John 1:9 he states, "To lose fellowship does not mean to lose sonship; but it certainly results in losing a reward." (47–48) He assumes 1 John 1:9 means the only sins judged were those not cleansed by confession (53). All of these concepts (claimed without evidence) by Sale-Harrison are currently held as firm biblical doctrine by certain Christian conservative evangelicals.

Lewis Sperry Chafer, founder and president of Dallas Theological Seminary, wrote his *Systematic Theology* in 1948. Chafer wrote, "Although his sins have been brought up at the cross and will not be brought up again, at the judgment seat of Christ his works or service must be judged."[6] Chafer cited C. I. Scofield, "The judgment of the believer's works, not sins, is in question here. These have been atoned for, and are 'remembered no more forever' (Heb.10:17)."[7] Chafer adds, "It cannot be too strongly emphasized that this judgment is unrelated to the problem of sin, that it is more for the bestowing of rewards than for the rejection of failure."[8]

J. Dwight Pentecost, professor at Dallas Theological Seminary, cited Sale-Harrison's *Judgment Seat of Christ* (twenty years after its publication) in his 1958 work *Things to Come.*[9] Pentecost appropriately cited a scholar and Thayer's Greek-English lexicon to demonstrate the *bema* as a judicial

---

[6] Lewis S. Chafer, *Systematic Theology*, Vol. 7 (Dallas Seminary Press: Dallas, Texas, 11th printing, 1973 edn.), IV.215.

[7] Chafer, *Systematic Theology*, IV.377, citing Cyrus I. Scofield, *The Scofield Reference Bible* (New York: Oxford University Press, 1909), 1233.

[8] Chafer, *Systematic Theology*, 406.

[9] J. Dwight Pentecost, *Things to Come: A Study in Biblical Eschatology* (Elkins, NH, Dunham Pub., 1958; Grand Rapids: Zondervan, 1964), 219–220. He cited Alfred Plummer on 1 Corinthians and Thayer's lexicon.

seat pronouncing judgment. But he then cited the non-scholar Sale-Harrison, repeating the undocumented and inaccurate claim about the *bema* in the Olympic games. Pentecost then writes, "Thus, associated with this word are the ideas of prominence, dignity, authority, honor, and reward rather than the idea of justice and judgment."[10] Therefore, Pentecost based his conclusion on Sale-Harrison's unverified and false Olympic game *bema* claim. Pentecost propagated an error. This error led to his opinion that the Judgment Seat of Christ evaluation could result in only two outcomes—either a loss of reward or a reward.[11]

The second DTS president, John Walvoord repeated this error: "Although some have attempted to make this a Protestant purgatory, i.e., a time of punishment for unconfessed sin, it seems clear from the general doctrine of justification by faith that no condemnation [Rom 8:1] is possible for one who is in Christ. ... The penalty is limited to the loss of reward."[12]

---

[10] Pentecost, *Things to Come*, 220.

[11] Ibid., 223–226.

[12] John Walvoord, "The Future Work of Christ Part II: The Church in Heaven," *BSac* 123:490 (Apr 66), p. 100. This phrase "no condemnation" appears in Rom 8:1, but has been misunderstood. This Christian "no condemnation" (κατάκριμα, "judicial pronouncement of guilty upon a person") can be temporal, not solely eternal damnation, and must be distinguished from κατάκρινα (pronounce a penalty or sentence after being found guilty; e.g., Rom 8:3–4). Κατάκρινα means serving a penalty/sentence, not damnation to hell. Christians who walk in the Spirit no longer must serve the sentence of sin while in the body but may fulfill the righteousness requirement of the law, thereby avoiding the temporal penalty. Cf., BDAG, 518–9.

Hoyt expressed similar views writing in the DTS journal *Bibliotheca Sacra*.

> There will be no need for forensic punishment, for Christ has forever borne all of God's wrath toward the believer's sins. ... However, Scripture teaches that for the believer God's *justice* has already been fully and forever satisfied at the Cross in relation to the believer's sins. If God were to punish the believer judicially for his sins for which Christ has already rendered payment, He would be requiring two payments for sin and would therefore be unjust.[13]

The Moody Handbook of Theology claims:

> The judgment seat of Christ is mentioned in Romans 14:10, 1 Corinthians 3:9-15, and 2 Corinthians 5:10. It does not denote a judgment concerning eternal destiny but rather rewarding church age believers for faithfulness. The term *judgment seat* (Gk. *bema*) is taken from the Grecian games where successful athletes were rewarded for victory in athletic contests. Paul used that figure to denote the giving of rewards to church age believers.[14]

---

[13] Samuel L. Hoyt, "The Judgment Seat of Christ in Theological Perspective—Part 1: The Judgment Seat of Christ and Unconfessed Sins," *BSac* 137 (Jan 80): 32–41.

[14] Paul Enns, *The Moody Handbook of Theology* (Chicago, IL: Moody Press, 1989), 392.

Therefore, the "rewards only" error originated with Scofield and Sale-Harrison. It was quickly propagated by authors from Moody Bible Institute and Dallas Theological Seminary. The lack of research by these authors to confirm or refute the validity of these erroneous claims confounds me.

Problems with a "Reward only" βῆμα

Significant difficulties arise from this viewpoint. First, neither Enns (*The Moody Handbook of Theology*) nor any previous author cites a single reference as evidence for Sale-Harrison's claim about the Olympic games βῆμα. In fact, of the twelve times βῆμα appears in the NT, receiving for the good (a benefit/reward) only appears in 2 Cor 5:10.[15] Eleven of twelve are judicial for punishment. Paul's only other use of βῆμα (Rom 14:10) arises in the context of warning believers of judgment, not reward. The earliest church fathers consistently used the term βῆμα only for a judicial seat of judgment—never of reward.[16] Neither Danker nor Brown mentions any concept of reward under the term βῆμα in their dictionaries.[17] The NA[27]

---

[15] Nine of the twelve appear in the Gospels where they refer to a governmental judicial seat, with only one reference to a small space (Acts 7:5). None refer to a "reward seat" or Olympic games.

[16] Of the approximately 54 occurrences prior to about 200 CE, none refer to reward or the Olympic games.

[17] BDAG, 175; See Colin Brown, ed., *The New International Dictionary of New Testament Theology*, Vol. 2 (Zondervan Publishing House: Grand Rapids, 1986; German original as *Theologishes Begriffslexikon Zum Neuen Testament* by Theologisher Verlag Rolf Brockhaus: Wuppertal, 1967), s.v.,

translates this text as the "law court" of Christ.[18] This author has been unable to identify even a single instance in early Greek literature where the word βῆμα can be found in the context of the Olympic games. In contrast, the raised platform at Olympic games seems to have been named an *exedra*. From this lack of evidence for reward, we should conclude that in 2 Cor 5:10, Paul expanded the analogy of the Roman judicial βῆμα by adding the Christian concept of rewards (payment) for obedient faithfulness in good deeds.

In contrast to the unsupported theory of the βῆμα being solely for rewards, no less a Protestant scholar than Berkhof supports the idea that the sins of Christians will be made public at Christ's judgment seat after death.

> But it is sometimes objected that the sins of believers, which are pardoned, certainly will not be published at that time; but Scripture leads us to expect that they will be, though they will, of course, be revealed as *pardoned* sins. Men will be judged for 'every idle word,' Matt. 12:36, and for 'every secret thing,' Rom 2:16'; 1 Cor 4:5, and there is no indication whatsoever that this will be limited to the wicked. Moreover, it is perfectly evident from such passages

---

"Judgment," βῆμα pp. 369–371: "a place of judicial judgment where legal cases are heard and a judgment pronounced."

[18] Kurt Aland, et. al. eds. *Nestle-Aland 27th Edition Greek New Testament with McReynolds English Interlinear* (Deutsche Bibelgesellschaft, 1993), Rom. 14:10.

as Matt. 13:30,40-43, 49; 25:14-23, 34-40, 46, that
the righteous will appear before the judgment seat of
Christ." (emphasis original)[19]

Total absolution

Forgiveness of sin through Christ's sacrificial death eliminates
eternal condemnation but does not unconditionally exempt us
from God's remembrance of our sin or from punishment for sin.
When Scripture declares that God no longer remembers our
sins, it must be interpreted in the context of current intimacy lest
Scripture contradict itself. How does God discipline or punish
(Heb 12:5–11) if he does not remember sin? The regenerate
Christian must confess sin in order to restore intimacy with God.
He or she must also repent of sin in order to escape the
impending temporal judgment of God. According to Scripture,
appealing to the cross of Christ in justification or propitiation
does not logically preclude God's future punishment upon his
children.

Theoretically, God could punish a Christian for sin in
any way he chooses as long as he did not send that child to
eternal damnation, in violation of Christ's sacrifice delivering
us from it. Interestingly, the Roman Catholic Church limits the
benefit of Christ's sacrifice in remitting *only* the penalty of
eternal death. Cardinal Wiseman taught the following in 1836:

---

[19] Berkhof, *Systematic Theology*, 732.

We believe that upon this forgiveness of sins, that is, after the remission of that eternal debt, which God in his justice awards to transgressions against his law, he has been pleased to reserve a certain degree of inferior or temporary punishment, appropriate to the guilt which had been incurred; and it is on this part of the punishment alone, that, according to the Catholic doctrine, satisfaction can be made to God. What the grounds of this belief are, I will state just now. At present, I wish to lay down the doctrine clearly and intelligibly; that it is only with regard to the reserved degree of temporal punishment that we believe the Christian can satisfy the justice of God. But is even this satisfaction any thing of his own ? Certainly not ; it is not of the slightest avail, except as united to the merits of Christ's passion, for it receives its entire efficacy from that complete and abundant purchase made by our Blessed Saviour. [20]

Not even this suffering of temporal punishment in purgatory would be a satisfaction to God's justice if not for "the merits of Christ's passion," from which the purging "receives its entire efficacy." The "Rewards Only" view trivializes sin, promotes sin, and tramples God's holy justice.

---

[20] Cardinal Nicholas Wiseman, *Lectures on the Principle Doctrines and Practices of the Catholic Church*, vol.2 (London: Booker, 1836), 41–2; https://archive.org/details/LecturesOnThePrincipalDoctrinesV2/page/n9/mode/2up ; Accessed 5 July 2023.

Conclusion

Therefore, the entire "Rewards Only" view was built upon the sand of erroneous unsubstantiated claims regarding the βῆμα (Judgment Seat) of Christ. It fails to adequately address the severe warning passages throughout scripture. Shame and loss of reward are insufficient to deter a Christian sinner who has been guaranteed "heaven." This error does injustice to the holy justice of God. It mocks God because persons do not reap what they sow (Gal 6:7–8). The funeral service and burial for this fraudulent doctrine cannot come too soon.

Works Cited

Achtemeier, Paul. *1 Peter* in Eldon J. Epp, ed. Hermeneia–A Critical and Historical Commentary. Minneapolis, MN: Fortress Press, 1996.

Adamson, James. *The Epistle of James* in F. F. Bruce, ed. New International Commentary on the New Testament. Grand Rapids: Eerdmans, 1976.

Aland, Kurt et. al. eds. *Nestle-Aland 27th Edition Greek New Testament with McReynolds English Interlinear.* Deutsche Bibelgesellschaft, 1993.

Allison, Dale Jr. and W. D. Davies in J.A. Emerton, C.E.B.

Cranfield, and G.N. Stanton, eds. *The Gospel According to St. Matthew*. International Critical Commentary. Vol. 1. Edinburgh: T&T Clark, 1988.

Anderson, Kelly and Daniel Keating. *James, First, Second, and Third John* in Peter Williamson and Mary Healy, eds. Catholic Commentary on Sacred Scripture. Grand Rapids, MI: Baker Academic, 2017.

Armstrong, Dave "The Biblical Roots and History of Indulgences," *National Catholic Register*, 25 May 2018; https://www.ncregister.com/blog/the-biblical-roots-and-history-of-Indulgences; Accessed 9 May 2023.

Attridge, Harold W. *The Epistle to Hebrews* in Helmet Koester, ed. Hermeneia–A Critical and Historical Commentary. Philadelphia, PA: Fortress Press, 1989.

Barnett, Paul. *The Second Epistle to the Corinthians* in Ned
    Stonehouse, F.F. Bruce, and Gordon Fee, eds. New
    International Commentary on the New Testament.
    Grand Rapids, MI: Eerdmans, 1997.

Barton, John and John Muddiman, eds. *The Oxford Bible
    Commentary*. Oxford: Oxford University Press, 2001.

Bateman, Herbert W. IV, ed. *Four Views on the Warning
    Passages in Hebrews*. Grand Rapids, MI: Kregel
    Publications, 2007.

Bauckham, Richard. *2 Peter and Jude* in David Hubbard,
    Glenn Barker, John Watts, and Ralph Martin, eds.
    WBC 50. Nashville, TN: Thomas Nelson, 1983.

_____. *The Jewish World Around the New
    Testament*. Grand Rapids, MI: Baker Academic, 2008.

Bellarmine, Robert. *Disputationes de Controversiis*. Three
    Volumes. Ingolstadt, Bavaria 1586, 1588, 1593;
    Venice, 1596. Reprint, *On Purgatory*. Translated by
    Ryan Grant. Post Falls, ID: Mediatrix Press, 2017.

Benware, Paul. *The Believer's Payday*. Chattanooga, TN:
    AMG Publishers, 2002.

Berkhof, Louis. *Systematic Theology*. Grand Rapids, MI:
    Eerdmans, 1932. Revised 1938. Reprint, Grand Rapids,
    MI: Eerdmans, 1982.

Bernard, Justin. "Purgatory and the Dilemma of
    Sanctification," *Faith and Philosophy* 26 (2009): 311–
    327.

Black, David. *Linguistics for Students of New Testament
    Greek*. 2nd edn. Grand Rapids, MI: Baker Books, 1995.

Bloesch, Donald. *The Last Things: Resurrection, Judgment,
    Glory*. Downers Grove, IL: InterVarsity Press, 2005.

Bock, Darrell. *Luke 9:51–24:53* in Moisés Silva, gen. ed. Exegetical Commentary on the New Testament Vol. 2. Grand Rapids, MI: Baker Academic, 1996.

Bréhier, Louis. "Attempts at Reunion of the Greek and Latin Churches," *Cambridge Medieval History* 4 (1936): 594-562.

Bray, Gerald, ed. and trans. *Commentaries on Romans and 1-2 Corinthians* in *Ancient Christian Texts*. Downers Grove, IL: Intervarsity, 2009.

Bruce, F.F. *Commentary on the Epistle to Hebrews* in F. F. Bruce, ed. Grand Rapids, MI: Eerdmans, 1963.

_____. *The Epistles to the Colossians, to Philemon, and to the Ephesians* in Ned Stonehouse, F.F. Bruce, and Gordon Fee, eds. New International Commentary on the New Testament. Grand Rapids, MI: Eerdmans, 1984.

Burns, J. Patout. "On Rebaptism: Social Organization in the Third Century Church," *JECS* 1 (1993): 367–403.

_____. Translator and editor. *Romans* in Robert L. Wilkin, gen. ed. The Church's Bible. Grand Rapids, MI: Eerdmans, 2012.

Burton, Ernest de Witt. *Spirit, Soul, and Flesh.* Chicago: University of Chicago Press, 1918.

Callaham, Scott N. "Blasphemy against the Holy Spirit: Rejecting the Sign of the Covenant," Horizons in Biblical Theology, Online April 20, 2023. Accessed 3 June 2023. https://brill.com/view/journals/hbth/45/1/article-p37_3.xml.

Calvin, John. *Calvin: Institutes of the Christian Religion in* John T. McNeill, ed. Library of Christian Classics. Translated by Ford L. Battles. Philadelphia, PA: The Westminster Press, 1960.

_____. Letter to Cardinal Sadoleto, September 1, 1539.

Chadwick, Henry. *The Early Church*. New York: Dorset Press, 1967.

Chafer, Lewis S. *Systematic Theology*. Vol. 7. Dallas Seminary Press: Dallas, Texas, edn. 1973.

Clapsis, Fr. Emmanuel. "Suffering and the Crucified Christ," Greek Orthodox Diocese of America 8/17/2015. https://www.goarch.org/-/suffering-and-the-crucified-christ. Accessed 5 June 2023.

Cross, F. L. and Elizabeth Livingston, eds. "Purgatory," in *The Oxford Dictionary of the Christian Church*. 3rd edn. Oxford University Press: Oxford, 2005.

Cohen, Shaye. *From the Maccabees to the Mishnah*. 2nd edn. Louisville, KY: Westminster John Knox Press, 2006.

Cranfield, C. E. B. *Romans* in John Emerton, C.E.B. Cranfield, and Graham Stanton, eds. International Critical Commentary. Vol.2. Edinburgh: T&T Clark, 1975.

Cranfield, Joseph. *The Incredible Scofield and His Book*. Vallecito, CA: Ross House Books, 1988; Chalcedon/Ross House Books, Second edition, 2005.

Crisp, Oliver. *Deviant Calvinism: Broadening Reformed Theology*. Minneapolis, MN: Fortress Press, 2014.

Daley, Brian E. *The Hope of the Early Church: A Handbook of Patristic Eschatology*. New York: Cambridge UP, 1991.

Danzinger, Eliezer. "Is there any sort of Purgatory or Satan in Jewish teachings?" *Chabad.org* https://www.chabad.org/library/article_cdo/aid/512017 /jewish/Is-there-any-sort-of-Purgatory-or-Satan-in-Jewish-teachings.htm#footnote1a512017 ; Accessed 15 May 2023.

Davids, Peter. *The Epistle of James* in I. Howard Marshall and W. Ward Gasque. New International Greek Testament Commentary. Grand Rapids, MI: Eerdmans, 1982.

Deferrari, Roy, ed. *Funeral Orations by Saint Gregory Nazianzen and Saint Ambrose.* Translated by Leo McCauley, John Sullivan, Martin McGuire, and Roy Deferrari. New York: Fathers of the Church,1953.

Dibelius, Martin. *James* in Helmut Koester, ed. Hermeneia–A Critical and Historical Commentary. Revised by Henrich Greeven. Translated by Michael Williams. Philadelphia, PA: Fortress Press, 1976.

Dodson, Kenneth. *The Prize of the Up-Calling.* Grand Rapids, MI: Baker, 1969.

Dorotheus of Mitylene. *The History of the Council of Florence* in J.M. Nealle, ed. Translated by Basil Popoff. London: Joseph Masters, 1861.

Dunn, James. *The Epistles to the Colossians and to Philemon* in I. Howard Marshall W. Ward Gasque, and Donald Hagner, eds. New International Greek Testament Commentary. Grand Rapids, MI: Eerdmans, 1996.

_____. "Response to Robert N. Wilkin," in Alan Stanley and Stanley Gundry, eds. *Four Views of the Role of Works at the Final Judgment.* Grand Rapids, MI: Zondervan, 2013.

Edwards, Jonathan. "The Portion of the Righteous," December, 1740 on Romans 2:10.

Ellingsworth, Paul. *The Epistle to Hebrews* in I. Howard
       Marshall and Donald A. Hagner, eds. The New
       International Greek Testament Commentary. Grand
       Rapids, MI: Eerdmans, 1993; Reprint, 2000.

Enns, Paul. *The Moody Handbook of Theology*. Chicago, IL:
       Moody Press, 1989.

Eubank, Nathan. "Prison, Penance or Purgatory: The
       Interpretation of Matthew 5.25–6 and Parallels," *New
       Testament Studies* 64.2 (April 2018): 162–177.

Fee, Gordon. *The First Epistle to the Corinthians* in F. F.
       Bruce, ed. New International Commentary on the New
       Testament. 2nd edn. Grand Rapids, MI: Eerdmans,
       2014.

Ferguson, Everett. *Baptism in the Early Church: History,
       Theology, and Liturgy in the First Five Centuries*.
       Grand Rapids, MI: Eerdmans, 2009.

Finkelstein, Louis. *Aktba: Scholar, Saint, and Martyr*.
       Cleveland, OH: Meridian Books, JP25 and
       Philadelphia, PA: Jewish Publication Society of
       America, 1962.

Fitzgerald, Allan. "Penance," in Susan Harvey and David
       Hunter, eds. *The Oxford Handbook of Christian
       Studies*. Oxford: Oxford University Press, 2008.

Fitzgerald, Rev. Fr. Thomas. "Teachings of the Orthodox
       Church," Greek Orthodox Diocese of America
       6/11/1990 https://www.goarch.org/-/teachings-of-the-
       orthodox-church Accessed 5 June 2023.

Forsyth, Peter. *This Life and the Next*. Boston, MA: The
       Pilgrim Press, 1948.

Frame, James. *The Epistles of St. Paul to the Thessalonians* in Alfred Plummer, ed. International Critical Commentary. New York: Charles Scribner's Sons, 1912.

France, R. T. *The Gospel of Matthew* in Gordon Fee, ed. New International Commentary on the New Testament. Grand Rapids, MI: Eerdmans, 2007.

Furnish, Victor. *II Corinthians* in William Albright and David Freedman, gen. eds. The Anchor Bible. Garden City, NY: Doubleday, 1984.

Gill, Joseph. "Florence, Council of," at 5:770–772 in *New Catholic Encyclopedia*. 2nd edn. Detroit, MI: Thomson Gale, 2003.

Gnilka, J. *1 Kor. 3:10–15 ein Schriftzeugnis für das Fegfeuer?* Düsseldorf: Triltsch, 1955.

Goodman, Martin. *A History of Judaism*. Princeton, NJ: Princeton University Press, 2018.

Grudem, Wayne. *Systematic Theology*. Grand Rapids, MI: Zondervan, 1994.

Harris, Murray J. *The Second Epistle to the Corinthians: A Commentary on the Greek Text* in I. Howard Marshall and Donald Hagner, eds. New International Greek Testament Commentary. Grand Rapids, MI: Eerdmans; and Milton Keynes, UK: Paternoster, 2005.

Helfferick, Tryntje ed. *The Essential Luther*. Translated by Tryntje Helfferick. Indianapolis, IN: Hackett, 2018.

Hodge, Charles. *Systematic Theology*. Vol. 3. New York, London and Edinburgh: C. Scribner, T. Nelson and sons, 1872–1873. Reprint, Grand Rapids, MI: Eerdmans, 1993.

Hogg, C.F. and W. E. Vine. *The Epistles to the Thessalonians.* Grand Rapids, MI: Kregel, 1959.

Hoyt, Samuel L., "The Judgment Seat of Christ in Theological Perspective—Part 1: The Judgment Seat of Christ and Unconfessed Sins," *BSac* 137 (Jan 80): 32–41.

Hunt, Dwight. "1–2 Corinthians" in Robert N. Wilkin, ed. *The Grace New Testament Commentary.* Vol.2. Denton, Texas: Grace Evangelical Society, 2010.

Instone-Brewer, David. "Chapter 14: Eternal Punishment in First Century Jewish Thought" in Christopher Date and Ron Highfield, eds. *A Consuming Passion:* Essays on Hell and Immortality in Honor of Edward Fudge. Eugene, OR: Pickwick Publications, 2015.

Jastrow, Marcus and S. Mendelsohn, sv. "Bet Hillel and Bet Shammai," in *Jewish Encyclopedia* https://jewishencyclopedia.com/articles/13499-shammaites; Accessed 19 May 2023.

Jewett, Robert. *Romans: A Commentary* in Eldon Epp, ed. Hermeneia. Minneapolis, MN: Augsburg Fortress, 2007.

Johnson, Luke Timothy. *The Letter of James* in William Albright and David Freedman, eds. Anchor Yale Bible Commentary Series. Vol. 37A. New York: Doubleday, 1995.

Johnson, Carl. *The Account Which We Must Give: Studies on the Judgment Seat of Christ.* Beckley, WV: np, 1989.

Jurgie, Martin. *Purgatory and the Means to Avoid It.* Translated by Malachy Carroll from the French 7th edn. Cork, Ireland: The Mercier Press, 1949.

Kent, William. "Indulgences," in *The Catholic Encyclopedia*, Vol. 7. New York: Robert Appleton Company, 1910. http://www.newadvent.org/cathen/07783a.htm. Accessed 16 November 2022.

Kittel, Gerhard and Gerhard Friedrich, eds. sv. *"κρίνω."* Vol. 3, *Theological Dictionary of the New Testament*. 10th edn. Grand Rapids, MI: Eerdmans, 1984.

Kittel, Gerhard, ed., *Theological Dictionary of the New Testament*. Translated by Geoffrey Bromiley. Vol.2. Grand Rapids, MI: Eerdmans, 2006.

Kohler, Kaufmann. "Purgatory," *Jewish Encyclopedia*, 1901–1906. https://jewishencyclopedia.com/articles/12446-purgatory. Accessed 12 December 2022.

Kruse, Colin G. *The Letters of John* in D.A. Carson, ed. Pillar New Testament Commentary. *2nd edn.* Grand Rapids, MI: Eerdmans, 2020.

Lambert, W. A. "Doctrines of Men..." Pages 431–455 in *Works of Martin Luther with Introduction and Notes*. Philadelphia, PA: Holman Co. and Castle Press, 1915.

Lampe, G.W.H. ed. *A Patristic Greek Lexicon*. Oxford: Clarendon Press, 1961; Reprint, 2008.

Lane, William. *Hebrews* in Ralph Martin, ed. Word Biblical Commentary. Vol. 47B. Word Books: Dallas, Texas, 1991.

Le Goff, Jacques. *The Birth of Purgatory*. Translated by Arthur Goldhammer. Chicago, IL: University of Chicago Press, 1984.

Lenski, R.C.H. *The Interpretation of St. Paul's First and Second Epistles to the Corinthians*. Minneapolis, MN: Augsburg, 1963.

Lewis, C.S. *Letters to Malcolm, Chiefly on Prayer*. United Kingdom: Harcourt Brace, 1963. Reprint New York: HarperCollins, 1991.

_____. *Mere Christianity*. United Kingdom: Geoffrey Bles, 1952. Reprint, San Francisco: Harper San Francisco, 2001.

Liftin, Duane. "Revisiting the Unpardonable Sin: Insight from an Unexpected Source," *JETS* 60.4 (2017): 713–32.

Longenecker, Richard. *The Epistle to the Romans: A Commentary on the Greek Text* in I. Howard Marshall and Donald Hagner, eds. New International Greek Testament Commentary. Grand Rapids, MI: Eerdmans, 2016.

_____. *Galatians* in Bruce Metzger, gen. ed. Word Biblical Commentary. Vol. 41. Nashville, TN: Thomas Nelson, 1990.

Lossky, Vladimir. *Essai sur la Théologie de L'Énglise d'Orient*. Paris: N.p., 1944. Translation to English, 1957. *The Mystical Theology of the Eastern Church*. Crestwood, NY: St. Vladimir's Seminary Press, 1976.

_____. *Orthodox Theology: An Introduction*. Translated by Ian and Ihita Kesarcodi-Watson. Crestwood, NY: St. Vladimir's Seminary Press, 2001.

Louth, Andrew. "Chapter 12: Eastern Orthodox Eschatology," in Jerry Walls, ed. *The Oxford Handbook of Orthodox Eschatology*. Oxford: Oxford University Press: 2008.

Luther, Martin. *Triglot Concordia: The Symbolical Books of the Evangelical Lutheran Church*. Translated by F. Bente and W. H. T. Dau. St. Louis: Concordia Publishing House, 1921.

Lutzer, Erwin. *Your Eternal Reward: Triumph and Tears at the Judgment Sat of Christ*. Chicago, IL: Moody Press, 1998.

MacArthur, John. "The False Hope of Purgatory," in Fulfilling the Promises. https://fulfillingthepromises.com/the-false-hope-of-purgatory-by-john-macarthur/. Accessed 26 November 2022.

MacCullough, Diarmond. *A History of Christianity*. London: Penguin Books, 2009.

Mares, Courtney. "Catholics can get an indulgence for the dead by praying at a cemetery any day this November," *Catholic News Agency*. Oct 28, 2021. https://www.catholicnewsagency.com/news/249426/catholics-can-get-an-indulgence-for-the-dead-by-praying-at-a-cemetery-any-day-this-november. Accessed 11 May 2023.

Marinis, Vasileios. *Death and the Afterlife in Byzantium: The Fate of the Soul in Theology, Liturgy, and Art*. New York: Cambridge University Press, 2017.

Marshall, I. Howard. *The Epistles of John* in F.F. Bruce, ed. New International Commentary on the New Testament. Grand Rapids, MI: Eerdmans, 1978.

Martin, Ralph. *James* in David Hubbard and Glenn Barker, eds. Word Biblical Commentary. Vol. 48. Grand Rapids, MI: Zondervan, 1988.

Metzger, Bruce and Michael Coogan, eds. *The Oxford Companion to the Bible*. New York: Oxford University Press, 1993.

Moreira, Isabel. *Heaven's Purge: Purgatory in Late Antiquity*. New York: Oxford University Press, 2010.

Meyendorff, John. *Byzantine Theology: Historical Trends and Doctrinal Themes*. New York: Fordham University Press, 1974. Reprint, 1979.

Meyer, A.W. *Meyer's New Testament Commentary*. Translated by Peter Christie. Revised, translated, and edited Frederick Crombie. Edinburgh: T & T Clark, 1880.

Moo, Douglas. *2 Peter, Jude* in Terry Muck, ed. The NIV Application Commentary. Grand Rapids, MI: Zondervan, 1997.

_____. *The Epistle to the Romans* in Terry Muck, ed. New International Commentary on the New Testament. Grand Rapids, MI: Eerdmans, 1996.

Morris, Leon. *The Epistle to the Romans*. PNTC. Grand Rapids, MI: Eerdmans, 1988.

Moule, C.F.D. *Idiom Book of the N.T. Greek*. 2nd edn. Cambridge: Cambridge University Press, 1979.

Muraoka, T. *A Greek-English Lexicon of the Septuagint*. Leuven: Peters, 2009.

Noll, Mark. *Turning Points: Decisive Moments in the History of Christianity*. 2nd edn. Grand Rapids: Baker Academic, 2000.

O'Brien, Peter. *Colossians, Philemon* in David Hubbard and Glenn Barker, eds. Word Biblical Commentary. Vol. 44 . Nashville, TN: Thomas Nelson, 1982.

Pannenberg, Wolfhart. *Systematic Theology*. Vol. 3. Translated by Geoffrey Bromiley. Grand Rapids, MI: Eerdmans, 1998.

Panton, D. M. *The Judgment Seat of Christ*. Hayesville, NC: Schoettle Publishing, 1984.

Pentecost, J. Dwight. *Things to Come: A Study in Biblical Eschatology*. Elkins, NH: Dunham Pub., 1958. Reprint, Grand Rapids: Zondervan, 1964.

Peterson, Robert and Michael Williams. *Why I Am Not an Arminian*. Downers Grove, IL: InterVarsity, 2004.

Pfeiffer, Charles. *The Epistle to the Hebrews* in Everyman's Bible Commentary. Moody Bible Institute: Chicago, 1962.

Pink, Arthur. *An Exposition of Hebrews*. Grand Rapids, MI: Baker Book House, 2004.

Piper, John. "What Does the Bible Say about Purgatory?" Ask Pastor John, May 17, 2021, Episode 1627 https://www.desiringgod.org/interviews/what-does-the-bible-say-about-purgatory. Accessed 14 June 2023.

Plested, Marcus. *Orthodox Readings of Aquinas*. Oxford: Oxford University Press, 2012.

Pomazansky, Michael. *Orthodox Dogmatic Theology: A Concise Exposition. Translated and edited by* Hieromonk Seraphim Rose *(1963 as Pravoslavnoye Dogmaticheskoye Bogoslaviye;. Revised 1973. Reprinted,* 2009. IntraText Edition CT) II.5 Accessed 5 June 2023. http://www.intratext.com/IXT/ENG0824/_P1J.HTM.

Pope Benedict XVI. *Spe salvi* Encyclical Letter of November 30, 2007.

Pope Paul VI. *Indulgentiarum Doctrina* 12 (1967). https://www.vatican.va/content/paul-vi/en/apost_constitutions/documents/hf_p-vi_apc_01011967_indulgentiarum-doctrina.html Accessed 19 February 2019.

Pope Paul VI. Enchiridion of Indulgences (1968).

Pope John Paul II. http://w2.vatican.va/content/john-paul-
      ii/en/audiences/1999/documents/hf_jp-
      ii_aud_04081999.html. Accessed 19 Feb 2019.

Price, Richard. "Informal Penance in Early Medieval
      Christendom," *Studies in Church History*, Vol.40:
      Retribution, Repentance, and Reconciliation (2004):
      29–38.

Ratzinger, Joseph (Pope Benedict XVI). *Eschatologie–Tod
      und ewiges Leben* (Regensburg: Friedrich Pustet, 1977.
      Reprint as *Eschatology: Death and the Eternal Life.* 2nd
      edn. Translated by Michael Waldstein. Washington,
      DC: Catholic University of America Press, 2007.

Richardson, Peter. *Israel in the Apostolic Church*. Cambridge:
      Cambridge University Press, 1969.

Robertson, A.T. and Alfred Plummer. *A Critical and
      Exegetical Commentary on the First Epistle of St. Paul
      to the Corinthians* in Samuel Driver, Alfred Plummer,
      and Charles Briggs, eds. The International Critical
      Commentary. Edinburgh: T. & T. Clark, 1914.

Rosenthal Rachel. "Between This World and the Next:
      Rabbinic Visions of Purgatory" Jewish Theological
      Seminary; https://www.jtsa.edu/torah/rabbinic-visions-
      of-purgatory/. Accessed 6 Feb 2023.

Rotelle, John, ed. *The Works of Saint Augustine: A Translation
      for the 21st Century*. Expositions of the Psalms 33–50,
      III/16. Translation and notes by Maria Boulding. Hyde
      Park, NY: New City Press, 2000.

Russell, Norman. *The Doctrine of Deification in the Greek
      Patristic Tradition*. Oxford: Oxford University Press,
      2004.

Ryrie, Charles. *Basic Theology*. Chicago, IL: Moody Press,
      1986. Reprint, 1999.

Sale-Harrison, Leonard. *The Judgment Seat of Christ: An Incentive and a Warning*. New York: Sale-Harrison Publications, 1938.

Sanders, E.P. *Judaism: Practice & Belief 63BCE–66CE*. London: SCM Press, 1992.

Schenck, Kenneth. *1 & 2 Corinthians: A Commentary for Bible Students*. Indianapolis, IN: Wesleyan Publishing House, 2006.

Schiffman, Lawrence. *From Text to Tradition: A History of Second Temple & Rabbinic Judaism* Hoboken, NJ: Ktav Publishing, 1991.

Schreiner, Thomas. *Commentary on Hebrews* in T. Desmond Alexander, Andreas Köstenberger, and Thomas Schreiner, eds. Biblical Theology for Christian Proclamation. Nashville, TN: B & H Publishing, 2015.

_____. *Romans* in Moisés Silva, ed. Baker Exegetical Commentary on the New Testament. Grand Rapids, MI: Baker Academic, 1998.

_____. "Response to James D.G. Dunn," in Alan Stanley, ed., *The Role of Works at the Final Judgment*. Grand Rapids: Zondervan, 2013.

Schwartz, Daniel R. *2 Maccabees. Commentaries on Early Jewish Literature*. Pages 85–96, "Reception and Text." Berlin/New York: Walter de Gruyter, 2008.

Scofield, Cyrus I. *The Scofield Reference Bible*. New York: Oxford University Press, 1909. Revised, 1917.

Sproul, R.C. *Faith Alone: The Evangelical Doctrine of Justification*. Grand Rapids, MI: Baker Books, 1995.

_____. *The Holiness of God*. Wheaton, IL: Tyndale House, 1985. Revised, 1998.

Stanley, Alan P. *Did Jesus Teach Salvation by Works?: The Role of Works in Salvation in the Synoptic Gospels.* 4th edn. Eugene, OR: Pickwick Publications, 2006.

Stavropoulos, Christoforos. *Partakers of the Divine Nature.* Translated by S. Harakas. Minneapolis, MN: Light and Life Publishing Co., 1976.

Stolk, Maarten. "Calvin and Rome" in Herman Selderhuis, ed. *The Calvin Handbook.* Translated by Gerrit Sheeres. Grand Rapids, MI: Eerdmans, 2009.

Steenberg, M.C. sv. "Original Sin," in John McGuckin, ed. *The Concise Encyclopedia of Orthodox Christianity.* Oxford: Wiley Blackwell, 2014.

Thielman, Frank. *Romans* in Clinton Arnold, gen. ed. Exegetical Commentary on the New Testament. Grand Rapids, MI: Zondervan Academic, 2018.

Thiselton, Anthony C. *The First Epistle to the Corinthians: A Commentary on the Greek Text* in I. Howard Marshall and Donald Hagner, eds. New International Greek Testament Commentary; Grand Rapids, MI: W.B. Eerdmans, 2000.

Torrance, Thomas F. *The Doctrine of Grace in the Apostolic Fathers.* Oliver and Boyd LTD: Edinburgh, 1948. Reprint, Wipf and Stock Publishers: Eugene, Oregon, 1996.

Townsend, John T. "1 Corinthians 3:15 and the School of Shammai," *HTR* 61.3 (July 1968): 500–504.

Travis, Stephen. *Christ and the Judgment of God: The Limits of Divine Retribution in New Testament Thought.* Np.: B.M. Pickering, 1986. Reprint, 2nd edn. Milton Keynes, UK: Paternoster, 2008.

Truglia, Craig. "The Orthodox Doctrine of Sin: A Comprehensive Treatment," at Orthodox Christian Theology, April 11, 2012. https://orthodoxchristiantheology.com/2021/04/11/the-orthodox-doctrine-of-original-sin-a-comprehensive-treatment/. Accessed 5 June 2023.

United States Conference of Catholic Bishops. "Bereavement and Funerals." https://www.usccb.org/prayer-and-worship/sacraments-and-sacramentals/bereavement-and-funerals ; Accessed 9 May 2023.

Viller, Marcel. "La Question de l'Union des Églises entre Grecs et Latins depuis le concile de Lyon jusqu'à celui de Florence (1274–1438)." Revue *d'histoire ecclésiastique* 17.2 (1921): 260–305, 515–532.

Vogel, Cyril. "Penitence," in Angelo Di Berardino, ed. *Encyclopedia of the Early Church*. Vol. 2. Translated by Adrian Walford. Cambridge: James Clarke & Co., 1992.

Wallace, Daniel. *Greek Grammar Beyond the Basics.* Grand Rapids: Zondervan, 1996.

Walls, Jerry. *Purgatory: The Logic of Total Transformation.* New York: Oxford University Press, 2012.

Walls, Jerry and Joseph Dongell. *Why I am Not a Calvinist.* Downers Grove, IL: InterVarsity, 2004.

Walvoord, John. "The Future Work of Christ Part II: The Church in Heaven in Heaven," *BSac* 123:490 (Apr 66): 99–100.

Wanamaker, Charles. *The Epistles to the Thessalonians* in I. Howard Marshall and Donald Hagner, eds. New International Greek Testament Commentary. Grand Rapids, MI: Eerdmans, 1990.

Wesley, John. *Brief thoughts on Christian perfection*. London, 1767. Sections 26–281.

White, L. Michael. "Penance," in Everett Ferguson, ed. *Encyclopedia of Early Christianity*, 2nd edn. New York: Routledge, 1999.

Wilkin, Bob. "Can Believers Get Away with Murder?" May 3, 2021 GES Blog. https://faithalone.org/blog/can-believers-get-away-with-murder/. Accessed 21 May 2023.

_____. "Will the Bad Deeds of Believers be Considered at the Judgement Seat of Christ?" *JOTGES* (Spring 2015): 17–36.

_____. "Christians will be Judged According to their Works at the *Rewards* Judgment, but *Not* at the *Final* Judgment." Pages 25–50 in Alan Stanley and Stanley Gundry, eds. *Four Views of the Role of Works at the Final Judgment*. Grand Rapids, MI: Zondervan, 2013.

Williams, David. *1 and 2 Thessalonians* in David Williams and W. Ward Gasque, eds. New International Biblical Commentary. Peabody, MA: Hendrickson, 1992.

Wilson, Kenneth. *Augustine's Conversion from Traditional Free Choice to "Non-free Free Will": A Comprehensive Methodology*. Studien Und Texte Zu Antike Und Christentum 111. Tübingen: Mohr Siebeck, 2018.

_____. "Reading James 2:18–20 with Anti-Donatist Eyes: Untangling Augustine's Exegetical Legacy," *Journal of Biblical Literature* 139.2 (2020): 389–410.

_____. "Augustine of Hippo's Tenuous Tension between Stoic Providence and Christian Free Will," *Studia Patristica* 119 (2021): 153–168.

_____. "Chapter 6: Calvinism is Augustinianism."
Pages 213–237 in David Allen and Steve Lemke, eds.
Calvinism: A Biblical and Theological Critique.
Nashville, TN: B & H Publishing, 2022.

Wiseman, Cardinal Nicholas. *Lectures on the Principle
Doctrines and Practices of the Catholic Church.* Vol.2.
London: Booker,1836. Accessed 5 July 2023 at
https://archive.org/details/LecturesOnThePrincipalDoct
rinesV2/page/n9/mode/2up.

Wolfson Ron."Yizkor: The Jewish Memorial Service."
Accessed 14 May 2023 at
https://www.myjewishlearning.com/article/yizkor-the-
memorial-service/.

Wright, N.T. *For All the Saints: Remembering the Christian
Departed.* Harrisburg, PA: Morehouse, 2004.

Yechiel, Bais. *Above All Else: The Chofetz Chaim Anthology
on TORAH STUDY.* Vol.2. Translated by Gavriel
Rubin. Jerusalem: Feldheim Publishers, 2006.

Zernov, Nicolas. *Eastern Christendom: A Study of the Origin
and Development of the Eastern Orthodox Church.*
London: Weidenfeld & Nicolson, 1961.

Scripture Index

Author Index

Subject Index

318 Subject Index

Lactantius 154
Polycarp xiii, 21, 150, 151, 152, 234
pseudo-Athanasias 44
Tertullian 19, 20, 21, 22, 33, 111, 152
Edwards, Jonathan 209, 210, 293
expiatory 102, 105
expiatory suffering 95, 102
faith 46, 71, 90, 188, 192, 194, 195, 226, 266, 267, 290, 303
faith alone 2, 6, 66, 67, 168, 173, 184, 185, 188, 193, 194, 206, 218, 231, 265, 269
faith and works 172, 184, 192
fear of God 167, 223, 226
Filioque 46
Finkelstein, Louis 124, 125, 294
forgive 15, 16, 104, 133, 285
Forsyth, Peter 86, 294
Gehenna 8, 9, 10, 11, 12, 14, 15, 18, 101, 112, 122, 124, 211, 262
Gnostic 195, 215, 267
grace 70, 71, 97, 217, 219, 296, 304
Hodge, Charles 69, 81, 295
Hoyt, Samuel L. 70, 281, 282, 296
indulgences 21, 29, 30, 34, 35, 49, 108, 109, 212, 289, 297
Enchiridion of Indulgences 34, 301
Manual of Indulgences 30
Raccolta 29, 30
injustice i, 217
Early Church Fathers 110, 159, 214
Jewish writings
2 Maccabees xii, 2, 16, 32, 67, 99, 109, 110, 111, 303
Chabad.org 12, 293
Jewish Encyclopedia 8, 124, 296, 297
Kel Maleh Rachamim 17, 18
Midrash Rabba 11

Midrash Sifré to Deuteronomy 15
Midrash, Tanna Devei Eliyahu 9
Mishnah, Berakhot 15
Talmud, Eruvin 19a 11, 12
Testament of Abraham xiii, 9, 10, 256
Tosephta Sanhedrin xiii, 8, 9, 13, 122
Zohar Chadash xiii, 10
Judgment Seat of Christ 69, 70, 77, 168, 183, 216, 222, 223, 233, 246, 265, 280, 282, 285
reward only error 277
Jurgie, Martin 102, 103, 171, 220, 296
justice ii, 130, 133, 165, 173, 209, 220
restorative 165, 173, 174
retributive 171, 173, 174
Kittel, Gerhard 3, 135, 180, 181, 216, 272, 297
life 34, 43, 44, 52, 75, 86, 213, 294, 302, 304
Luther, Martin ix, 1, 29, 40, 56, 57, 59, 62, 295, 297, 298
mercy ix, x, 1, 4, 17, 24, 55, 57, 60, 112, 136, 155, 160, 205, 207, 208, 209, 221, 222, 225, 226, 241, 265
Moody Handbook of Theology 69, 282, 283, 294
Newman, John Henry 30, 173
Orthodox Church 40, 41, 42, 46, 48, 49, 52, 89, 90, 110, 121, 212, 213, 221, 294, 307
Palamas, Gregory 53
Pannenberg, Wolfhart 179, 180, 300
penalty 81, 120, 281
penance 21, 22, 23, 27, 28, 35, 108, 112, 294, 302, 305, 306
Pew Research Center 66

www.ingramcontent.com/pod-product-compliance
Lightning Source LLC
La Vergne TN
LVHW052014080426
835513LV00018B/2026